C-1939

CAREER EXAMINATION SERIES

THIS IS YOUR **PASSBOOK**® FOR ...

POLICE OFFICER

NLC®

NATIONAL LEARNING CORPORATION®
passbooks.com

PASSBOOK® SERIES

THE *PASSBOOK® SERIES* has been created to prepare applicants and candidates for the ultimate academic battlefield – the examination room.

At some time in our lives, each and every one of us may be required to take an examination – for validation, matriculation, admission, qualification, registration, certification, or licensure.

Based on the assumption that every applicant or candidate has met the basic formal educational standards, has taken the required number of courses, and read the necessary texts, the *PASSBOOK® SERIES* furnishes the one special preparation which may assure passing with confidence, instead of failing with insecurity. Examination questions – together with answers – are furnished as the basic vehicle for study so that the mysteries of the examination and its compounding difficulties may be eliminated or diminished by a sure method.

This book is meant to help you pass your examination provided that you qualify and are serious in your objective.

The entire field is reviewed through the huge store of content information which is succinctly presented through a provocative and challenging approach – the question-and-answer method.

A climate of success is established by furnishing the correct answers at the end of each test.

You soon learn to recognize types of questions, forms of questions, and patterns of questioning. You may even begin to anticipate expected outcomes.

You perceive that many questions are repeated or adapted so that you can gain acute insights, which may enable you to score many sure points.

You learn how to confront new questions, or types of questions, and to attack them confidently and work out the correct answers.

You note objectives and emphases, and recognize pitfalls and dangers, so that you may make positive educational adjustments.

Moreover, you are kept fully informed in relation to new concepts, methods, practices, and directions in the field.

You discover that you arre actually taking the examination all the time: you are preparing for the examination by "taking" an examination, not by reading extraneous and/or supererogatory textbooks.

In short, this PASSBOOK®, used directedly, should be an important factor in helping you to pass your test.

POLICE OFFICER

DUTIES:

Performs general police work in the enforcement of laws and the protection of life and property; patrols a specific district or beat on foot, in radio cruising car, or on a motorcycle; checks doors and windows of unoccupied business and residential property to determine security and the possible commission of a crime; investigates suspicious activities and complaints and makes arrests for violations of Federal and State laws and local ordinances; investigates at the scene of accidents, aids the injured, determines if any criminal offenses have been committed, and prepares reports; directs traffic at scenes of accidents, fires, public assemblages, and at busy thoroughfares and intersections; patrols parking areas and issues summonses for parking violations; when assigned to desk duty, receives complaints, dispatches officers and keeps appropriate records in accordance with well-defined procedures; watches for and makes investigations of wanted and missing persons and stolen cars and property; escorts prisoners to jail and to court, has them booked, and prepares arrest reports; testifies in court or before a grand jury; answers questions for and directs the public; makes daily reports of activities.

SCOPE OF EXAMINATION

The written test will be designed to test for knowledge, skills, and/or abilities in such areas as:

1. **Applying written information (rules, regulations, policies, procedures, directives, etc.) in police situations** - These questions test for the ability to apply written rules in given situations similar to those typically experienced by police officers.
2. **Memory for facts and information** - These questions test for the ability to remember facts and information presented in written form. You will be given 5 minutes to read and study the information in the Memory Booklet. After the 5-minute period, the Memory Booklet will be taken away. You will then be required to answer questions about the material that was presented in the Memory Booklet.
3. **Reading, understanding and interpreting written information** - These questions test for the ability to read, understand, and interpret the kinds of written information that police officers are required to read during their formal training period and on the job.
4. **Preparing written material in a police setting** - These questions test for the ability to prepare the types of reports that police officers write. You will be presented with a page of notes followed by several questions. Each question will consist of four restatements of the information given in the notes. From each set of four, you must choose the version that presents the information most clearly and accurately.

HOW TO TAKE A TEST

I. YOU MUST PASS AN EXAMINATION

A. *WHAT EVERY CANDIDATE SHOULD KNOW*

Examination applicants often ask us for help in preparing for the written test. What can I study in advance? What kinds of questions will be asked? How will the test be given? How will the papers be graded?

As an applicant for a civil service examination, you may be wondering about some of these things. Our purpose here is to suggest effective methods of advance study and to describe civil service examinations.

Your chances for success on this examination can be increased if you know how to prepare. Those "pre-examination jitters" can be reduced if you know what to expect. You can even experience an adventure in good citizenship if you know why civil service exams are given.

B. *WHY ARE CIVIL SERVICE EXAMINATIONS GIVEN?*

Civil service examinations are important to you in two ways. As a citizen, you want public jobs filled by employees who know how to do their work. As a job seeker, you want a fair chance to compete for that job on an equal footing with other candidates. The best-known means of accomplishing this two-fold goal is the competitive examination.

Exams are widely publicized throughout the nation. They may be administered for jobs in federal, state, city, municipal, town or village governments or agencies.

Any citizen may apply, with some limitations, such as the age or residence of applicants. Your experience and education may be reviewed to see whether you meet the requirements for the particular examination. When these requirements exist, they are reasonable and applied consistently to all applicants. Thus, a competitive examination may cause you some uneasiness now, but it is your privilege and safeguard.

C. *HOW ARE CIVIL SERVICE EXAMS DEVELOPED?*

Examinations are carefully written by trained technicians who are specialists in the field known as "psychological measurement," in consultation with recognized authorities in the field of work that the test will cover. These experts recommend the subject matter areas or skills to be tested; only those knowledges or skills important to your success on the job are included. The most reliable books and source materials available are used as references. Together, the experts and technicians judge the difficulty level of the questions.

Test technicians know how to phrase questions so that the problem is clearly stated. Their ethics do not permit "trick" or "catch" questions. Questions may have been tried out on sample groups, or subjected to statistical analysis, to determine their usefulness.

Written tests are often used in combination with performance tests, ratings of training and experience, and oral interviews. All of these measures combine to form the best-known means of finding the right person for the right job.

II. HOW TO PASS THE WRITTEN TEST

A. NATURE OF THE EXAMINATION

To prepare intelligently for civil service examinations, you should know how they differ from school examinations you have taken. In school you were assigned certain definite pages to read or subjects to cover. The examination questions were quite detailed and usually emphasized memory. Civil service exams, on the other hand, try to discover your present ability to perform the duties of a position, plus your potentiality to learn these duties. In other words, a civil service exam attempts to predict how successful you will be. Questions cover such a broad area that they cannot be as minute and detailed as school exam questions.

In the public service similar kinds of work, or positions, are grouped together in one "class." This process is known as *position-classification*. All the positions in a class are paid according to the salary range for that class. One class title covers all of these positions, and they are all tested by the same examination.

B. FOUR BASIC STEPS

1) Study the announcement

How, then, can you know what subjects to study? Our best answer is: "Learn as much as possible about the class of positions for which you've applied." The exam will test the knowledge, skills and abilities needed to do the work.

Your most valuable source of information about the position you want is the official exam announcement. This announcement lists the training and experience qualifications. Check these standards and apply only if you come reasonably close to meeting them.

The brief description of the position in the examination announcement offers some clues to the subjects which will be tested. Think about the job itself. Review the duties in your mind. Can you perform them, or are there some in which you are rusty? Fill in the blank spots in your preparation.

Many jurisdictions preview the written test in the exam announcement by including a section called "Knowledge and Abilities Required," "Scope of the Examination," or some similar heading. Here you will find out specifically what fields will be tested.

2) Review your own background

Once you learn in general what the position is all about, and what you need to know to do the work, ask yourself which subjects you already know fairly well and which need improvement. You may wonder whether to concentrate on improving your strong areas or on building some background in your fields of weakness. When the announcement has specified "some knowledge" or "considerable knowledge," or has used adjectives like "beginning principles of..." or "advanced ... methods," you can get a clue as to the number and difficulty of questions to be asked in any given field. More questions, and hence broader coverage, would be included for those subjects which are more important in the work. Now weigh your strengths and weaknesses against the job requirements and prepare accordingly.

3) Determine the level of the position

Another way to tell how intensively you should prepare is to understand the level of the job for which you are applying. Is it the entering level? In other words, is this the position in which beginners in a field of work are hired? Or is it an intermediate or advanced level? Sometimes this is indicated by such words as "Junior" or "Senior" in the class title. Other jurisdictions use Roman numerals to designate the level – Clerk I, Clerk II, for example. The word "Supervisor" sometimes appears in the title. If the level is not indicated by the title, check the description of duties. Will you be working under very close supervision, or will you have responsibility for independent decisions in this work?

4) Choose appropriate study materials

Now that you know the subjects to be examined and the relative amount of each subject to be covered, you can choose suitable study materials. For beginning level jobs, or even advanced ones, if you have a pronounced weakness in some aspect of your training, read a modern, standard textbook in that field. Be sure it is up to date and has general coverage. Such books are normally available at your library, and the librarian will be glad to help you locate one. For entry-level positions, questions of appropriate difficulty are chosen – neither highly advanced questions, nor those too simple. Such questions require careful thought but not advanced training.

If the position for which you are applying is technical or advanced, you will read more advanced, specialized material. If you are already familiar with the basic principles of your field, elementary textbooks would waste your time. Concentrate on advanced textbooks and technical periodicals. Think through the concepts and review difficult problems in your field.

These are all general sources. You can get more ideas on your own initiative, following these leads. For example, training manuals and publications of the government agency which employs workers in your field can be useful, particularly for technical and professional positions. A letter or visit to the government department involved may result in more specific study suggestions, and certainly will provide you with a more definite idea of the exact nature of the position you are seeking.

III. KINDS OF TESTS

Tests are used for purposes other than measuring knowledge and ability to perform specified duties. For some positions, it is equally important to test ability to make adjustments to new situations or to profit from training. In others, basic mental abilities not dependent on information are essential. Questions which test these things may not appear as pertinent to the duties of the position as those which test for knowledge and information. Yet they are often highly important parts of a fair examination. For very general questions, it is almost impossible to help you direct your study efforts. What we can do is to point out some of the more common of these general abilities needed in public service positions and describe some typical questions.

1) General information

Broad, general information has been found useful for predicting job success in some kinds of work. This is tested in a variety of ways, from vocabulary lists to questions about current events. Basic background in some field of work, such as sociology or economics, may be sampled in a group of questions. Often these are principles which have become familiar to most persons through exposure rather than through formal training. It is difficult to advise you how to study for these questions; being alert to the world around you is our best suggestion.

2) Verbal ability

An example of an ability needed in many positions is verbal or language ability. Verbal ability is, in brief, the ability to use and understand words. Vocabulary and grammar tests are typical measures of this ability. Reading comprehension or paragraph interpretation questions are common in many kinds of civil service tests. You are given a paragraph of written material and asked to find its central meaning.

3) Numerical ability

Number skills can be tested by the familiar arithmetic problem, by checking paired lists of numbers to see which are alike and which are different, or by interpreting charts and graphs. In the latter test, a graph may be printed in the test booklet which you are asked to use as the basis for answering questions.

4) Observation

A popular test for law-enforcement positions is the observation test. A picture is shown to you for several minutes, then taken away. Questions about the picture test your ability to observe both details and larger elements.

5) Following directions

In many positions in the public service, the employee must be able to carry out written instructions dependably and accurately. You may be given a chart with several columns, each column listing a variety of information. The questions require you to carry out directions involving the information given in the chart.

6) Skills and aptitudes

Performance tests effectively measure some manual skills and aptitudes. When the skill is one in which you are trained, such as typing or shorthand, you can practice. These tests are often very much like those given in business school or high school courses. For many of the other skills and aptitudes, however, no short-time preparation can be made. Skills and abilities natural to you or that you have developed throughout your lifetime are being tested.

Many of the general questions just described provide all the data needed to answer the questions and ask you to use your reasoning ability to find the answers. Your best preparation for these tests, as well as for tests of facts and ideas, is to be at your physical and mental best. You, no doubt, have your own methods of getting into an exam-taking mood and keeping "in shape." The next section lists some ideas on this subject.

IV. KINDS OF QUESTIONS

Only rarely is the "essay" question, which you answer in narrative form, used in civil service tests. Civil service tests are usually of the short-answer type. Full instructions for answering these questions will be given to you at the examination. But in case this is your first experience with short-answer questions and separate answer sheets, here is what you need to know:

1) Multiple-choice Questions

Most popular of the short-answer questions is the "multiple choice" or "best answer" question. It can be used, for example, to test for factual knowledge, ability to solve problems or judgment in meeting situations found at work.

A multiple-choice question is normally one of three types—

- It can begin with an incomplete statement followed by several possible endings. You are to find the one ending which *best* completes the statement, although some of the others may not be entirely wrong.
- It can also be a complete statement in the form of a question which is answered by choosing one of the statements listed.
- It can be in the form of a problem – again you select the best answer.

Here is an example of a multiple-choice question with a discussion which should give you some clues as to the method for choosing the right answer:

When an employee has a complaint about his assignment, the action which will *best* help him overcome his difficulty is to
- A. discuss his difficulty with his coworkers
- B. take the problem to the head of the organization
- C. take the problem to the person who gave him the assignment
- D. say nothing to anyone about his complaint

In answering this question, you should study each of the choices to find which is best. Consider choice "A" – Certainly an employee may discuss his complaint with fellow employees, but no change or improvement can result, and the complaint remains unresolved. Choice "B" is a poor choice since the head of the organization probably does not know what assignment you have been given, and taking your problem to him is known as "going over the head" of the supervisor. The supervisor, or person who made the assignment, is the person who can clarify it or correct any injustice. Choice "C" is, therefore, correct. To say nothing, as in choice "D," is unwise. Supervisors have and interest in knowing the problems employees are facing, and the employee is seeking a solution to his problem.

2) True/False Questions

The "true/false" or "right/wrong" form of question is sometimes used. Here a complete statement is given. Your job is to decide whether the statement is right or wrong.

SAMPLE: A roaming cell-phone call to a nearby city costs less than a non-roaming call to a distant city.

This statement is wrong, or false, since roaming calls are more expensive.

This is not a complete list of all possible question forms, although most of the others are variations of these common types. You will always get complete directions for answering questions. Be sure you understand *how* to mark your answers – ask questions until you do.

V. RECORDING YOUR ANSWERS

Computer terminals are used more and more today for many different kinds of exams.

For an examination with very few applicants, you may be told to record your answers in the test booklet itself. Separate answer sheets are much more common. If this separate answer sheet is to be scored by machine – and this is often the case – it is highly important that you mark your answers correctly in order to get credit.

An electronic scoring machine is often used in civil service offices because of the speed with which papers can be scored. Machine-scored answer sheets must be marked with a pencil, which will be given to you. This pencil has a high graphite content which responds to the electronic scoring machine. As a matter of fact, stray dots may register as answers, so do not let your pencil rest on the answer sheet while you are pondering the correct answer. Also, if your pencil lead breaks or is otherwise defective, ask for another.

Since the answer sheet will be dropped in a slot in the scoring machine, be careful not to bend the corners or get the paper crumpled.

The answer sheet normally has five vertical columns of numbers, with 30 numbers to a column. These numbers correspond to the question numbers in your test booklet. After each number, going across the page are four or five pairs of dotted lines. These short dotted lines have small letters or numbers above them. The first two pairs may also have a "T" or "F" above the letters. This indicates that the first two pairs only are to be used if the questions are of the true-false type. If the questions are multiple choice, disregard the "T" and "F" and pay attention only to the small letters or numbers.

Answer your questions in the manner of the sample that follows:

32. The largest city in the United States is
  A. Washington, D.C.
  B. New York City
  C. Chicago
  D. Detroit
  E. San Francisco

1) Choose the answer you think is best. (New York City is the largest, so "B" is correct.)
2) Find the row of dotted lines numbered the same as the question you are answering. (Find row number 32)
3) Find the pair of dotted lines corresponding to the answer. (Find the pair of lines under the mark "B.")
4) Make a solid black mark between the dotted lines.

VI. BEFORE THE TEST

Common sense will help you find procedures to follow to get ready for an examination. Too many of us, however, overlook these sensible measures. Indeed, nervousness and fatigue have been found to be the most serious reasons why applicants fail to do their best on civil service tests. Here is a list of reminders:

- Begin your preparation early – Don't wait until the last minute to go scurrying around for books and materials or to find out what the position is all about.
- Prepare continuously – An hour a night for a week is better than an all-night cram session. This has been definitely established. What is more, a night a week for a month will return better dividends than crowding your study into a shorter period of time.
- Locate the place of the exam – You have been sent a notice telling you when and where to report for the examination. If the location is in a different town or otherwise unfamiliar to you, it would be well to inquire the best route and learn something about the building.
- Relax the night before the test – Allow your mind to rest. Do not study at all that night. Plan some mild recreation or diversion; then go to bed early and get a good night's sleep.
- Get up early enough to make a leisurely trip to the place for the test – This way unforeseen events, traffic snarls, unfamiliar buildings, etc. will not upset you.
- Dress comfortably – A written test is not a fashion show. You will be known by number and not by name, so wear something comfortable.
- Leave excess paraphernalia at home – Shopping bags and odd bundles will get in your way. You need bring only the items mentioned in the official notice you received; usually everything you need is provided. Do not bring reference books to the exam. They will only confuse those last minutes and be taken away from you when in the test room.
- Arrive somewhat ahead of time – If because of transportation schedules you must get there very early, bring a newspaper or magazine to take your mind off yourself while waiting.
- Locate the examination room – When you have found the proper room, you will be directed to the seat or part of the room where you will sit. Sometimes you are given a sheet of instructions to read while you are waiting. Do not fill out any forms until you are told to do so; just read them and be prepared.
- Relax and prepare to listen to the instructions
- If you have any physical problem that may keep you from doing your best, be sure to tell the test administrator. If you are sick or in poor health, you really cannot do your best on the exam. You can come back and take the test some other time.

VII. AT THE TEST

The day of the test is here and you have the test booklet in your hand. The temptation to get going is very strong. Caution! There is more to success than knowing the right answers. You must know how to identify your papers and understand variations in the type of short-answer question used in this particular examination. Follow these suggestions for maximum results from your efforts:

1) Cooperate with the monitor

The test administrator has a duty to create a situation in which you can be as much at ease as possible. He will give instructions, tell you when to begin, check to see that you are marking your answer sheet correctly, and so on. He is not there to guard you, although he will see that your competitors do not take unfair advantage. He wants to help you do your best.

2) Listen to all instructions

Don't jump the gun! Wait until you understand all directions. In most civil service tests you get more time than you need to answer the questions. So don't be in a hurry. Read each word of instructions until you clearly understand the meaning. Study the examples, listen to all announcements and follow directions. Ask questions if you do not understand what to do.

3) Identify your papers

Civil service exams are usually identified by number only. You will be assigned a number; you must not put your name on your test papers. Be sure to copy your number correctly. Since more than one exam may be given, copy your exact examination title.

4) Plan your time

Unless you are told that a test is a "speed" or "rate of work" test, speed itself is usually not important. Time enough to answer all the questions will be provided, but this does not mean that you have all day. An overall time limit has been set. Divide the total time (in minutes) by the number of questions to determine the approximate time you have for each question.

5) Do not linger over difficult questions

If you come across a difficult question, mark it with a paper clip (useful to have along) and come back to it when you have been through the booklet. One caution if you do this – be sure to skip a number on your answer sheet as well. Check often to be sure that you have not lost your place and that you are marking in the row numbered the same as the question you are answering.

6) Read the questions

Be sure you know what the question asks! Many capable people are unsuccessful because they failed to *read* the questions correctly.

7) Answer all questions

Unless you have been instructed that a penalty will be deducted for incorrect answers, it is better to guess than to omit a question.

8) Speed tests

It is often better NOT to guess on speed tests. It has been found that on timed tests people are tempted to spend the last few seconds before time is called in marking answers at random – without even reading them – in the hope of picking up a few extra points. To discourage this practice, the instructions may warn you that your score will be "corrected" for guessing. That is, a penalty will be applied. The incorrect answers will be deducted from the correct ones, or some other penalty formula will be used.

9) Review your answers

If you finish before time is called, go back to the questions you guessed or omitted to give them further thought. Review other answers if you have time.

10) Return your test materials

If you are ready to leave before others have finished or time is called, take ALL your materials to the monitor and leave quietly. Never take any test material with you. The monitor can discover whose papers are not complete, and taking a test booklet may be grounds for disqualification.

VIII. EXAMINATION TECHNIQUES

1) Read the general instructions carefully. These are usually printed on the first page of the exam booklet. As a rule, these instructions refer to the timing of the examination; the fact that you should not start work until the signal and must stop work at a signal, etc. If there are any *special* instructions, such as a choice of questions to be answered, make sure that you note this instruction carefully.

2) When you are ready to start work on the examination, that is as soon as the signal has been given, read the instructions to each question booklet, underline any key words or phrases, such as *least, best, outline, describe* and the like. In this way you will tend to answer as requested rather than discover on reviewing your paper that you *listed without describing*, that you selected the *worst* choice rather than the *best* choice, etc.

3) If the examination is of the objective or multiple-choice type – that is, each question will also give a series of possible answers: A, B, C or D, and you are called upon to select the best answer and write the letter next to that answer on your answer paper – it is advisable to start answering each question in turn. There may be anywhere from 50 to 100 such questions in the three or four hours allotted and you can see how much time would be taken if you read through all the questions before beginning to answer any. Furthermore, if you come across a question or group of questions which you know would be difficult to answer, it would undoubtedly affect your handling of all the other questions.

4) If the examination is of the essay type and contains but a few questions, it is a moot point as to whether you should read all the questions before starting to answer any one. Of course, if you are given a choice – say five out of seven and the like – then it is essential to read all the questions so you can eliminate the two that are most difficult. If, however, you are asked to answer all the questions, there may be danger in trying to answer the easiest one first because you may find that you will spend too much time on it. The best technique is to answer the first question, then proceed to the second, etc.

5) Time your answers. Before the exam begins, write down the time it started, then add the time allowed for the examination and write down the time it must be completed, then divide the time available somewhat as follows:

- If 3-1/2 hours are allowed, that would be 210 minutes. If you have 80 objective-type questions, that would be an average of 2-1/2 minutes per question. Allow yourself no more than 2 minutes per question, or a total of 160 minutes, which will permit about 50 minutes to review.
- If for the time allotment of 210 minutes there are 7 essay questions to answer, that would average about 30 minutes a question. Give yourself only 25 minutes per question so that you have about 35 minutes to review.

6) The most important instruction is to *read each question* and make sure you know what is wanted. The second most important instruction is to *time yourself properly* so that you answer every question. The third most important instruction is to *answer every question*. Guess if you have to but include something for each question. Remember that you will receive no credit for a blank and will probably receive some credit if you write something in answer to an essay question. If you guess a letter – say "B" for a multiple-choice question – you may have guessed right. If you leave a blank as an answer to a multiple-choice question, the examiners may respect your feelings but it will not add a point to your score. Some exams may penalize you for wrong answers, so in such cases *only*, you may not want to guess unless you have some basis for your answer.

7) Suggestions
    a. Objective-type questions
        1. Examine the question booklet for proper sequence of pages and questions
        2. Read all instructions carefully
        3. Skip any question which seems too difficult; return to it after all other questions have been answered
        4. Apportion your time properly; do not spend too much time on any single question or group of questions
        5. Note and underline key words – *all, most, fewest, least, best, worst, same, opposite*, etc.
        6. Pay particular attention to negatives
        7. Note unusual option, e.g., unduly long, short, complex, different or similar in content to the body of the question
        8. Observe the use of "hedging" words – *probably, may, most likely*, etc.
        9. Make sure that your answer is put next to the same number as the question
        10. Do not second-guess unless you have good reason to believe the second answer is definitely more correct
        11. Cross out original answer if you decide another answer is more accurate; do not erase until you are ready to hand your paper in
        12. Answer all questions; guess unless instructed otherwise
        13. Leave time for review

    b. Essay questions
        1. Read each question carefully
        2. Determine exactly what is wanted. Underline key words or phrases.
        3. Decide on outline or paragraph answer

4. Include many different points and elements unless asked to develop any one or two points or elements
5. Show impartiality by giving pros and cons unless directed to select one side only
6. Make and write down any assumptions you find necessary to answer the questions
7. Watch your English, grammar, punctuation and choice of words
8. Time your answers; don't crowd material

8) Answering the essay question

Most essay questions can be answered by framing the specific response around several key words or ideas. Here are a few such key words or ideas:

M's: manpower, materials, methods, money, management
P's: purpose, program, policy, plan, procedure, practice, problems, pitfalls, personnel, public relations

a. Six basic steps in handling problems:
1. Preliminary plan and background development
2. Collect information, data and facts
3. Analyze and interpret information, data and facts
4. Analyze and develop solutions as well as make recommendations
5. Prepare report and sell recommendations
6. Install recommendations and follow up effectiveness

b. Pitfalls to avoid
1. *Taking things for granted* – A statement of the situation does not necessarily imply that each of the elements is necessarily true; for example, a complaint may be invalid and biased so that all that can be taken for granted is that a complaint has been registered
2. *Considering only one side of a situation* – Wherever possible, indicate several alternatives and then point out the reasons you selected the best one
3. *Failing to indicate follow up* – Whenever your answer indicates action on your part, make certain that you will take proper follow-up action to see how successful your recommendations, procedures or actions turn out to be
4. *Taking too long in answering any single question* – Remember to time your answers properly

IX. AFTER THE TEST

Scoring procedures differ in detail among civil service jurisdictions although the general principles are the same. Whether the papers are hand-scored or graded by machine we have described, they are nearly always graded by number. That is, the person who marks the paper knows only the number – never the name – of the applicant. Not until all the papers have been graded will they be matched with names. If other tests, such as training and experience or oral interview ratings have been given, scores will be combined. Different parts of the examination usually have different weights. For example, the written test might count 60 percent of the final grade, and a rating of training and experience 40 percent. In many jurisdictions, veterans will have a certain number of points added to their grades.

After the final grade has been determined, the names are placed in grade order and an eligible list is established. There are various methods for resolving ties between those who get the same final grade – probably the most common is to place first the name of the person whose application was received first. Job offers are made from the eligible list in the order the names appear on it. You will be notified of your grade and your rank as soon as all these computations have been made. This will be done as rapidly as possible.

People who are found to meet the requirements in the announcement are called "eligibles." Their names are put on a list of eligible candidates. An eligible's chances of getting a job depend on how high he stands on this list and how fast agencies are filling jobs from the list.

When a job is to be filled from a list of eligibles, the agency asks for the names of people on the list of eligibles for that job. When the civil service commission receives this request, it sends to the agency the names of the three people highest on this list. Or, if the job to be filled has specialized requirements, the office sends the agency the names of the top three persons who meet these requirements from the general list.

The appointing officer makes a choice from among the three people whose names were sent to him. If the selected person accepts the appointment, the names of the others are put back on the list to be considered for future openings.

That is the rule in hiring from all kinds of eligible lists, whether they are for typist, carpenter, chemist, or something else. For every vacancy, the appointing officer has his choice of any one of the top three eligibles on the list. This explains why the person whose name is on top of the list sometimes does not get an appointment when some of the persons lower on the list do. If the appointing officer chooses the second or third eligible, the No. 1 eligible does not get a job at once, but stays on the list until he is appointed or the list is terminated.

X. HOW TO PASS THE INTERVIEW TEST

The examination for which you applied requires an oral interview test. You have already taken the written test and you are now being called for the interview test – the final part of the formal examination.

You may think that it is not possible to prepare for an interview test and that there are no procedures to follow during an interview. Our purpose is to point out some things you can do in advance that will help you and some good rules to follow and pitfalls to avoid while you are being interviewed.

What is an interview supposed to test?
The written examination is designed to test the technical knowledge and competence of the candidate; the oral is designed to evaluate intangible qualities, not readily measured otherwise, and to establish a list showing the relative fitness of each candidate – as measured against his competitors – for the position sought. Scoring is not on the basis of "right" and "wrong," but on a sliding scale of values ranging from "not passable" to "outstanding." As a matter of fact, it is possible to achieve a relatively low score without a single "incorrect" answer because of evident weakness in the qualities being measured.

Occasionally, an examination may consist entirely of an oral test – either an individual or a group oral. In such cases, information is sought concerning the technical knowledges and abilities of the candidate, since there has been no written examination for this purpose. More commonly, however, an oral test is used to supplement a written examination.

Who conducts interviews?

The composition of oral boards varies among different jurisdictions. In nearly all, a representative of the personnel department serves as chairman. One of the members of the board may be a representative of the department in which the candidate would work. In some cases, "outside experts" are used, and, frequently, a businessman or some other representative of the general public is asked to serve. Labor and management or other special groups may be represented. The aim is to secure the services of experts in the appropriate field.

However the board is composed, it is a good idea (and not at all improper or unethical) to ascertain in advance of the interview who the members are and what groups they represent. When you are introduced to them, you will have some idea of their backgrounds and interests, and at least you will not stutter and stammer over their names.

What should be done before the interview?

While knowledge about the board members is useful and takes some of the surprise element out of the interview, there is other preparation which is more substantive. It *is* possible to prepare for an oral interview – in several ways:

1) Keep a copy of your application and review it carefully before the interview

This may be the only document before the oral board, and the starting point of the interview. Know what education and experience you have listed there, and the sequence and dates of all of it. Sometimes the board will ask you to review the highlights of your experience for them; you should not have to hem and haw doing it.

2) Study the class specification and the examination announcement

Usually, the oral board has one or both of these to guide them. The qualities, characteristics or knowledges required by the position sought are stated in these documents. They offer valuable clues as to the nature of the oral interview. For example, if the job involves supervisory responsibilities, the announcement will usually indicate that knowledge of modern supervisory methods and the qualifications of the candidate as a supervisor will be tested. If so, you can expect such questions, frequently in the form of a hypothetical situation which you are expected to solve. NEVER go into an oral without knowledge of the duties and responsibilities of the job you seek.

3) Think through each qualification required

Try to visualize the kind of questions you would ask if you were a board member. How well could you answer them? Try especially to appraise your own knowledge and background in each area, *measured against the job sought*, and identify any areas in which you are weak. Be critical and realistic – do not flatter yourself.

4) Do some general reading in areas in which you feel you may be weak

For example, if the job involves supervision and your past experience has NOT, some general reading in supervisory methods and practices, particularly in the field of human relations, might be useful. Do NOT study agency procedures or detailed manuals. The oral board will be testing your understanding and capacity, not your memory.

5) Get a good night's sleep and watch your general health and mental attitude

You will want a clear head at the interview. Take care of a cold or any other minor ailment, and of course, no hangovers.

What should be done on the day of the interview?

Now comes the day of the interview itself. Give yourself plenty of time to get there. Plan to arrive somewhat ahead of the scheduled time, particularly if your appointment is in the fore part of the day. If a previous candidate fails to appear, the board might be ready for you a bit early. By early afternoon an oral board is almost invariably behind schedule if there are many candidates, and you may have to wait. Take along a book or magazine to read, or your application to review, but leave any extraneous material in the waiting room when you go in for your interview. In any event, relax and compose yourself.

The matter of dress is important. The board is forming impressions about you – from your experience, your manners, your attitude, and your appearance. Give your personal appearance careful attention. Dress your best, but not your flashiest. Choose conservative, appropriate clothing, and be sure it is immaculate. This is a business interview, and your appearance should indicate that you regard it as such. Besides, being well groomed and properly dressed will help boost your confidence.

Sooner or later, someone will call your name and escort you into the interview room. *This is it.* From here on you are on your own. It is too late for any more preparation. But remember, you asked for this opportunity to prove your fitness, and you are here because your request was granted.

What happens when you go in?

The usual sequence of events will be as follows: The clerk (who is often the board stenographer) will introduce you to the chairman of the oral board, who will introduce you to the other members of the board. Acknowledge the introductions before you sit down. Do not be surprised if you find a microphone facing you or a stenotypist sitting by. Oral interviews are usually recorded in the event of an appeal or other review.

Usually the chairman of the board will open the interview by reviewing the highlights of your education and work experience from your application – primarily for the benefit of the other members of the board, as well as to get the material into the record. Do not interrupt or comment unless there is an error or significant misinterpretation; if that is the case, do not hesitate. But do not quibble about insignificant matters. Also, he will usually ask you some question about your education, experience or your present job – partly to get you to start talking and to establish the interviewing "rapport." He may start the actual questioning, or turn it over to one of the other members. Frequently, each member undertakes the questioning on a particular area, one in which he is perhaps most competent, so you can expect each member to participate in the examination. Because time is limited, you may also expect some rather abrupt switches in the direction the questioning takes, so do not be upset by it. Normally, a board member will not pursue a single line of questioning unless he discovers a particular strength or weakness.

After each member has participated, the chairman will usually ask whether any member has any further questions, then will ask you if you have anything you wish to add. Unless you are expecting this question, it may floor you. Worse, it may start you off on an extended, extemporaneous speech. The board is not usually seeking more information. The question is principally to offer you a last opportunity to present further qualifications or to indicate that you have nothing to add. So, if you feel that a significant qualification or characteristic has been overlooked, it is proper to point it out in a sentence or so. Do not compliment the board on the thoroughness of their examination – they have been sketchy, and you know it. If you wish, merely say, "No thank you, I have nothing further to add." This is a point where you can "talk yourself out" of a good impression or fail to present an important bit of information. Remember, *you close the interview yourself.*

The chairman will then say, "That is all, Mr. _____, thank you." Do not be startled; the interview is over, and quicker than you think. Thank him, gather your belongings and take your leave. Save your sigh of relief for the other side of the door.

How to put your best foot forward

Throughout this entire process, you may feel that the board individually and collectively is trying to pierce your defenses, seek out your hidden weaknesses and embarrass and confuse you. Actually, this is not true. They are obliged to make an appraisal of your qualifications for the job you are seeking, and they want to see you in your best light. Remember, they must interview all candidates and a non-cooperative candidate may become a failure in spite of their best efforts to bring out his qualifications. Here are 15 suggestions that will help you:

1) Be natural – Keep your attitude confident, not cocky

If you are not confident that you can do the job, do not expect the board to be. Do not apologize for your weaknesses, try to bring out your strong points. The board is interested in a positive, not negative, presentation. Cockiness will antagonize any board member and make him wonder if you are covering up a weakness by a false show of strength.

2) Get comfortable, but don't lounge or sprawl

Sit erectly but not stiffly. A careless posture may lead the board to conclude that you are careless in other things, or at least that you are not impressed by the importance of the occasion. Either conclusion is natural, even if incorrect. Do not fuss with your clothing, a pencil or an ashtray. Your hands may occasionally be useful to emphasize a point; do not let them become a point of distraction.

3) Do not wisecrack or make small talk

This is a serious situation, and your attitude should show that you consider it as such. Further, the time of the board is limited – they do not want to waste it, and neither should you.

4) Do not exaggerate your experience or abilities

In the first place, from information in the application or other interviews and sources, the board may know more about you than you think. Secondly, you probably will not get away with it. An experienced board is rather adept at spotting such a situation, so do not take the chance.

5) If you know a board member, do not make a point of it, yet do not hide it

Certainly you are not fooling him, and probably not the other members of the board. Do not try to take advantage of your acquaintanceship – it will probably do you little good.

6) Do not dominate the interview

Let the board do that. They will give you the clues – do not assume that you have to do all the talking. Realize that the board has a number of questions to ask you, and do not try to take up all the interview time by showing off your extensive knowledge of the answer to the first one.

7) Be attentive

You only have 20 minutes or so, and you should keep your attention at its sharpest throughout. When a member is addressing a problem or question to you, give him your undivided attention. Address your reply principally to him, but do not exclude the other board members.

8) Do not interrupt

A board member may be stating a problem for you to analyze. He will ask you a question when the time comes. Let him state the problem, and wait for the question.

9) Make sure you understand the question

Do not try to answer until you are sure what the question is. If it is not clear, restate it in your own words or ask the board member to clarify it for you. However, do not haggle about minor elements.

10) Reply promptly but not hastily

A common entry on oral board rating sheets is "candidate responded readily," or "candidate hesitated in replies." Respond as promptly and quickly as you can, but do not jump to a hasty, ill-considered answer.

11) Do not be peremptory in your answers

A brief answer is proper – but do not fire your answer back. That is a losing game from your point of view. The board member can probably ask questions much faster than you can answer them.

12) Do not try to create the answer you think the board member wants

He is interested in what kind of mind you have and how it works – not in playing games. Furthermore, he can usually spot this practice and will actually grade you down on it.

13) Do not switch sides in your reply merely to agree with a board member

Frequently, a member will take a contrary position merely to draw you out and to see if you are willing and able to defend your point of view. Do not start a debate, yet do not surrender a good position. If a position is worth taking, it is worth defending.

14) Do not be afraid to admit an error in judgment if you are shown to be wrong

The board knows that you are forced to reply without any opportunity for careful consideration. Your answer may be demonstrably wrong. If so, admit it and get on with the interview.

15) Do not dwell at length on your present job

The opening question may relate to your present assignment. Answer the question but do not go into an extended discussion. You are being examined for a *new* job, not your present one. As a matter of fact, try to phrase ALL your answers in terms of the job for which you are being examined.

Basis of Rating

Probably you will forget most of these "do's" and "don'ts" when you walk into the oral interview room. Even remembering them all will not ensure you a passing grade. Perhaps you did not have the qualifications in the first place. But remembering them will help you to put your best foot forward, without treading on the toes of the board members.

Rumor and popular opinion to the contrary notwithstanding, an oral board wants you to make the best appearance possible. They know you are under pressure – but they also want to see how you respond to it as a guide to what your reaction would be under the pressures of the job you seek. They will be influenced by the degree of poise you display, the personal traits you show and the manner in which you respond.

ABOUT THIS BOOK

This book contains tests divided into Examination Sections. Go through each test, answering every question in the margin. At the end of each test look at the answer key and check your answers. On the ones you got wrong, look at the right answer choice and learn. Do not fill in the answers first. Do not memorize the questions and answers, but understand the answer and principles involved. On your test, the questions will likely be different from the samples. Questions are changed and new ones added. If you understand these past questions you should have success with any changes that arise. Tests may consist of several types of questions. We have additional books on each subject should more study be advisable or necessary for you. Finally, the more you study, the better prepared you will be. This book is intended to be the last thing you study before you walk into the examination room. Prior study of relevant texts is also recommended. NLC publishes some of these in our Fundamental Series. Knowledge and good sense are important factors in passing your exam. Good luck also helps. So now study this Passbook, absorb the material contained within and take that knowledge into the examination. Then do your best to pass that exam.

———

EXAMINATION SECTION

POLICE SCIENCE

EXAMINATION SECTION
TEST 1

DIRECTIONS: Each question or incomplete statement is followed by several suggested answers or completions. Select the one that BEST answers the question or completes the statement. *PRINT THE LETTER OF THE CORRECT ANSWER IN THE SPACE AT THE RIGHT.*

Questions 1-5.

DIRECTIONS: Make use of the following Police Department rule when answering questions 1 to 5: A description of persons or property wanted by the Police Department, which is to be given to the police force through the medium of a general alarm, if not distinctive, is of no value.

1. Mrs. R. Jones reported the theft of a valuable brooch from her apartment. The brooch was of gold and consisted of a very large emerald surrounded by 50 small diamonds. The one of the following additional pieces of information which would be MOST helpful to you in identifying the brooch is that

    A. the value of the brooch is $50,000
    B. there are 48 small diamonds and 2 slightly larger diamonds
    C. the emerald is carved in the form of a woman's head
    D. the brooch is made of gold with a slightly green cast
    E. the brooch is circular with the emerald in the center and the diamond around it

1.____

2. Assume that you have stopped a 1983 Dodge four-door sedan which you suspect is a car which had been reported as stolen the day before.
    The one of the following items of information which would be of GREATEST value in determining whether this is the stolen car is that the

    A. stolen car's license number was QA 2356; this car's license number is U 21375
    B. stolen car's engine number was AB 6231; this car's engine number is CS 2315
    C. windshield of the stolen car was not cracked; this car's windshield is cracked
    D. stolen car had no dents; this car has numerous dents
    E. stolen car had white walled tires; this car does not have white walled tires

2.____

3. Assume that you are questioning a woman who, you suspect, is wanted by the Department.
    Of the characteristics listed below, the one which would be of GREATEST value in determining whether this is the wanted person, is

    A. *age*: about 30; height: 5'8"; weight: 160 lbs.
    B. *eyes:* blue; hair: blonde; complexion: fair
    C. that she frequently drinks to excess
    D. *scars:* two thin, half-moon scars just on right cheek bone and below eye
    E. that when last seen she was wearing a dark, gray wool dress and was accompanied by the prize fighter, Mohammed Bali

3.____

1

4. You are watching a great number of people leave the stadium after a boxing match.   4.____
    Of the characteristics listed below, the one which would be of GREATEST value to you
    in spotting a man wanted by the Department is

    A. *height:* 5'3"; weight: 200 lbs
    B. *eyes:* brown; hair: black wavy; complexion: sallow
    C. that he frequents bars and grills and customarily associates with females
    D. *soars:* thin 1/2" scar on left upper lip; tattoos: on right forearm-"Pinto"
    E. *mustache:* when last seen August,1980, he wore a small black mustache

5. Assume that on a hot summer day you are stationed on the grass of the' south bank of a   5.____
    busy parkway looking at east-bound traffic for a light blue 1983 Ford two-door sedan.
    If traffic is very heavy, the one of the following additional pieces of information which
    would be MOST helpful to you in identifying the car is that

    A. all chrome is missing from the left side of the car
    B. there is a bullet hole in the left front window
    C. motor number is 22674 A H
    D. the front bumper is missing
    E. the paint on the right side of the car is somewhat faded

6. While you are on patrol, you notice that the lone occupant of a car parked at the top of a   6.____
    long, steep hill is a boy about 7 years old. The boy is playing with the steering wheel and
    other controls.
    The FIRST action for you to take is to

    A. make sure that the car is safely parked
    B. test the car's emergency brake to make sure it will hold
    C. drive the car to the bottom of the hill and park it there
    D. test the car's controls to make sure that the boy has not changed anything
    E. order the boy to leave the car for his own safety

7. The proprietor of a tavern summons a police officer and turns over to him a loaded   7.____
    revolver that was found in one of the tavern's booths.
    Of the following, the LEAST appropriate action for the patrolman to take is to

    A. close off the booth from use by other patrons
    B. determine exactly when the revolver was found
    C. obtain the names or descriptions of the persons who occupied the booth before the
        revolver was found
    D. question the proprietor very closely concerning the matter
    E. unload the gun and place it in an inside pocket

8. The traditional method of training a patrolman - equipping him and putting him on the   8.____
    street with an experienced man -- is no longer adequate.
    The one of the following which is the MOST probable reason for this change in view-
    point is that

    A. patrolmen are no longer simply guardians of the peace but each one is a specialist
    B. the kind of recruit that the Police Department gets has changed
    C. the former belief that "the best way to learn is to do" is no longer accepted
    D. there has been a great change in police problems and methods
    E. more money has been made available for training purposes

9. A police officer overhears a business man complain that his sales of tires had fallen off sharply because a new competitor has suddenly appeared in his territory and is underselling him at unbelievably low prices. The patrolman recalls that a large shipment of tires had been reported stolen a short time ago. It is ADVISABLE for the police officer to

    9.____

    A. forget the matter as it is probably a coincidence
    B. tell the businessman to report the new competitor to the Better Business Bureau for unfair practices
    C. check to see if there is any connection between the two sets of circumstances
    D. inform the businessman about the robbery and ask him if he thinks that there is a connection
    E. arrest the owner of the new store as he is obviously involved in the robbery

10. While patrolling his post late Saturday night, a police officer notices a well-dressed man break a car window with a rock, open a front door and enter. He is followed into the car by a woman companion.
Of the following, the MOST essential action for the police officer to take is to

    10.____

    A. point his gun at the man, enter the car, and order the man to drive to the station house to explain his action
    B. approach the car and ask the man why it was necessary to break the car window
    C. take down the license number of the car and note the description of both the man and the woman in the event that the car is later reported as stolen
    D. "bawl the man out" for endangering himself by breaking the window
    E. request proof of ownership of the car from the man

11. Juveniles who rob do not usually use the money they obtain in this manner for essentials but rather to indulge in spending to impress others.
This observation indicates that clues leading to the apprehension of juvenile delinquents may be found by noting

    11.____

    A. family requirements and needs
    B. the recreation habits of young people
    C. which young people have a tendency to commit robbery
    D. the relationships which exist in criminal gangs between criminals who commit crimes to satisfy essential needs and those who do not
    E. what objects are taken in robberies

12. A storekeeper complains to a patrolman that his store window has been broken by a gang of neighborhood hoodlums. The police officer tells the storekeeper to notify headquarters.
This action is

    12.____

    A. *desirable*; the storekeeper will be able to tell the proper official his story first hand
    B. *undesirable*; the problem is so minor, that there is no need to bother headquarters
    C. *desirable*; the storekeeper will be more confident if his case is handled by a sergeant or lieutenant
    D. *undesirable*; buck passing of this type makes for inefficiency and poor public relations
    E. *desirable*; investigation of the case would take the patrolman away from his post for too long a period

13. In order to reduce the amount of contradictory testimony, the witnesses to a crime should   13.____
be allowed to discuss, as a group, What had happened before they are questioned. The
procedure suggested is

   A. *bad*; a witness is less likely to commit himself if other witnesses to the event are
   present
   B. *good*; the need to sift stories will be considerably reduced
   C. *bad*; a witness is less likely to blurt out the truth if other witnesses are present to
   give him moral backing
   D. *good*; witnesses will be more apt to recall exactly what happened
   E. *bad*; the views of the strongest personalities may be obtained rather than the truth

14. A police officer positively recognizes a man on a busy street as one wanted for passing   14.____
worthless checks.
Of the following, the MOST appropriate action for the officer to take is to

   A. approach and then arrest the man
   B. follow the man until a place is reached where there are few people; then take out
   his gun and arrest the man
   C. immediately take out his gun, stop the man and search him
   D. follow the man until he stops long enough for the patrolman to summon aid from
   his precinct
   E. follow the man as he may lead the way to associates

15. It is generally agreed that criminal tendencies are present in every person.   15.____
A BASIC difference, however, between the normal person and the criminal is that the

   A. normal person, sometimes, commits trivial crimes but the criminal commits crimes
   of a major nature
   B. criminal is unable to understand the possible results of antisocial acts he commits
   C. normal person is able to control his antisocial tendencies and direct his activity in
   socially approved channels
   D. criminal believes that he is not different from the person who does not commit
   crimes
   E. normal person believes that he is not different from the person who commits
   crimes

16. It has been claimed that a person who commits a crime sometimes has an unconscious   16.____
wish to be punished, which is caused by strong unconscious feelings of guilt.
The one of the following actions by a criminal which may be partly due to an unconscious desire for punishment is

   A. claiming that he doesn't know anything about the crime when he is questioned by
   the police
   B. running away from the state where he committed the crime
   C. revisiting the place where he committed the crime
   D. his care not to leave any clues at the scene of the crime
   E. accusing someone else when he is captured by the police

17. Experience has shown that many crimes have been planned in prison. From this finding, it is REASONABLE to assume that

17.____

    A. the principal motive for the commission of first crimes is the wish to take revenge on society
    B. some criminals may be influenced to continue their careers of crime because they associate with other criminals
    C. the real motives for the commission of most crimes originate in punishment for criminal acts
    D. fear of imprisonment will make a criminal who has been in jail plan his second crime more carefully
    E. the criminal mind is sharpened by maturity

18. Any change in insurance coverage immediately prior to a fire should be considered. Strange as it may seem, most such changes made by convicted arsonists are made to a smaller amount.
The MOST probable reason for such changes is that the arsonist

18.____

    A. usually is not a rational person
    B. decided to set the fire after the change was made
    C. did not have enough money to pay for the full amount
    D. reduced the insurance to the amount he expected to be lost in the fire
    E. was trying to divert suspicion

19. Suppose that you are a police officer whose tour of duty extends from 12 midnight to 8:00 A.M. While on the first round of your tour, you notice that the night light in the front of a small candy store is out. In the past the proprietor has always left the light on. The door to the store is locked,
Of the following, the *most* appropriate action for you to take FIRST is to

19.____

    A. use your flashlight to light the store interior so that you may inspect it for unusual conditions
    B. continue on your beat, since the light probably burned out
    C. break open the door lock so that you may conduct a thorough search of the store
    D. call the storekeeper to notify him that the night light is out
    E. call your precinct and report this unusual condition

20. A criminal becomes either a thief, an assailant, or a sexual offender, never an all-around criminal. Of the following, an IMPORTANT reason for these basic differences in criminal behavior is probably that

20.____

    A. to be an all-around criminal requires more intelligence than the average criminal has
    B. crime syndicates have gained control over certain branches of crime and have made it difficult for a beginner to break in
    C. criminal acts are an expression of the criminal's whole personality
    D. all-around crime is not as profitable as specialization in crime
    E. most crimes are committed on the spur of the moment and without previous thought

21. A young man who was arrested for smashing a store window and stealing a portable   21.____
    radio was asked why he did it.
    He answered: "Well, I wanted a radio and I just took it." If this answer is characteristic
    of the behavior of the young criminal, it is MOST reasonable to believe that

    A. the young criminal has a well-organized personality
    B. he sizes up each new situation in terms of his past experiences
    C. his decision to commit a crime is made after careful consideration of its possible
       effect on his future
    D. his temptation to commit a crime is an isolated situation, having, in his mind, little
       relation to his life as a whole
    E. he hesitates to commit a crime unless he thinks he can get away with it

22. When the bodies of two women were found stabbed in an inner room of an apartment, it   22.____
    was first believed that it was a case of mutual homicide.
    Of the following clues found at the scene, the one which indicates that it was *more
    likely* a case of murder by a third party is the fact that

    A. the door to the apartment was found locked
    B. there were blood stains on the outer door of the apartment
    C. there was a switch-blade knife in each body
    D. no money could be found in the room where the bodies were
    E. both women were fully clothed

23. A radio crime program dramatizing a different police case every week, showed the cap-   23.____
    ture or death of the criminal and ended with the slogan "Crime Does Not Pay." It was
    found that a gang of teen-age boys listened to this program every week in order to see
    what mistake was made by the criminal, and then duplicated the crime, trying to avoid
    the same mistake.
    This case illustrates that

    A. all criminal minds work the same way
    B. attempts to keep young people out of crime by frightening them into obeying the
       law are not always successful
    C. it is not possible to commit the perfect crime unless care is taken
    D. radio crime programs should not be permitted as they lead to an increase in the
       number of unsolved crimes
    E. most criminals learn from their own mistakes

24. While on patrol at 2 A.M., you notice a man and a woman walking down the street talking   24.____
    together in low tones. They do not see you as you are standing in the shadow. The pair
    stop in front of a large apartment house. The man takes a bunch of keys from his pocket
    and tries several before he finds one which will open the door. While he is doing this, the
    woman taps her foot impatiently.
    At this point, as the two are entering the apartment house, you should

    A. notify precinct headquarters of the incident
    B. permit them to enter but follow close behind them to see what they do
    C. ignore the incident and continue on your patrol
    D. force them to show their identification papers
    E. arrest them on suspicion of illegal entry

25. The one of the following which is the PROBABLE reason for restricting parking to alternate sides of some streets on successive days is that, without this restriction, the parked cars make it difficult for the

    A. Police Department to direct traffic
    B. Department of Water Supply, Gas and Electricity to service hydrants
    C. Traffic Department to plan the flow of traffic
    D. Sanitation Department to clear the streets
    E. Fire Department to put out fires

25._____

KEY (CORRECT ANSWERS)

1.	C		11.	B
2.	B		12.	D
3.	D		13.	E
4.	A		14.	A
5.	D		15.	C
6.	A		16.	C
7.	E		17.	B
8.	D		18.	E
9.	C		19.	A
10.	E		20.	C

21.	D
22.	B
23.	B
24.	C
25.	D

TEST 2

DIRECTIONS: Each question or incomplete statement is followed by several suggested answers or completions. Select the one that BEST answers the question or completes the statement. *PRINT THE LETTER OF THE CORRECT ANSWER IN THE SPACE AT THE RIGHT.*

1. Suppose that, while you are on traffic duty at about 8:30 o'clock one morning, a large trailer truck breaks down on a narrow street running north and south. The truck completely blocks one side of the street, so that there is room only for southbound traffic to pass. At this hour of day, traffic going towards the south is very heavy, while traffic towards the north is light. Of the following, the BEST action for you to take is to

    A. detour all northbound traffic around the block in which the truck has broken down
    B. halt all southbound traffic until the truck can be repaired
    C. halt only northbound traffic so that emergency vehicles and fire trucks may operate freely
    D. halt traffic in both directions until the truck can be repaired
    E. alternate the flow of traffic around the truck for about five minutes in each direction

1.____

2. Suppose that a hit-and-run driver has struck and seriously injured a little girl. Witnesses are able to furnish only part of the license number of the automobile which struck the girl. It is, therefore, necessary to interrogate a number of drivers and to inspect their automobiles. The day after the accident, you inspect an automobile belonging to Mr. T. You observe several unusual features about Mr. T.'s automobile.
The one of the following which should suggest MOST strongly to you that Mr. T.'s car might have been involved in the accident is the fact that

    A. the mileage reading on the speedometer has evidently been set back recently
    B. the right front fender has evidently been freshly repainted
    C. there is a dark stain on the rear seat upholstery
    D. there are no tools in the trunk
    E. there are new tires on the rear wheels

2.____

3. While patrolling your post, you observe a civilian exhibiting a revolver to a large group of children. The revolver appears to be of German make.
Your action in this situation should be governed CHIEFLY by the consideration that

    A. the children may be juvenile delinquents
    B. a permit should be obtained to carry a revolver
    C. the group may be obstructing the sidewalk
    D. the revolver may be loaded
    E. the revolver may have been stolen

3.____

4. Suppose that, while you are on duty as a patrolman, a woman informs you that a man has been found murdered in a rooming house. You proceed to the scene of the crime and find a large number of other tenants crowded into the dead man's room. For you to clear these people out of the room would be *wise* CHIEFLY because

    A. one patrolman may sometimes be insufficient to handle a large group of people
    B. valuable evidence may be inadvertently destroyed by the people in the room
    C. some of the tenants may have important information concerning the crime
    D. confusion usually attracts a crowd
    E. no further proof concerning the cause of death is needed

4.____

5. At 10:30 P.M., Robert Thomas was held up in the hallway of his apartment house. The robber took a gold watch and $300 in cash. At 10:40 P.M., James Green was seen loitering outside a jewelry shop two blocks from the scene of the holdup. Green was taken into custody and $150 was found in his wallet. On the basis of the above facts, the MOST valid conclusion that can be drawn concerning Green's guilt or innocence is that   5.____

    A. Green may or may not have committed the crime
    B. Green was the man who held up Thomas
    C. Green could not possibly have perpetrated the holdup
    D. Green would certainly have been loitering at the jewelry store if he had robbed Thomas
    E. the time of the crime provides Green with an effective alibi

6. Mr. B. stated that, when he answered the doorbell, two masked men armed with revolvers forced their way into his apartment. Without speaking, they went directly to his bedroom and immediately tore open the mattress, where Mr. B. had secreted $4600 in cash and jewelry valued at $2000. The men then tied and gagged Mr. B. and departed with their loot. According to Mr. B., he had displayed his valuables the evening before at a small party and had mentioned the hiding place. The one of the following which indicates MOST strongly that the robbers had been informed of the existence of the valuables is that the robbers   6.____

    A. compelled Mr. B. to disclose the hiding place
    B. neglected to tie and gag their victim
    C. neglected to make a thorough search of the apartment
    D. were masked
    E. took only the jewelry

7. A gaily wrapped parcel attracted the attention of a tenant because it had lain unclaimed in the entry for several days and had not come through the mails. He examined it and heard a loud ticking sound, whereupon he gingerly unwrapped the package and found two flashlight batteries, an alarm clock, and a soup can containing a whitish powder, later found to be bicarbonate of soda.
As a police officer, you should realize that the tenant's behaviour was *unwise* CHIEFLY because   7.____

    A. the package would have been claimed if it were harmless
    B. bicarbonate of soda is harmless
    C. there is a severe penalty for tampering with the mails
    D. the package was evidently addressed to him
    E. he had no way of knowing that the contents were harmless

8. The receptionist told the police that a man had been sitting in her office, waiting for an interview. While he sat there, the receptionist opened and sorted the mail. One letter contained a five-dollar bill, which she laid aside on the desk. The man seized a desk lamp, struck the receptionist over the head, and fled with the money.
This incident BEST illustrates a crime   8.____

    A. committed with little previous planning by the criminal
    B. in which there was collusion between the criminal and the victim
    C. in which the choice of weapon furnishes a clue as to the identity of the criminal
    D. which required precise advance knowledge of the time schedule followed by the intended victim
    E. involving the use of fraudulent means

9. On December 28th, the Police Department announced its plans for handling pedestrian 9._____
and automobile traffic in the main area on New Year's Eve.
The formulation of such plans beforehand is *wise* CHIEFLY because

    A. hindsight is better than foresight
    B. few violations of the law occur spontaneously
    C. some police problems are created by publicity
    D. the main area is an important industrial area
    E. many police problems can be foreseen

10. Suppose that, as a leader of a boys' club, you have succeeded in establishing friendly 10._____
relations with teenage boys in your own neighborhood. There are rumors that marijuana cigarettes have been appearing in the neighborhood. You decide to attempt to discourage the youths from smoking marijuana cigarettes.
Of the following, the argument which is likely to be MOST effective is that

    A. marijuana, as a drug, is considerably less potent than opium or cocaine
    B. the individual who flagrantly violates social codes may sometimes be accepted as
       a leader by some groups
    C. marijuana cigarettes may be more expensive than ordinary cigarettes
    D. smoking even a few marijuana cigarettes may lead to drug addiction
    E. the sale of marijuana cigarettes is a crime and the vendor may be subject to pun-
       ishment

11. Storekeepers are advised to remove partitions which obstruct free view from the street 11._____
into all parts of the premises.
The MOST accurate of the following statements is that such advice is

    A. *sensible*; criminals contemplating a holdup would be unable to survey the premises
       beforehand
    B. *unwise*; the probability that a holdup could be perpetrated without interruption
       would be increased
    C. *sensible*; it would be more difficult for criminals to perpetrate a holdup unseen by
       passers-by
    D. *unwise*; a patrolman passing by could determine at a glance any unusual occur-
       rence in the store
    E. *sensible*; obstruction of the doorway would prevent rapid escape by the criminal
       after a holdup

12. While on patrol at night, a patrolman should investigate all suspicious circumstances that 12._____
may present themselves to him.
Of the following, the circumstances which you would consider LEAST suspicious
would be that

    A. several typewriters are being carried out of an un-lighted store at about 3:00 M.
    B. the lights in a one-family dwelling are still visible at about 2:00 A.M.
    C. a stranger on your post tries the door of a clothing store at about 3:00 A.M.
    D. a woman denies ownership of an expensive handbag which she has just dropped
       near you at about 2:00 A.M.
    E. at about 2:00 A.M., two youths, each about fifteen years of age, lift the hood of an
       expensive parked automobile

13. If you are appointed to the Police Department as a probationary police officer, you may   13.____
be assigned to accompany a regular patrolman on his tour of duty.
Of the following, the BEST reason for assigning probationary police officers to accompany regular officers is that

    A. usually the more remote the supervision the greater the responsibility
    B. increasing the number of men assigned to a task increases efficiency
    C. every probationary police officer probably has some experience in police work
    D. there are relatively few probationary police officers
    E. learning under active supervision is more effective than unguided learning

14. The police officer is constantly advised to exercise caution in the preservation of possible   14.____
clues at the scene of a crime.
Of the following, the CHIEF point for the officer to keep in mind concerning the nature of clues is that

    A. clues are most obvious when the criminal has taken the precaution to conceal them
    B. an object found at the point where the crime was actually committed can hardly be considered a clue
    C. the complete significance of clues is sometimes not immediately apparent
    D. a clue which points to the identity of the criminal should usually be viewed with suspicion
    E. the significance of a clue depends largely upon its transitory nature

15. Patrol of the parks is an important phase of police work in a large city because parks   15.____
afford an excellent opportunity for certain types of criminals to perpetrate their crimes.
Of the following, the BEST justification for this statement is that

    A. criminals utilize park facilities less frequently than other individuals
    B. vehicular traffic in parks is usually no heavier than street traffic
    C. most modern cities provide at least some recreational facilities for their citizens
    D. there are usually many isolated spots in parks
    E. some parks in the city are quite small

16. Casual observers ignore many details. The patrolman must develop the habit of con-   16.____
stantly noting minute details, although they may seem perfectly ordinary at the time.
Of the following, the BEST justification for this statement is that

    A. circumstances must frequently be recalled which did not seem unusual when they occurred
    B. unusual circumstances are so minute that little effort is necessary for accurate recall
    C. casual observers are the most accurate observers
    D. ordinary details are usually easiest to recall
    E. the trained observer must frequently ignore casual details

17. The experienced police officer knows that his mere appearance on a scene is usually   17.____
sufficient to halt a dispute or to quell a disturbance.
This statement implies MOST accurately that

    A. disturbances are difficult to quell
    B. disputes usually develop from disturbances
    C. a patrolman is not always easy to identify
    D. a patrolman has prestige in the community
    E. disputes are rarely halted by a police officer

18. Many good cases of detection have been attributed to careful study of evidences of the   18.____
means criminals used in traveling away from the scene of the crime.
The one of the following which BEST illustrates this statement is the

    A. examination of the markings on bullets found at the scene of the crime
    B. study of the fingerprints found on articles not taken by the criminals
    C. examination of the tracks left by the tires of an automobile at the scene of the crime
    D. matching of fragments of cloth found at the scene of the crime with samples of fabric
    E. analysis of the handwriting characteristics of any written notes found at the scene of the crime

19. In a recent address, a police commissioner said: Many juvenile offenses, which are con-   19.____
sidered delinquent or potentially delinquent, are but evidences of misdirected play.
This statement emphasizes CHIEFLY that the solution to many of youth's problems lies
in

    A. providing opportunities to youth for the constructive use of leisure time
    B. securing better evidence in cases of juvenile delinquency
    C. increasing the severity of punishment for juvenile offenses
    D. considering juvenile offenders as delinquent rather than potentially delinquent
    E. avoiding direction of play activities of juveniles by adults

20. In taking the ante-mortem statement of the dying victim in a homicide case, the police   20.____
officer is to ask the victim, "Have you any hope of recovery from the effects of the injury
you have received?"
This instruction is MOST likely based on the theory that the dying victim in a homicide
case

    A. is probably too upset mentally to make any coherent statement
    B. will probably be more anxious to tell the truth if convinced he is about to die
    C. will probably be more anxious to tell the truth if he is convinced the police officer is anxious to help him recover
    D. will probably be more anxious to tell the truth if convinced he will live to testify against his assailant
    E. is usually not very eager to help the police to solve the crime

21. Blackmail is an especially troublesome problem for the police.   21.____
Of the following, the BEST justification for this statement is that the

    A. victim of a blackmail plot usually hesitates to cooperate with the police for fear of publicity
    B. blackmailer is usually a hardened criminal who will not hesitate to murder his victim

C. facts constituting the subject matter of a blackmail are seldom known to the victim
D. victim of a blackmail plot is usually anxious to expose all details to the police
E. blackmailer is usually well acquainted with the most modern techniques of criminology

22. In some states, statutes forbid the payment of ransom to kidnappers.
Such statutes are

     22._____

A. actually in violation of the due process of law clause of the Federal Constitution
B. necessary to encourage kidnappers to return the kidnapped person unharmed
C. harmful because kidnapping is encouraged by such legislation
D. examples of laws which protect society although sometimes working hardships on individuals
E. useful in pointing out new ways of coping with problems of penology

23. Criminals are frequently known to commit extraordinary acts not associated with the purposes of the crime.
An *extraordinary* act of this type is BEST demonstrated when

     23._____

A. criminals leave a loft building just looted by them and rush into a waiting automobile
B. a criminal, after plundering the apartment of a wealthy banker, sits down in the apartment to smoke a cigar
C. a criminal who intends to forge the signature of a well-known author requests him to sign a copy of his most recent book
D. a counterfeiter attempts to pass a counterfeit five-dollar bill by paying for a meal in a crowded restaurant
E. a shoplifter enters a retail store and requests the proprietor, who is alone, to show some merchandise which the shoplifter knows is kept behind a partition at the rear of the store

24. You suspect that a house on your patrol post is being used for gambling purposes.
Of the following, the BEST reason for reporting your suspicions to your superior officer rather than investigating the matter yourself is that

     24._____

A. law-breakers frequently use innocent guises to mask their activities
B. suspicions sometimes require investigation before being reported to superior officers
C. specialized detection procedures are frequently needed to apprehend law-breakers
D. gambling frequently offers the young a ready avenue to further criminal activity
E. acquaintance with the people living on a patrol post frequently renders police work easier

25. The fact that thousands of servicemen are returning to this country with souvenir weap-   25.____
ons creates a problem for law enforcement agencies. Strict supervision of such weapons
must be exercised.
Of the following, the CHIEF argument for supervising souvenir weapons in the possession of veterans is that

    A. souvenir weapons ordinarily possess strong sentimental value
    B. the incidence of crime is related to the availability of weapons
    C. souvenir weapons are a form of private property
    D. most weapons are difficult to conceal
    E. souvenir weapons must be rendered unserviceable before they can be brought into
       the country

KEYS (CORRECT ANSWERS)

1.	A	11.	C
2.	B	12.	B
3.	D	13.	E
4.	B	14.	C
5.	A	15.	D
6.	C	16.	A
7.	E	17.	D
8.	A	18.	C
9.	E	19.	A
10.	D	20.	B

21.	A
22.	D
23.	B
24.	C
25.	B

TEST 3

1. Assume that you are a police officer. A woman has complained to you about a man's indecent exposure in front of a house. As you approach the house, the man begins to run.
   You *should*

   A. shoot to kill as the man may be a dangerous maniac
   B. fire a warning shot to try to halt the man
   C. summon other patrolmen in order to apprehend him
   D. question the woman regarding the man's identity

   1.____

2. You are patrolling a parkway in a radio car with another police officer. A maroon car coming from the opposite direction signals you to stop and the driver informs you that he was robbed by three men speeding ahead of him in a black sedan. Your radio car cannot cross the center abutment.
   You *should*

   A. request the driver to make a report to the nearest precinct as your car cannot cross over to the other side
   B. make a U turn in your radio car and give chase on the wrong side of the parkway
   C. fire warning shots in the air to summon other patrolmen
   D. flash borough headquarters over your radio system

   2.____

3. You are on patrol duty in a crowded part of the city. You hear the traffic patrolman fire four shots in the air and cry, "Get out of his way. He's got a gun." You see a man tearing along the street, dodging traffic.
   You *should*

   A. fire several shots in the air to alert other policemen
   B. give chase to the man and shoot, as it is possible that one of your shots may hit him
   C. wait for an opening in the crowds and then shoot at the man from one knee
   D. wade through the crowds and then shout at the man to stop

   3.____

4. Assume that you have been assigned to a traffic post at a busy intersection. A car bearing out-of-town license plates is about to turn into a one-way street going in the opposite direction. You blow your whistle and stop the car.
   You *should then*

   A. hand out a summons to the driver in order to make an example of him, since out-of-town drivers notoriously disregard our traffic regulations
   B. pay no attention to him and let him continue to the proper direction
   C. ask him to pull over to the curb and advise him to drive to the nearest precinct to get a copy of the latest city traffic regulations
   D. call his attention to the fact that he was violating a traffic regulation and permit him to continue in the proper direction

   4.____

5. A storekeeper has complained to you that every day at noon several peddlers congre-
gate outside his store in order to sell their merchandise.
You *should*

    A. inform him that such complaints must be made directly to the Police Commissioner
    B. inform him that peddlers have a right to earn their living, too
    C. make it your business to patrol that part of your post around noon
    D. pay no attention to him as this storekeeper is probably a crank inasmuch as
nobody else has complained

5.____

6. You notice that a man is limping hurriedly, leaving a trail of blood behind him. You question him and his explanation is that he was hurt accidentally while he was watching a
man clean a gun. You *should*

    A. let him go as you have no proof that his story is not true
    B. have him sent to the nearest city hospital under police escort so that he may be
questioned again after treatment
    C. ask him whether the man had a license for his gun
    D. ask him to lead you to the man who cleaned his gun so that you may question him
further about the accident

6.____

7. There have been a series of burglaries in a certain residential area consisting of one-
family houses. You have been assigned to select a house in this area in which detectives
can wait secretly for the attempt to burglarize that house so that the burglars can be
apprehended in the act.
Which of the following would be the BEST house to select for this purpose? The house

    A. that was recently burglarized and from which several thousand dollars worth of
clothing and personal property were taken
    B. whose owner reports that several times the telephone has rung but the person
making the call hung up as soon as the telephone was answered
    C. that is smaller and looks much less pretentious than other houses in the same area
    D. that is occupied by a widower who works long hours but who lives with an invalid
mother requiring constant nursing service

7.____

8. The two detectives noticed the man climb a ladder to the roof of a loft building. The
detectives followed the same route. They saw him break a skylight and lower himself into
the building. Through the broken skylight, one of the detectives covered the man with his
gun and told him to throw up his hands.
The action of the detectives in this situation was *faulty* CHIEFLY because

    A. one of the detectives should have remained on the ladder
    B. criminals should be caught red-handed
    C. the detectives should have made sure of the identity of the man before following
him
    D. the possibility of another means of escape from the building should have been
foreseen

8.____

9. Suppose that, while you are patrolling your post, a middle-aged woman informs you that three men are holding up a nearby express office. You rush immediately to the scene of the holdup. While you are still about 75 feet away, you see the three men, revolvers in their hands, emerge from the office and make for what is apparently their getaway car, which is pointed in the opposite direction.
    Of the following, your FIRST consideration in this situation should be to

    A. enter the express office in order to find out what the men have taken
    B. maneuver quickly so as to get the getaway car between you and the express office
    C. make a mental note of the descriptions of the escaping men for immediate alarm
    D. attempt to overtake the car in which the holdup men seek to escape

10. Which of the following situations, if observed by you while on patrol, should you consider MOST suspicious and deserving of further investigation?

    A. A shabbily dressed youth is driving a 1995 Buick
    B. A 1993 Plymouth has been parked without lights outside an apartment house for several hours
    C. A light is on in the rear of a one-family, luxurious residence
    D. Two well-dressed men are standing at a bus stop at 2 A.M. and arguing heatedly

---

KEY (CORRECT ANSWERS)

1.	C
2.	D
3.	D
4.	D
5.	C
6.	B
7.	B
8.	D
9.	C
10.	D

POLICE SCIENCE

EXAMINATION SECTION
TEST 1

DIRECTIONS: Each question or incomplete statement is followed by several suggested answers or completions. Select the one that *BEST* answers the question or completes the statement. *PRINT THE LETTER OF THE CORRECT ANSWER IN THE SPACE AT THE RIGHT.*

1. Of the following, the *MOST ESSENTIAL* function *common* to the four jobs of Police Officer, Transit Patrolman, Correction Officer, and Bridge and Tunnel Officer is: 1._____

    A. Observation of dangerous conditions
    B. Prevention of accidents
    C. Protection of the public
    D. Handling of criminals

2. Assume that a person you have taken into custody has broken away from you and is attempting to escape.   2._____
    Of the following, the *CHIEF* precaution for you to observe before firing your revolver at the escaping prisoner is to make certain that

    A. the person attempting to escape was taken into custody lawfully
    B. the person attempting to escape is actually guilty of a serious crime
    C. there are no bystanders in the line of fire
    D. there are no accomplices in the vicinity

3. Assume that, while you are off duty, you see a man holding a revolver run out of a retail store, leap into an automobile, and drive quickly away. You make a mental note of important information to transmit to headquarters.   3._____
    Of the following, the information which will *probably* be of *LEAST* value in apprehending the criminal is the

    A. color of the automobile
    B. direction which the automobile took
    C. license number of the automobile
    D. type and make of the automobile

4. As a newly appointed member of the uniformed force, you may be changed from one type of assignment to another every few weeks.   4._____
    The *CHIEF* justification for such regular rotation of assignment is, in general, to

    A. discourage future requests for transfer from one type of assignment to another
    B. develop traits of initiative and independence
    C. encourage greater specialization of interest in a limited area
    D. provide a better understanding of the functioning of the organization as a whole

5. Of the following, the *LEAST* important rule for you to keep in mind concerning the handling and care of a revolver is to   5._____

    A. point the revolver at somebody only if you actually intend to use it
    B. check the revolver frequently to make certain that it is clean and well oiled
    C. store the revolver, when you are not on duty, in an inaccessible place where children cannot possibly reach it
    D. examine the revolver each time before you use it to make certain that it is loaded

6. An officer in a position of authority may often find that a warning will be more effective than punishment.
Of the following, the *BEST* justification for this statement is that   6._____

    A. most punishment is intended to create fear
    B. warnings are usually ineffective
    C. the sharper the punishment, the better the lesson learned
    D. many violations are committed without intent

7. Suppose that, while you are on duty alone, it becomes necessary for you to search two men who have been acting suspiciously.
Of the following, the *MOST* important point for you to keep in mind is that   7._____

    A. both men should be kept constantly under observation while you search each man in turn
    B. the smaller and weaker appearing man should be searched first and as a precautionary measure
    C. dangerous weapons are easily detected even without careful search
    D. each man should be questioned at length before he is searched

8. In any uniformed service, strict discipline is essential. Of the following, the *BEST* justification for requiring that subordinates follow the orders of superior officers without delay is that   8._____

    A. not all orders can be carried out quickly
    B. it is more important that an order be obeyed accurately than promptly
    C. prompt obedience makes for efficient action in emergencies
    D. some superior officers are too strict

9. Suppose that, in the course of your duties, you are called to the scene of a disturbance in which some seven or eight men are involved.
Of the following, the action *most likely* to end the disturbance quickly and effectively is for you to   9._____

    A. divide the disorderly group immediately into three approximately equal sections
    B. take the nearest person promptly into custody and remove him from the scene
    C. announce your authority and call for order in a firm and decisive manner
    D. question a bystander in detail about the reasons for the disorder

10. The police officer who fails to understand completely an order issued by his superior should ask to have the order explained *CHIEFLY* because   10._____

    A. his superior may not be aware of all the facts involved
    B. acting on an erroneous impression may lead to serious mistakes
    C. police officers are expected to be able to exercise initiative
    D. asking questions frequently is a sign of application to duty

11. Of the following, the *CHIEF* justification for requiring newly-appointed officers to attend a training course before they are assigned to regular duty is that

    A. training in a military type of organization can be obtained only by actual performance of duties
    B. even the most intelligent newly-appointed officer is likely to be ignorant of specific departmental procedures
    C. competence on the job will almost certainly increase with years of service
    D. persons who have passed a competitive examination can reasonably be expected to have a good knowledge of the job

11.____

12. Police officers are expected to be observant.
Of the following, the *MOST* accurate statement concerning proper methods of observation is that

    A. observation which is casual tends to be highly accurate
    B. the object observed last tends to be forgotten first
    C. the more things observed at a time, the longer they will be remembered
    D. observation is most effective when it is approached purposefully

12.____

13. Of the following, the *MOST* accurate statement concerning punishment of law violators, according to modern penology, is that

    A. certainty of punishment is a greater deterrent to crime than severity of punishment
    B. the more severe the penalty, the less likely the occurrence of crime
    C. the more youthful the offender, the greater the value of harsh punishment
    D. punishment should be adapted to the nature of the crime rather than the criminal

13.____

14. There is evidence that some men commit violations of the law after they have been paroled.
Of the following, the *BEST* justifications for parole, in view of the above statement , is that

    A. parole violators constitute a majority of all criminals
    B. relatively few men are granted parole
    C. parole violators are only a fraction of all parolees
    D. parole is granted only to the most deserving persons

14.____

15. A member of the uniformed force shall properly mark all articles of value that come into his possession in connection with a case.
Of the following, the *BEST* justification for this regulation is that

    A. the article may be lost
    B. the articles coming into the possession of an officer in connection with a case are not private property
    C. unless the mark made is a simple one the officer may not recognize his own mark
    D. it may be necessary for the officer to identify the evidence in court

15.____

16. Officers are required to submit written reports of all unusual occurrences.
Of the following, the *BEST* justification for making written notes as soon as possible after the unusual occurrence is that

16.____

A. the experienced officer has had long experience with and can easily handle all types of unusual occurrences
B. reports written after a long delay tend to be excessively long
C. proper perspective of an incident increases with the passage of time
D. memory of specific events is more accurate when the event is fresh in mind

17. Suppose that you are required to write a report of an accident which occurred while you were on duty.
Of the following, the LEAST valuable principle for you to observe in preparing the report is to

A. present the facts exactly in the order in which you recall them
B. include in the report a statement of what you thought was the cause of the accident
C. describe clearly and exactly what action you took
D. include in the report all the facts which you believe to be pertinent

17.____

18. A newly appointed officer may LEAST reasonably expect his immediate supervising officer to

A. help him avoid errors
B. give him specific instructions
C. check on the progress he is making
D. make all necessary decisions for him

18.____

19. A thorough knowledge of his printed departmental regulations will help a police officer to know

A. how to tell whether a man is a forger
B. when it is proper to make an arrest
C. how to take care of his uniform
D. when to expect vandalism on his post

19.____

20. If a police officer is called upon to eject a disorderly person from a railroad station, his MOST important consideration must necessarily be to

A. avoid damaging railroad system property
B. earn good public opinion
C. avoid endangering other passengers
D. get the person off the property

20.____

21. If a police officer has to telephone for an ambulance for an injured person, the MOST important information he must transmit is

A. how the accident occurred
B. whether the injured person is male or female
C. what the injured person complains of
D. where the ambulance is needed

21.____

22. When reporting a robbery to headquarters over a police system telephone, a police officer should make the report as brief as possible to avoid

A. long entries in the record book
B. confusing the listener
C. errors in fact
D. tying up the line

22.____

22

23. If a police officer sees a passenger fall on a station platform, his first action should be to   23.____

    A. maintain order
    B. determine the cause of the accident
    C. call for an ambulance
    D. render practical assistance

24. Because a police officer wears a police uniform, people are likely to recognize his author-   24.____
    ity when he gives orders.
    A police officer should, therefore, avoid

    A. calling for assistance in controlling a crowd
    B. using force when a person resists arrest
    C. wearing a raincoat over his uniform
    D. ordering people around unnecessarily

25. When a police officer arrives at his assigned post, his *first* move must *CLEARLY* be to   25.____

    A. see whether other police officers in the area are performing their duties
    B. unlimber his gun
    C. inspect the post
    D. check with the men on the adjoining posts

KEY (CORRECT ANSWER)

1.	C		11.	B
2.	C		12.	D
3.	B		13.	A
4.	D		14.	C
5.	D		15.	D
6.	D		16.	D
7.	A		17.	A
8.	C		18.	D
9.	C		19.	B
10.	B		20.	C

21.	D
22.	D
23.	D
24.	D
25.	C

TEST 2

Each question or incomplete statement is followed by several suggested answers or completions. Select the one that *BEST* answers the question or completes the statement. *PRINT THE LETTER OF THE CORRECT ANSWER IN THE SPACE AT THE RIGHT.*

1. Police officers are constantly urged to consider every revolver loaded until proven other-wise.
   Of the following, the *BEST* justification for this recommendation is that

   A. no time is lost when use of the revolver is required
   B. police revolvers have safety devices
   C. less danger is involved when facing armed thugs
   D. ammunition deteriorates unless replaced periodically
   E. there are many accidents involving apparently empty revolvers

   1._____

2. A dog bites a woman on a railroad station and runs onto the tracks. The woman insists on leaving after you take her name and address.
   Your *subsequent* action in this situation should be governed by the consideration that

   A. the dog must have escaped from a nearby house
   B. there may have been provocation for the dog's attack
   C. the dog should be caught and examined by health authorities
   D. the woman evidently does not wish to prosecute
   E. the dog apparently belongs to the woman, who is attempting to conceal the fact

   2._____

3. As a rule, a police officer is not permitted to engage in any other business or calling.
   Of the following, the *most probable* reason for this prohibition is that

   A. most citizens object to a civil servant holding a second job
   B. such other activity may affect the manner in which he performs his regular duties
   C. the uniformed officer would be unable to devote adequate time to such other busi-ness
   D. a uniformed officer may be called on at any time to perform special police work
   E. the whereabouts of a uniformed officer must be known at all times

   3._____

4. Law enforcement has undergone an important change in recent times.
   Of the following, the *MOST* accurate statement of this change is that there has been

   A. increased use of scientific means of crime detection
   B. greater application of principles of military discipline
   C. decentralization of authority and greater reliance on local knowledge
   D. more careful training of men before recruitment into law enforcement work
   E. considerably less emphasis on breaking law enforcement into specialized fields

   4._____

5. The officer, with revolver drawn, ordered the criminals to lie face down on the ground after having taken a lead pipe from one and an unloaded automatic from another. Then he sent a bystander to summon help.
   The action of this officer in having the men lie down is *BEST* described as

   A. *foolish;* the men had already been disarmed
   B. *sensible;* valuable evidence was then preserved

   5._____

C. *foolish;* valuable evidence was thus destroyed
D. *foolish;* additional help was obviously unnecessary
E. *sensible;* the men might otherwise have broken away or attacked the officer

6. You become suspicious of a man carrying a valise and you believe it necessary to search the valise.
   Of the following, the *BEST* reason for you to ask the suspect to place the valise on the ground and have him take out the contents, rather than for you to open the valise yourself, is that

   A. the valise is obviously too heavy to hold up
   B. the suspect may have noticed that you were suspicious of him
   C. you probably have no legal right to search the valise
   D. the suspect may strike you as you bend over the valise
   E. the contents of the valise may well be loot from a burglary

   6.____

7. The police officer must go out on duty alone regardless of how well he has been trained and instructed.
   Of the following, the *CHIEF* implication of the above statement is that

   A. every uniformed officer should realize that the full weight of law enforcement does not rest on his shoulders alone
   B. the competent uniformed officer seeks the advice of his superiors before reaching an important decision
   C. training cannot be expected to supplant cooperation
   D. the competent uniformed officer must have a high degree of self-reliance
   E. behind every uniformed officer is a well-trained force, poised for action

   7.____

8. If some criminals are arrested, and some persons arrested are innocent, it follows *MOST* logically that

   A. a criminal is a person who is arrested
   B. if a person is not arrested, he is not a criminal
   C. no innocent persons are arrested
   D. at least some criminals are innocent
   E. not all persons arrested are criminals

   8.____

9. There are two important elements which are usually present in order to constitute a crime. They are, first, the criminal act or omission, and, second, the mental element or criminal intent.
   Of the following, the *most* accurate statement *SOLELY* on the basis of the above is:

   A. Mental element enters into a crime only when there has been an overt act
   B. Criminal intent determines whether a crime has been committed, but not the degree of the crime
   C. Either an act or failure to act may constitute a crime
   D. A crime is constituted when there is a criminal intent
   E. Mental element refers to a criminal act, whereas criminal intent refers to an omission

   9.____

10. Most departments insist that a written notation be made immediately of each telephone message received by an officer on desk duty.
Of the following, the *BEST* justification for following this procedure is that a written message

    A. is less likely to be overlooked or forgotten
    B. can more easily be filed
    C. bears greater authority
    D. is less likely to include all the pertinent information
    E. is often incomplete

10.____

11. Suppose that you receive from your supervisor directions that you do not altogether understand.
Of the following, the *BEST* action for you to take is to

    A. request a more experienced employee to assist you in your work
    B. go ahead and do the best you can
    C. do nothing until your supervisor speaks to you again about the matter
    D. ask your supervisor to repeat those instructions which are not clear
    E. follow out only those directions which you understand completely

11.____

12. Members of semi-military organizations are required to wear uniforms in the performance of their duties.
Of the following, the *LEAST* valid justification for this practice is that uniforms

    A. enable members of the force to be recognized easily,
    B. give members of the force an appearance of authority
    C. are supplied to members of the force free of charge
    D. tend to develop high morale among members of the force
    E. aid in developing a sense of discipline and duty

12.____

13. If you are appointed to the uniformed force before Brown, and Brown was appointed after Smith, then the *MOST* accurate of the following statements is that

    A. you were appointed before Smith
    B. Smith was appointed before Brown
    C. Brown was appointed before you
    D. Smith was appointed before you
    E. Brown was appointed before Smith

13.____

14. An "arsonist" is a person who

    A. studies methods of fire prevention
    B. investigates the causes of fire
    C. is guilty of larceny connected with fires
    D. underwrites fire damage
    E. maliciously sets a fire

14.____

15. A member of the force assigned to investigate a complaint should visit the complainant and obtain a direct account of the condition complained of *MAINLY* because

    A. this gives the police officer more time to plan his procedure
    B. most complaints are fictitious

15.____

C. important details may have been omitted in the original complaint
D. a complainant will sometimes withdraw his complaint when faced by the investigator

16. Inspections of critical points on a post are purposely made at irregular intervals to   16._____

A. permit leaving the post when arrests are necessary
B. make it difficult for wrongdoers to time police officers
C. allow for delays due to unusual occurrences at other points
D. simplify the scheduling of lunch reliefs and rest periods

17. A police officer is required to report to headquarters hourly by telephone, and then wait   17._____
one minute at the location from which he telephoned.
The *logical* reason for this wait is to give

A. the police officer time for relief if required
B. headquarters time to call back to the police officer if necessary
C. the police officer time to jot down any instructions received
D. the police officer a chance to think of any errors or omissions

18. Investigating the area from which you heard a shot, you find a man sitting on the steps   18._____
and holding one hand to a bloody spot on his arm.
It would be *LEAST* important for you to

A. try to find the bullet
B. examine the wound
C. ask the man whether he knows who shot at him
D. take the names and addresses of any witnesses

19. If the man in the previous question were bleeding heavily, you should *FIRST*   19._____

A. administer a stimulant   B. apply an antiseptic
C. apply a tourniquet   D. treat him for shock

20. A woman excitedly tells a police officer that a man seized her arm as she was getting off   20._____
the local train which just left the station, but that she broke away and the man remained
on the train.
The *BEST* action for the police officer is to

A. commandeer a taxicab and make check-ups at the next few stations
B. board the next express to overtake the man
C. sympathize with the woman, but tell her it is too late to do anything
D. telephone the information to his headquarters immediately

21. Official inspection of police officers' winter uniforms is made at the end of the winter sea-   21._____
son rather than at the beginning.
The *most likely* reason for this practice is that

A. it gives patrolmen ample time to make necessary repairs and replacements
B. weather conditions are not so changeable in the spring
C. moth damage is more easily detected at this time of year
D. clothing prices are lowest at the end of a season

22. A police officer in uniform is prohibited from carrying any package or bundle unless it is needed in the performance of his duty.
The *LEAST* probable reason for this prohibition is that

    A. it might interfere with his freedom of action
    B. it would look as if he accepted favors
    C. a trim appearance while in uniform is important
    D. the article may damage or soil the uniform

22.____

23. Police officers must wear their uniforms securely buttoned at all times because

    A. the streets are drafty
    B. a neat appearance commands respect
    C. the uniforms will last longer
    D. loose clothing is likely to catch on trains

23.____

24. The marks left on a bullet by a gun barrel are different from those left by any other gun barrel.
This fact is *MOST* useful in directly identifying the

    A. direction from which a shot was fired
    B. person who fired a particular gun
    C. gun from which a bullet was fired
    D. bullet which caused a fatal wound

24.____

25. A police officer sent to arrest a minor would expect to take into custody a

    A. member of a minority race
    B. person who is less than voting age
    C. man who works underground with a pick
    D. child who has a low I.Q.

25.____

———————

KEY (CORRECT ANSWER)

1.	E		11.	D
2.	C		12.	C
3.	B		13.	B
4.	A		14.	E
5.	E		15.	C
6.	D		16.	B
7.	D		17.	B
8.	E		18.	A
9.	C		19.	C
10.	A		20.	D

21.	A
22.	B
23.	B
24.	C
25.	B

EXAMINATION SECTION
TEST 1

DIRECTIONS: Each question or incomplete statement is followed by several suggested answers or completions. Select the one that BEST answers the question or completes the statement. *PRINT THE LETTER OF THE CORRECT ANSWER IN THE SPACE AT THE RIGHT.*

1. Upon arriving at the scene of an accident in which a pedestrian was struck and killed by an automobile, an officer's FIRST action was to clear the scene of spectators.
   Of the following, the PRINCIPAL reason for this action is that   1._____

   A. important evidence may be inadvertently destroyed by the crowd
   B. this is a fundamental procedure in first aid work
   C. the operator of the vehicle may escape in the crowd
   D. witnesses will speak more freely if other persons are not present

2. In questioning witnesses, an officer is instructed to avoid leading questions or questions that will suggest the answer. Accordingly, when questioning a witness about the appearance of a suspect, it would be BEST for him to ask: 2._____

   A. What kind of hat did he wear?
   B. Did he wear a felt hat?
   C. What did he wear?
   D. Didn't he wear a hat?

3. The only personal description the police have of a particular criminal was made several years ago. Of the following, the item in the description that will be MOST useful in identifying him at the present time is the   3._____

   A. color of his eyes   B. color of his hair
   C. number of teeth   D. weight

4. Crime statistics indicate that property crimes such as larceny, burglary and robbery, are more numerous during winter months than in summer.
   The one of the following explanations that MOST adequately accounts for this situation is that   4._____

   A. human needs, such as clothing, food, heat and shelter, are greater in winter
   B. criminal tendencies are aggravated by climatic changes
   C. there are more hours of darkness in winter and such crimes are usually committed under cover of darkness
   D. urban areas are more densely populated during winter months, affording greater opportunity for such crimes

5. When automobile tire tracks are to be used as evidence, a plaster cast is made of them. Before the cast is made, however, a photograph of the tracks is taken.
   Of the following, the MOST probable reason for taking a photograph is that   5._____

   A. photographs can be duplicated more easily than castings
   B. less skill is required for photographing than casting
   C. the tracks may be damaged in the casting process
   D. photographs are more easily transported than castings

6. It is generally recommended that an officer, in lifting a revolver that is to be sent to the police laboratory for ballistics tests and fingerprint examination, do so by insetting a pencil through the trigger guard rather than into the barrel of the weapon.
The reason for preferring this procedure is that

    A. every precaution must be taken not to eliminate fingerprints on the weapon
    B. there is a danger of accidentally discharging the weapon by placing the pencil in the barrel
    C. the pencil may make scratches inside the barrel that will interfere with the ballistics tests
    D. a weapon can more easily be lifted by the trigger guard

6.____

7. PHYSICIAN is to PATIENT as ATTORNEY is to

    A. court   B. client
    C. counsel   D. judge

7.____

8. JUDGE is to SENTENCE as JURY is to

    A. court   B. foreman
    C. defendant   D. verdict

8.____

9. REVERSAL is to AFFIRMANCE as CONVICTION is to

    A. appeal   B. acquittal
    C. error   D. mistrial

9.____

10. GENUINE is to TRUE as SPURIOUS is to

    A. correct   B. conceived
    C. false   D. speculative

10.____

11. ALLEGIANCE is to LOYALTY as TREASON IS TO

    A. felony   B. faithful
    C. obedience   D. rebellion

11.____

12. CONCUR is to AGREE as DIFFER is to

    A. coincide   B. dispute
    C. join   D. repeal

12.____

13. A person who has an uncontrollable desire to steal without need is called a

    A. dipsomaniac   B. kleptomaniac
    C. monomaniac   D. pyromaniac

13.____

14. In the sentence, "The placing of any inflammable substance in any building or the placing of any device or contrivence capable of producing fire, for the purpose of causing a fire is an attempt to burn," the MISSPELLED word is

    A. inflammable   B. substance
    C. device   D. contrivence

14.____

15. In the sentence, "The word 'break' also means obtaining an entrance into a building by   15.____
any artifice used for that purpose, or by colussion with any person therein," the MIS-
SPELLED word is

    A. obtaining   B. entrance
    C. artifice   D. colussion

16. In the sentence, "Any person who with intent to provoke a breech of the peace causes a   16.____
disturbance or is offensive to others may be deemed to have committed disorderly conduct," the MISSPELLED word is

    A. breech   B. disturbance
    C. offensive   D. committed

17. In the sentence, "When the offender inflicts a grevious harm upon the person from whose   17.____
possession, or in whose presence, property is taken, he is guilty of robbery," the MIS-
SPELLED word is

    A. offender   B. grevious
    C. possession   D. presence

18. In the sentence, "A person who willfully encourages or advises another person in   18.____
attempting to take the latter's life is guilty of a felony," the MISSPELLED word is

    A. willfully   B. encourages
    C. advises   D. attempting

19. The treatment to be given the offender cannot alter the fact of his offense; but we can   19.____
take measures to reduce the chances of similar acts in the future. We should banish the
criminal, not in order to exact revenge nor directly to encourage reform, but to deter him
and others from further illegal attacks on society.
According to this paragraph, the PRINCIPAL reason for punishing criminals is to

    A. prevent the commission of future crimes
    B. remove them safely from society
    C. avenge society
    D. teach them that crime does not pay

20. Even the most comprehensive and best substantiated summaries of the total volume of   20.____
criminal acts would not contribute greatly to an understanding of the varied social and
biological factors which are sometimes assumed to enter into crime causation, nor would
they indicate with any degree of precision the needs of police forces in combating crime.
According to this statement,

    A. crime statistics alone do not determine the needs of police forces in combating
       crime
    B. crime statistics are essential to a proper understanding of the social factors of
       crime
    C. social and biological factors which enter the crime causation have little bearing on
       police needs
    D. a knowledge of the social and biological factors of crime is essential to a proper
       understanding of crime statistics

21. The policeman's art consists in applying and enforcing a multitude of laws and ordinances in such degree or proportion and in such manner that the greatest degree of
social protection will be secured. The degree of enforcement and the method of application will vary with each neighborhood and community.
According to the foregoing paragraph,

    A. each neighborhood or community must judge for itself to what extent the law is to
be enforced
    B. a policeman should only enforce those laws which are designed to give the great-
est degree of social protection
    C. the manner and intensity of law enforcement is not necessarily the same in all
communities
    D. all laws and ordinances must be enforced in a community with the same degree of
intensity

21._____

22. Police control in the sense of regulating the details of police operations involves such
matters as the technical means for so organizing the available personnel that competent
police leadership, when secured, can operate effectively. It is concerned not so much
with the extent to which popular controls can be trusted to guide and direct the course of
police protection as with the administrative relationships which should exist between the
component parts of the police organism.
According to the foregoing statement, police control is

    A. solely a matter of proper personnel assignment
    B. the means employed to guide and direct the course of police protection
    C. principally concerned with the administrative relationships between units of a
police organization
    D. the sum total of means employed in rendering police protection

22.___ _

23. Two patrol cars hurry to the scene of an accident from different directions. The first proceeds at the rate of 45 miles per hour and arrives in four minutes. Although the second
car travels over a route which is three-fourths of a mile longer, it arrives at the scene only
a half minute later. The speed of the second car, expressed in miles per hour, is

    A. 50   B. 55   C. 60   D. 65

23._____

24. A motorcycle policeman issued 72 traffic summonses in January, 60 in February and 83
in March. In order to average 75 summonses per month for the four months of January,
February, March and April, during April he will have to issue _____ summonses.

    A. 80   B. 85   C. 90   D. 95

24._____

25. In a unit of the Police Department to which 40 patrolmen are assigned, the sick report
record during 1983 was as follows:

1 was absent 8 days   5 were absent 3 days each
4 were absent 5 days each   10 were absent 2 days each
8 were absent 4 days each   5 were absent 1 day each

The *average* number of days on sick report for all the members of this unit is *most
nearly*

    A. 1/2   B. 1   C. 2 1/2   D. 3

25._____

QUESTIONS 26-30.

Column I lists various statements of fact. Column II is a list of crimes. Next to the numbers corresponding to the number preceding the statements of fact in Column I, place the letter preceding the crime listed in Column II with which Jones should be charged. In answering these questions, the following definitions of crimes should be applied, bearing mind that ALL elements contained in the definitions must be present in order to charge a person with that crime.

BURGLARY is breaking and entering a building with intent to commit some crime therein.

EMBEZZLEMENT is the appropriation to one's own use of another's property which has been entrusted to one's care or which has come lawfully into one's possession.

EXTORTION is taking or obtaining property from another with his consent. induced by a wrongful use of force or fear.

LARCENY is taking and carrying away the personal property of another with intent to deprive or defraud the true owner of the use and benefit of such property.

ROBBERY is the unlawful taking of the personal propety of another from his person or in his presence by force or violence, or fear of injury.

Column I	Column II	
26. Jones, believing Smith had induced his wife to leave him, went to Smith's home armed with a knife with which he intended to assault Smith. When his knock was unanswered, he forced open the door of Smith's home and entered but, finding the house empty, he threw away the knife and left.	A. burglary B. embezzlement C. extortion D. larceny E. robbery F. no crime	26._____
27. Jones was employed as a collection agent by Smith. When Smith refused to reimburse him for certain expenses he claimed to have incurred in connection with his work, Jones deducted this amount from sums he had collected for Smith.		27._____
28. Jones spent the night in a hotel. During the night he left his room, went downstairs to the desk, stole money and returned to his room.		28._____
29. Jones, a building inspector, found that the elevators in Smith's building were being operated without a permit. He threatened to report the matter and have the elevators shut down unless Smith paid him a sum of money. Smith paid the amount demanded.		29._____
30. Jones held-up Smith on the street and, pointing a revolver at him, demanded his money. Smith, without resisting, handed Jones his money. When Jones was apprehended it was discovered that the revolver was a toy.		30._____

QUESTIONS 31-40.

Questions 31-40 consist of statements from which a term is missing. Each of these statements can be completed correctly with one of the terms in the following list. In the space opposite the number corresponding to the number of the question, place the LETTER preceding the term in the following list, which most accurately completes the statement.

A. affidavit	B. appeal
C. arraignment	D. arrest
E. E. bench warrant	F. habeas corpus
G. indictment	H. injunction
J. sentence	K. subpoena

31. A _____ is a writ calling witnesses to court.   31._____

32. _____ is a method used to obtain a review of a case in court of superior jurisdiction.   32._____

33. A judgment passed by a court on a person on trial as a criminal offender is called a   33._____
_____.

34. _____ is a writ or order requiring a person to refrain from a particular act.   34._____

35. _____ is the name given to a writ commanding the bringing of the body of a certain per-   35._____
son before a certain court.

36. A _____ is a court order directing that an offender be brought into court.   36._____

37. The calling of a defendant before the court to answer an accusation is called _____.   37._____

38. The accusation in writing, presented by the grand jury to a competent court charging a   38._____
person with a public offense is an _____.

39. A sworm declaration in writing is an _____.   39._____

40. _____ is the taking of a person into custody for the purpose of holding him to answer a   40._____
criminal charge.

QUESTIONS 41-55.

Questions 41-55 consist of statements from which a term is missing. Each of these statements can be completed correctly with one of the terms in the following list. In the space opposite the number corresponding to the number of the question, place the LETTER preceding the term in the following list, which MOST accurately completes the statement.

A. accessory
C. alibi
E. ballistics
G. confidence man
J. conspiracy
L. grand jury
N. misdemeanors
P. perjury

B. accomplice
D. autopsy
F. capital
H. commission
K. corroborated
M. homicide
O. penology

41. _____ is the dissection of a dead human body to determine the cause of death.   41._____

42. The general term which means the killing of one person by another is _____.   42._____

43. _____ is the science of the punishment of crime.   43._____

44. False swearing constitutes the crime of _____.   44._____

45. A combination of two or more persons to accomplish a criminal or unlawful act is called   45._____
_____.

46. By _____ is meant evidence showing that a defendant was in another place when the   46._____
crime was committed.

47. _____ is a term frequently used to describe a person engaged in a kind of swindling   47._____
operation.

48. A _____ offense is one for which a life sentence or death penalty is prescribed by law.   48._____

49. A violation of a law may be either an act of omission or an act of _____.   49._____

50. An _____ is a person who is liable to prosecution for the identical offense charged   50._____
against a defendant on trial.

51. A person would be an _____ who after the commission of a crime aided in the escape   51._____
of one he knew to be an offender.

52. An official body called to hear complaints and to determine whether there is ground for   52._____
criminal prosecution is known as the _____.

53. Crimes are generally divided into two classes, namely felonies and _____.   53._____

54. _____ is the science of the motion of projectiles.   54._____

55. Testimony of a witness which is confirmed by another witness is _____.   55._____

QUESTIONS 56-60.

Next to the question number which corresponds with the number of each item in Column I, place the letter preceding the adjective in Column II which BEST describes the persons in Column I.

Column I		Column II	
56. a talkative woman	A.	abstemious	56._____
	B.	pompous	
57. a person on a reducing diet	C.	erudite	57._____
	D.	benevolent	
58. a scholarly professor	E.	docile	58._____
	F.	loquacious	
59. a man who seldom speaks	G.	indefatigable	59._____
	H.	taciturn	
60. a charitable person			60._____

QUESTIONS 61-65.

Next to the question number which corresponds with the number preceding each profession in Column I, place the letter preceding the word in Column II which BEST explains the subject matter of that profession.

Column I		Column II	
61. geologist	A.	animals	61._____
	B.	eyes	
62. oculist	C.	feet	62._____
	D.	fortune-telling	
63. podiatrist	E.	language	63._____
	F.	rocks	
64. palmist	G.	stamps	64._____
	H.	woman	
65. zoologist			65._____

QUESTIONS 66-70.

Next to the question number corresponding to the number of each of the words in Column I, place the letter preceding the word in Column II that is most nearly OPPOSITE to it in meaning.

Column I		Column II	
66. comely	A.	beautiful	66._____
	B.	cowardly	
67. eminent	C.	kind	67._____
	D.	sedate	
68. frugal	E.	shrewd	68._____
	F.	ugly	
69. gullible	G.	unknown	69._____
	H.	wasteful	
70. valiant			70._____

KEY (CORRECT ANSWERS)

1.	A	16.	A	31.	K	46.	C	61.	F
2.	C	17.	B	32.	B	47.	G	62.	B
3.	A	18.	A	33.	J	48.	F	63.	C
4.	C	19.	A	34.	H	49.	H	64.	D
5.	C	20.	A	35.	F	50.	B	65.	A
6.	C	21.	C	36.	E	51.	A	66.	F
7.	B	22.	C	37.	C	52.	L	67.	G
8.	D	23.	A	38.	G	53.	N	68.	H
9.	B	24.	B	39.	A	54.	E	69.	E
10.	C	25.	C	40.	D	55.	K	70.	B
11.	D	26.	A	41.	D	56.	F		
12.	B	27.	B	42.	M	57.	A		
13.	B	28.	D	43.	O	58.	C		
14.	D	29.	C	44.	P	59.	H		
15.	D	30.	E	45.	J	60.	D		

EXAMINATION SECTION

TEST 1

DIRECTIONS: Each question or incomplete statement is followed by several suggested answers or completions. Select the one that BEST answers the question or completes the statement. These questions are designed to test your judgment in situations similar to those encountered by police officers on duty. *PRINT THE LETTER OF THE CORRECT ANSWER IN THE SPACE AT THE RIGHT.*

1. A man comes out of a store and complains to a police officer that he has been overcharged $50 by the storeowner. He wants the storeowner arrested. The police officer should FIRST
    A. advise the man to hire a lawyer
    B. go inside and ask the store owner to give the money back
    C. go inside the store and find out what happened
    D. tell the man that there is nothing the police can do

    1._____

2. A teenage boy stops a passing patrol car. He tells the police officers that a pipe has broken in the basement of a nearby apartment house and "everything is getting flooded." The officers should
    A. tell the boy to find a plumber
    B. look for some tools to fix the leak
    C. radio the stationhouse for assistance
    D. investigate the matter and then decide what to do

    2._____

3. A very old man walks slowly from a bus stop to a patrol car that happens to be parked nearby. He tells the police officers that he has been visiting a friend and wants to go home now. But he says that he cannot remember his home address or how to get there. The FIRST thing the officers should do is
    A. find out if he is carrying any identification
    B. find out if he is listed as a missing person
    C. tell him to go back to his friend's house
    D. take him to a hospital

    3._____

4. In general, a police officer dealing with teenagers should
    A. establish two-way communication with them
    B. show them that he can solve their problems
    C. force them to respect the law
    D. avoid face-to-face contact

    4._____

5. Occasionally, a police officer may be required to deal with a mentally disturbed person. In such a situation, the officer should, as a rule,
    A. try not to frighten or excite the person
    B. take no action unless a doctor is present
    C. avoid speaking to the person
    D. consider the person harmless

5._____

6. While a man is being booked at a police station for attempted robbery, his wife enters the station. She screams and curses at the police officers there and threatens to tear up the police forms which are being filled out. The officers on duty should
    A. give her a cup of coffee
    B. tell her they will lock her up too
    C. ignore the woman and continue what they are doing
    D. take the woman into another room and try to calm her down

6._____

7. A patrol car is stopped on the street by a man who wants help for his sick son. The man tells the officers that he thinks his son may be ill from an overdose of drugs. On reaching the family's apartment, the police find the son unconscious. The FIRST thing they should do is
    A. place the son under arrest
    B. question the father about his son's use of drugs
    C. call for an ambulance
    D. search for drugs

7._____

8. In response to a call one night, a patrol car is sent to a private house. On arriving, the officers find that the house is dark and the owner is waiting for them at the front door. She explains that all of the lights suddenly went out and she does not know how to get them back on. The officers should
    A. replace the light bulbs
    B. tell the woman that the police do not have the time to fix lights
    C. tell the woman to call the utility company
    D. check the fuse box as a possible source of trouble

8._____

9. A police officer is asked to talk to a neighborhood group about the use of force in making arrests. One person in the meeting says, "The trouble with you pigs is that you always want to beat a man's brains out." The police officer should say,
    A. "With most criminals you must use force."
    B. "Some people may think that, but that's not the way it is."
    C. "Only idiots call us pigs."
    D. "I won't talk with people who hate the police."

9._____

10. A police officer is on foot patrol near a supermarket when a young mother pushing a baby carriage stops him. She asks him to watch her child for a few minutes while she goes in to buy a couple of things. The officer should

    A. tell her she could be arrested for interfering with a police officer's duties

    B. agree to the request, since the delay will probably not amount to more than five or ten minutes

    C. agree to the request to avoid argument, then continue on patrol after the woman has entered the store

    D. refuse the request, since he should continue with his patrol

10._____

11. In the course of a barroom argument one Saturday night, Pete Smith seriously injures three police officers. He then agrees to go quietly to the police station. This is not the first time that the local police have been injured by Smith. On the way to the station, the arresting officers should

    A. offer to let Smith go if he will promise to give up fighting

    B. give Smith a bruise or two so that he will think twice about striking police officers

    C. use only as much physical force as needed to bring Smith in

    D. try to talk Smith into giving up drinking

11._____

12. Police officers are assigned to duty at a school where parents are picketing to get the principal removed. When the police accompany the principal as he leaves the building, some of the parents scream insults at the police and yell, "We'll get him tomorrow!" The BEST course of action for the police to take is to

    A. give summonses to the leaders of the pickets for threatening the principal

    B. warn them that picketing will be forbidden if the insults continue

    C. ignore the insults but watch out for any violent actions

    D. arrest the leader of the pickets to make an example of him

12._____

13. Two police officers respond to a complaint of an argument between a man and his wife in their apartment. The door is opened by one of their children, and the police officers find the man and wife in the kitchen of their three-room apartment loudly threatening one another. The FIRST course of action for the officers to follow is to

    A. handcuff the man before he has a chance to strike the woman

    B. get the husband and wife into separate rooms for a while

    C. ask the man and wife to explain why they are upset

    D. arrest the angriest one of the two

13._____

14. A police officer on patrol one night sees a woman standing alone in a   14._____
    vacant lot. The officer should
    A. ignore the woman since she can do no harm there
    B. ask the woman whether she needs assistance
    C. order her to leave the lot since she has no business being there
    D. greet her courteously and continue on his way

15. An officer on foot patrol hears a siren and looks up to see a care   15._____
    speeding in his direction. Several blocks behind is a patrol car,
    apparently giving chase. As the speeding car goes by him, the officer
    should
    A. fire his gun at the tires
    B. attempt to flag it down
    C. fire his gun at the driver
    D. get as good a description of it as he can

16. One Sunday, the police receive a complaint that a small local tavern is   16._____
    open in violation of the Sunday closing law. In line with routine police
    procedure, a patrol officer is sent to close the store and issue a summons
    to the owner. When the officer arrives at the store, the owner says that
    his shop is open because he badly needs the money. The officer should
    A. issue a summons but allow the owner to remain open for a little
        while
    B. close the store and forget about the summons
    C. issue a summons and close the store
    D. close the store and warn the owner that next time a summons will
        be issued

17. The police receive a report one night that a ground-floor apartment is   17._____
    being burglarized. One of the two officers responding to the call enters
    the front door of the apartment house. The other officer, with gun in
    hand, goes into an alley in the back of the apartment building. A few
    yards ahead of him, he sees someone crouching in the shadows. The
    officer orders the person to come out slowly. Whoever is there jumps up
    and dashes down the alley. The officer should
    A. fire his gun at the fleeing person
    B. ignore the person since there is no proof that he has done
        anything wrong
    C. chase after the person and try to catch him
    D. let the person go, but notify other police units to be on the lookout
        for him

18. When a police officer responds to a call, a woman tells him that she is
    afraid her teenage daughter will run away while she (the mother) is in the
    hospital. She asks the police officer for help. The officer should
        A. take the daughter into protective custody
        B. tell the woman that she should not waste a police officer's time on
            such things
        C. explain to the woman that this is not a police matter, and tell he
            where she may be able to get help
        D. give the daughter a lecture and threaten to arrest her if she runs
            away

18._____

19. One evening, paint is sprayed on the window of a ground-floor apartment.
    The next morning the tenant of the apartment stops a passing police
    officer and shows the officer the painted window. The tenant believes the
    spraying was done by a boy who lives in the apartment building, and asks
    the officer to make the boy remove the paint. The officer should
        A. tell the tenant to discuss the matter with the boy's parents
        B. tell the boy's parents that they are responsible for having the paint
            removed
        C. tell the boy's parents to punish their son
        D. tell the tenant to forget it – that "boys will be boys"

19._____

20. Late one night, an officer on foot patrol observes a middle-aged man
    standing outside a bar counting a large roll of bills. He knows the man as
    someone who lives a block away. As the officer gets closer, he realizes
    that the man is very drunk. The officer would be MOST helpful if he said,
        A. "Get that money out of sight and learn to hold your liquor."
        B. "If you have to count your money, do it inside the bar."
        C. "You'd better tell me where all that money came from."
        D. "Better put the money away and let me walk you home."

20._____

21. A police officer chases a suspected burglar down a street that is crowded
    with people and cars. Suddenly, the suspect turns and fires, narrowly
    missing the officer. The officer should
        A. continue the chase with caution
        B. stop the chase before someone gets hurt
        C. shoot back before the suspect gets away
        D. fire a warning shot over the suspect's head

21._____

22. Patrolman Thompson, who is stationed in a city precinct, has recently moved his family to a home in a different county. Several of his new neighbors tell Thompson that for many years an illegal betting parlor has been operating in the rear of a nearby stationery store. According to his neighbors, the police are aware of the betting parlor, but do not interfere with its operation. Thompson has been regularly buying newspapers and magazines at the store. On the basis of what he has learned, he should

    22._____

    A. stay away from the store, and report what he has been told to the local police station
    B. stay away from the store, but take no other action
    C. continue to visit the store, and personally investigate the truth of the information
    D. say away from the store, and report what he has been told to his own superiors

23. A police officer sees a young man throw a brick through the front window of a jewelry store and disappear into a crowd at the end of the block. The BEST course of action for the officer to take is to

    23._____

    A. get into the crowd as quickly as possible in search of the young man
    B. try to find persons who can identify the young man
    C. request help by radio and remain near the broken window to prevent burglary
    D. yell to nearby pedestrians to go after the escaping man

24. A police officer on foot patrol on a Sunday night observes two men he does not recognize carrying supplies from an unfinished building to a parked car. The officer should

    24._____

    A. stop the two men and ask for an explanation
    B. stay out of sight so he can observe them unnoticed
    C. arrest the two men and give them a chance to explain in the stationhouse
    D. call the police station for instructions

25. A hysterical woman rushes up to a police officer and says she is afraid her baby has been kidnapped. She had left her baby outside a supermarket while she shopped, and it was gone when she came out. The FIRST thing the police should do is

    25._____

    A. tell the woman to call her husband at work
    B. hail a passing car to search the neighborhood
    C. call the police station for assistance
    D. make sure the baby is not at the supermarket

26. In general, police officers should make a point of getting personally acquainted with the storekeepers, businessmen, and people who live in the area which they patrol. In making themselves known, police officers should

    A. warn that they will not allows any complaints in their area
    B. make it plain that the police officer's job is to serve the community
    C. make it clear that they will help the community only if the community will help them
    D. mention that "inside information" is always worth money to the police

26._____

27. While on patrol downtown, two police officers see a well-dressed woman standing by a late-model car. She calls to them as they drive by. When they stop, the woman explains that in the course of a day of shopping she has lost her car keys. She gives her name and an address in a city ten miles away. The car is locked, and she asks the officers if they can open the car and start it for her without a key. The FIRST thing the officers should do is

    A. verify ownership of the car
    B. start the car by jumping the ignition wires
    C. pry open a window and release the door lock
    D. accompany the woman to the stores where she may have lost the keys

27._____

28. A child calls the police emergency number and screams that her father is beating her mother to death. On responding to the call for help, two police officers find that the fight is over. The woman is unharmed and unwilling to press charges against her husband, who is present. The officers should

    A. take no action, but make it clear to the woman that they are angry with her for refusing to press charges against her husband
    B. offer their assistance and, if it is not accepted, leave
    C. arrest the husband and take the wife to the precinct house to sign a complaint against her husband
    D. apologize for bothering them unnecessarily, and leave

28._____

29. While off duty in a neighborhood bar, a police officer overhears a man who has had too much to drink. The man threatens to break a chair over another person's head. If the man who is drunk picks up the chair, the police officer should

    A. avoid interfering in the matter, since it is none of his business
    B. draw his gun, and force the man to drop the chair
    C. call the nearest precinct house and request police assistance
    D. identify himself as a police officer and tell the man to leave the bar and go home

29._____

30. Two police officers on patrol come upon a large and disorderly mob of
men, women and children. The crowd is throwing bricks and bottles and
several store windows have been broken. The officers should
    A. fire one or two warning shots over the heads of the crowd
    B. radio the precinct house and ask for assistance
    C. mingle with the crowd in order to find out what is going on
    D. identify and arrest the leaders of the mob

30._____

KEY (CORRECT ANSWERS)

1. C	11. C	21. A
2. D	12. C	22. D
3. A	13. B	23. C
4. A	14. B	24. A
5. A	15. D	25. D
6. D	16. C	26. B
7. C	17. C	27. A
8. D	18. C	28. B
9. B	19. A	29. D
10. D	20. D	30. B

TEST 2

DIRECTIONS: Each question or incomplete statement is followed by several suggested answers or completions. Select the one that BEST answers the question or completes the statement. These questions are designed to test your judgment in situations similar to those encountered by police officers on duty. *PRINT THE LETTER OF THE CORRECT ANSWER IN THE SPACE AT THE RIGHT.*

1. A police station receives a report that a man plans to shoot himself. Two police officers are sent to the address given, which is in a neighborhood where most of the people speak Spanish. The officers find the man's wife frightened and in tears. A neighbor who does not speak Spanish tells them that the man has locked himself in the bathroom and that neither the man nor his wife speak English. The officers are not able to speak more than a few words of Spanish. The FIRST thing they should do is

    1._____

    A. send for tear gas which can be used to drive the man from the bathroom
    B. find someone who speaks both English and Spanish so they can talk with the man and his wife
    C. force their way into the bathroom and quickly disarm the man
    D. get everyone out of the apartment and allow the man an hour or two to calm down

2. Two police officers stop for lunch at a diner which has just opened under new management. After the officers have been served, the manager of the diner walks over to their table and introduces himself. He hopes they will eat often at his diner and tells them that this first lunch is "on the house." The officers should

    2._____

    A. thank him for his offer, but insist on paying for their lunch
    B. accept his offer, but make it clear that they will pay for their lunch in the future
    C. warn the manager about offering bribes to police officers
    D. accept his offer, and thank him for being friendly to the local police

3. After breaking up a fight at a party, two police officers find it necessary to arrest a man. While taking him to their patrol car, they find that a small crowd has gathered on the street. The people in the crowd are friends and neighbors of the man and they angrily demand that he be set free. The FIRST action that the officers should take is to

    3._____

    A. draw their guns to prevent the crowd from getting out of hand
    B. offer to go back inside and discuss the matter with the leaders of the crowd
    C. threaten the crowd with arrest if anyone tries to get in their way
    D. tell them the man is under arrest and let them know where he is being taken

4. A man runs out of a movie theater and calls to a police officer. He tells the officer that there may be a bomb in a telephone booth inside the theater. The officer hurries to the theater and finds a length of pipe wedged under a phone booth seat. Visible at one end of the pipe are some electrical tape and wires. The FIRST thing the officer should do is

    A. tell the people in the theater that there is a bomb and that they should leave at once
    B. try to remove the pipe so that he can get a better look at it
    C. tell the manager to have the theater emptied quickly and quietly
    D. call the Police Bomb Squad

4._____

5. A small store has been broken into and money has been stolen from the cash register. The owner of the store tells one of the investigating police officers that an employee forgot to turn on the burglar alarm system the night the crime occurred. The officer should

    A. suggest ways of preventing future burglaries
    B. urge that the forgetful employee be fired
    C. point out that the store is responsible for the crime
    D. arrest the employee on suspicion of being involved in the crime

5._____

6. A patrol car stops a truck that is being driven at night without lights. The driver of the truck is a large, powerfully built man who is slightly drunk. He climbs down from the truck cab and waits as the two police officers approach him. Suddenly, he swings at one of the officers, but misses him. He then turns and lunges at the second officer. The officers should

    A. keep out of the truck driver's reach until he cools off
    B. use physical force to stop the driver's attack
    C. fire a warning shot over his head to stop him
    D. call for police assistance on the patrol car radio

6._____

7. The "Saints," a neighborhood street gang, had had trouble from time to time with the police. The police think that the gang may have been responsible for the recent burglary of a pawn shop, and have questioned the gang members about that crime. Shortly after 9:00 one night, two officers driving on patrol see three members of the Saints standing by themselves on a corner. The officers should

    A. drive slowly by the gang members in order to let them know that the police are watching them
    B. take the gang members to the police station for further questioning
    C. park the patrol car and prepare to follow the gang members on foot
    D. search the gang members for possession of stolen goods

7._____

8. The police receive a call from the owner of a delicatessen who reports that a man is hanging around outside his store. Two police officers promptly respond to the call and find a young soldier in uniform standing outside the delicatessen. From inside the store the owner points to the soldier, indicating that he is the person under suspicion. The officers should
    8._____
   A. remain in their car and watch the soldier until he leaves
   B. tell the soldier to move along or they will arrest him
   C. ask the soldier his name and what he is doing there
   D. ignore the soldier and tell the owner he should not be so nervous

9. Police Officer Helen Murphy is directing traffic at a busy intersection when she sees two men fighting on the sidewalk about half a block away. A crowd is already beginning to gather. She hurries to the scene of the fight and finds one of the men lying unconscious with blood on his face. The second man, a six-footer, brushes off his jacket and turns to leave. Officer Murphy, who is 5'3" tall, tells him to stay where he is. The man stops, stares at her, and says, "No lady cop can tell me what to do." The FIRST thing Officer Murphy should do is
    9._____
   A. tend to the injured person and allow the second man to leave if he wants to
   B. place the second man under arrest
   C. draw her gun and tell the second man she will shoot if he refuses to obey her
   D. ask some of the bystanders to grab the second man and stop him from leaving

10. Late one night, the police receive a telephone call from a man who complains that a loud party in his apartment building is disturbing the peace. The man will not give his name. When two officers arrive at the address given, the street is quiet except for the faint sound of drums coming from someone's apartment. The officers should
    10._____
   A. locate the source of the drums and arrest the tenant for disturbing the peace
   B. knock on several doors and ask whether the drums are bothering anyone in the apartment building
   C. continue on patrol without taking any action regarding the drums
   D. locate the source of the drums and ask the tenant to lower the volume of the music

Questions 11-20: BASIC ARITHMETIC

DIRECTIONS: Questions 11 through 20 test your ability to perform basic
arithmetical operations. Each question is followed by four
choices. *PRINT THE LETTER OF THE CORRECT ANSWER IN
THE SPACE AT THE RIGHT.*

Use the calendar below to answer questions 11 and 12:

AUGUST						
S	M	T	W	T	F	S
				1	2	3	4
5	6	7	8	9	10	11
12	13	14	15	16	17	18
19	20	21	22	23	24	25
26	27	28	29	30	31	

11. The first day of a special duty assignment was the third Monday of   11._____
    August. The assignment lasted two weeks and one day. The FINAL day
    of the assignment was on
    A. September 4   B. September 3
    C. September 11   D. September 10

12. A man works for five days each week, Tuesday through Saturday. How   12._____
    many days did he work in August?
    A. 22   B. 23   C. 24   D. 25

13. The diagram below shows an automobile fuel gauge. The arrow on the   13._____
    gauge indicates that the gas tank is _____ full.

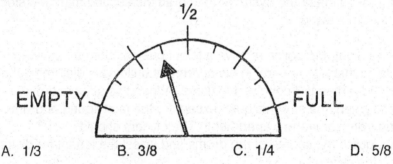

A. 1/3   B. 3/8   C. 1/4   D. 5/8

14. If the time shown on the clock below represents the present time, the time   14._____
    in twenty-five minutes will be

A. 2:55   B. 4:55   C. 3:50   D. 3:25

15. Five pounds of uncut heroin are found by police in the trunk of a car. One ounce of uncut heroin is enough to make approximately 500 bags which sell for five dollars each on the street. How many five-dollar bags could have been made from the five pounds of heroin?

    A. 50,000   B. 40,000   C. 25,000   D. 2,500

15._____

Questions 16 through 18 are based on the passage below:

In the Police Department, the time of day is given by a four-digit number between 0000 and 2400. The first two digits represent the hours from 00 to 24. The last two digits express minutes from 00 to 59. For example, 0326 hours is 3:26 a.m.; 1200 hours is noon; 1443 is 2:43 p.m.; and 2400 hours is midnight.

16. If a patrol car passed a store at 0100 and returned every two hours and 10 minutes after that, it would also pass the store at

    A. 0710   B. 0330   C. 0930   D. 0520

16._____

17. The time is now 2027 hours. How many hours and minutes is it before midnight?

    A. 3 hours, 33 minutes   B. 3 hours, 3 minutes
    C. 4 hours, 13 minutes   D. 4 hours, 3 minutes

17._____

18. The time at which a crime occurred was 0142 hours. The police were notified of the crime a half-hour later. They arrived at the scene a quarter of an hour after that. They stayed there for one hour. What time did the police leave the scene?

    A. 0732 hours   B. 0723 hours
    C. 0327 hours   D. 0237 hours

18._____

Questions 19 and 20 are based on the table below:

	Population	
Borough	2000	1990
Bronx	1,471,701	1,424,815
Brooklyn	2,602,012	2,627,319
Manhattan	1,539,233	1,698,281
Queens	1,987,174	1,809,578
Richmond	295,443	221,991
TOTAL	7,895,563	7,781,984

19. For which borough was the change in NUMBER of residents GREATEST between 1990 and 2000?

    A. Manhattan   B. Bronx   C. Richmond   D. Queens

19._____

20. In 2000, the population of Queens was APPROXIMATELY what fraction   20._____
    of the total population of New York City?
        A. one-half   B. one-eighth   C. one-third   D. one-fourth

Questions 21-25: WORD MEANING

DIRECTIONS: Questions 21 through 25 test your understanding of some words
                 commonly found in newspapers and magazines, and often used
                 in police work. Each question is followed by four choices. *PRINT*
                 THE LETTER OF THE CORRECT ANSWER IN THE SPACE AT
                 THE RIGHT.

21. An auto and a truck were in an accident. An inspector who tested the   21._____
    truck's brakes reported that they were <u>defective</u>.
    By this, he meant that the brakes
        A. were not working properly
        B. were in good shape
        C. had been relined
        D. had nothing to do with the accident

22. When taken to the stationhouse, the woman said that she had been   22._____
    <u>previously</u> arrested.
    She meant that she had
        A. never been arrested
        B. been arrested illegally
        C. been arrested by mistake
        D. been arrested before

23. The prisoner claimed that the wallet found in his pocket when he was   23._____
    arrested was his wife's. His story was <u>verified</u> when
        A. the wallet was found to be empty
        B. his wife could not be found
        C. his wife's name was found in the wallet
        D. his wife said she had her wallet

24. A police officer watched a young woman cross from one side of the   24._____
    avenue to the other and was sure that she <u>disregarded</u> the traffic light.
    The officer believed that the woman
        A. looked at the light
        B. crossed with the light
        C. paid no attention to the light
        D. responded to the light

25. During a heavy rainstorm one night, a car went off the road and hit a pole.   25._____
    The police officer who investigated wrote in his report that the weather
    <u>contributed</u> to the accident.
    The officer meant that the weather
    - A. caused the accident
    - B. was partly responsible for the accident
    - C. was the only explanation for the accident
    - D. had nothing to do with the accident

KEY (CORRECT ANSWERS)

1. B	11. B	21. A
2. A	12. B	22. D
3. D	13. B	23. C
4. C	14. C	24. C
5. A	15. B	25. B
6. B	16. D	
7. A	17. A	
8. C	18. C	
9. B	19. D	
10. D	20. D	

TEST 3

Each question or incomplete statement is followed by several suggested answers or completions. Select the one that BEST answers the question or completes the statement. *PRINT THE LETTER OF THE CORRECT ANSWER IN THE SPACE AT THE RIGHT.*

Answer questions 1 and 2 on the basis of the passage below:

From time to time, a police officer may have to appear in court as a witness in a criminal case. The content of the officer's statement is very important. The way he or she gives the testimony may create a favorable or an unfavorable impression in court. The officer should be able to talk about the kind of evidence he or she has and where the evidence came from; otherwise, cross-examination may confuse the officer and reduce the value of what he or she has to say. If the officer reviews the facts before testifying, he or she will be better prepared to carry out the assignment – which is to provide accurate information in such a way that its meaning will be understood by the court.

1. When testifying on court, the CHIEF responsibility of a police officer is to   1._____
    A. prepare his case ahead of time
    B. make a favorable impression
    C. avoid becoming confused during cross-examination
    D. present factual evidence in a clear manner

2. Which one of the following statements regarding testimony by a police   2._____
    officer may be inferred from the passage?
    A. What the officer says in the testimony should make the case stronger
    B. Not only what the officer says in court is important, but also how the officer says it
    C. The officer should memorize all of the facts which he or she may be asked to give
    D. How the officer gives the testimony is more important that what is said

Answer questions 3 and 4 on the basis of the passage below:

According to a report on police corruption, some police officers collected "pad" payments on a regular basis. These were bribes from people whose businesses would have suffered if they or their customers had received parking tickets. For example, some bar owners paid the police to allow their customers to double- or triple-park without being ticketed. Payoffs were made by construction companies and businesses that made pickups and deliveries in crowded areas. Some small companies used unlicensed drivers during rush seasons and wanted to make sure that the police did not bother them. Police corruption also took the form of "scores." "Scores" were one-time payments to police officers to overlook moving traffic violations. Taxi drivers, truck drivers and other motorists whose livelihoods depended on having a driver's license were often willing to make such payments.

3. On the basis of the information given above, which of the following statements is CORRECT?　　　　3._____
    A. Police corruption was supported by law-breaking citizens
    B. In general, "pad" payments involved less money than "scores"
    C. The police should have overlooked minor violations
    D. Taxi drivers were more likely than businessmen to bribe police officers

4. According to the passage, "pad" payments and "scores" both involved　　　　4._____
    A. unlicensed drivers
    B. payoffs which were made on a regular basis
    C. police officers who were willing to be bribed
    D. seasonal city traffic conditions

Answer questions 5 though 7 on the basis of the passage below:

As a rule, police officers arriving at the scene of an automobile accident should first care for victims who need immediate medical treatment. If necessary, the officers should ask bystanders to help warn approaching cars and keep traffic moving. People should be kept out of traffic lanes and at a safe distance from the damaged cars. This will help to avoid additional accidents at the scene, and will allow faster movement of emergency vehicles. Such action will also protect any evidence that might be important later.

5. Among the following actions that officers might take at the scene of an accident, which one should be taken FIRST?　　　　5._____
    A. Warn approaching cars of the accident
    B. Keep the bystanders moving
    C. Find out which driver was responsible for the accident
    D. Get the license plate numbers of the cars involved

6. The FIRST thing that police officers should do when they get to the scene of an accident is to
   A. take care of the injured who need immediate help
   B. ask for the help of bystanders
   C. warn oncoming cars and keep traffic moving
   D. protect evidence which shows how the accident happened

   6._____

7. An IMPORTANT reason for keeping people out of the traffic lane is to
   A. allow ambulances to get through
   B. allow photographers to get a picture of the accident
   C. keep crowds from forming
   D. keep souvenir hunters away from the scene

   7._____

Answer questions 8 and 9 on the basis of the passage below:

Many factors must be considered when a police officer is deciding whether or not to make an arrest. If an arrest is not considered legal, it could mean that some evidence will not be allowed in court. At other times, an arrest may tip off a suspect before evidence can be found. In all cases, an arrest takes away from a person they very important right to liberty. It is very upsetting to a person, causing worry and possibly loss of money. On the other hand, an officer must also realize that if an arrest is delayed too long, the suspect may run away or the evidence may be destroyed.

8. A judge may refuse to accept evidence of a crime if
   A. it interfered with the suspect's right to liberty
   B. it was found after the suspect was tipped off
   C. the suspect was able to get away
   D. it was collected during an illegal arrest

   8._____

9. In deciding whether to make an arrest, a police officer should
   A. consider whether the suspect is a known criminal
   B. realize that an innocent person could be very upset by being arrested
   C. not delay since evidence can be found later
   D. not worry about the innocent person because the courts will free him

   9._____

Answer questions 10 and 11 on the basis of the passage below:

The sergeant in command of a team of police officers on special assignment gave extra instructions only to the inexperienced officers in the group. Each of the experienced officers was to guard one of the four exits from a building, while the sergeant led the remaining three men through the front door.

10. The plan to be followed   10._____
   - A. required the participation of all members of the team
   - B. is standard operating procedure
   - C. was known only to the experienced police officers
   - D. did not require the sergeant to take part

11. The total number of inexperienced officers in the group was   11._____
   A. 8   B. 7   C. 4   D. 3

Answer questions 12 and 13 on the basis of the passage below:

A factory hires an armed guard for its front gate. He is given the following instructions:

"Do not let anyone enter the factory after 6 p.m. unless they have a company identification card with their photograph on it. If a person does not have such identification, check with the Security Office for instructions. If an alarm goes off in the factory at any time, no one is allowed to leave through the front gate. Stay at your post unless the Security Office orders you to leave it."

12. A visitor arrives at 6:15 p.m. in a chauffeur-driven car. The visitor   12._____
   explains that he had an appointment at 5:45 with a company official but
   was delayed in traffic. The guard should
   - A. allow the man to enter, since his appointment was for 5:45
   - B. ask him to wait while he checks with the Security Office
   - C. ask the man to please make another appointment
   - D. permit the man to go in, since he is clearly an important person

13. At 5:15 p.m. an alarm is sounded in the factory. Shortly afterwards, a   13._____
   man who the guard recognizes as a company vice president runs up and
   tells him to find out what the trouble is. The vice president offers to watch
   the gate while the guard is in the factory. The guard should
   - A. remain at the front gate and prevent anyone from leaving
   - B. follow the instructions of the vice president
   - C. enter the factory with the vice president to investigate the alarm
   - D. assume the alarm went off by accident since it is before 6 p.m.

Answer questions 14 through 16 on the basis of the passage below:

A recent newspaper story reported that in New York City four of the seven major types of crime increased during the first half of this year, with the rate of increase greater than ten percent for rapes, assaults and homicides. However, larcenies, robberies and burglaries decreased, and the overall rate for the seven major crimes went down. Auto theft is the seventh type of major crime. The Police Commissioner noted that the rise in homicides was related to the illegal weapons that were available. He estimated that about 80 percent of 8,000 confiscated weapons were pistols that could easily be concealed.

14. It appears that the number of concealable pistols that were confiscated during the six months of this year was about
   A. 800   B. 1,600   C. 6,400   D. 8,000

14._____

15. The rate of auto thefts _____ than ten percent.
   A. increased less
   B. decreased more
   C. increased more
   D. decreased less

15._____

16. According to the paragraph, the rate of killings in New York City
   A. was not included in the report
   B. decreased the same as the rate for burglaries
   C. did not change for the half-year
   D. increased during the first half of this year

16._____

Questions 17-26:

DIRECTIONS: Questions 17 through 26 test your ability to fill out forms correctly. Two incidents are described, each requiring that a police form be filled out. Read the questions that apply to each form. *PRINT THE LETTER OF THE CORRECT ANSWER IN THE SPACE AT THE RIGHT.*

Answer questions 17 through 21 by using the passage below and the Report of Aid Given that follows:

Police Officers Margaret Firestone and Harry Davis are partners on patrol. They see a man lying on his back on the southwest corner of Second Avenue and Sixth Street. Officer Firestone leaves the patrol car to look at him more closely. The man is dressed in clean clothes and seems to have stopped breathing. Officer Firestone bends over him, makes a quick inspection, and tells Officer Davis to send for an ambulance. She begins to administer mouth-to-mouth resuscitation. At this point the man becomes fully conscious and states that this has happened before. He insists that all he needs is a glass of water. He does not want to go to the hospital, nor does he want to be driven home.

Officer Davis gets a glass of water for the man from a nearby store. The man refuses to give his name and will not wait for the ambulance. He drinks the water, thanks the officers for their help, and walks north on Second where he disappears from view.

Officer Firestone then fills out a *Report of Aid Given*, shown on below.

```
┌─────────────────────────────────────────────────────────────────┐
│                      REPORT OF AID GIVEN                          │
│                                                                   │
│  Identification                                                   │
│       Date _____  Time _____  Place _____    │
│       Name of Person Aided _____ ___ Unknown     │
│  - - - - - - - - - - - - - - - - - - - - - - - - - - - - - - -    │
│                                                                   │
│  Nature of Problem                                                │
│       ____ Abandoned          ____ Destitute      ____ Ill        │
│       ____ Neglected          ____ Lost           ____ Injured    │
│  - - - - - - - - - - - - - - - - - - - - - - - - - - - - - - -    │
│                                                                   │
│  Nature of Illness or Injury                                      │
│       ____ Mental             ____ Physical       ____ Unknown    │
│  - - - - - - - - - - - - - - - - - - - - - - - - - - - - - - -    │
│                                                                   │
│  Aid Given                                                        │
│       ____ Artificial Respiration   ____ Food or Water            │
│       ____ Control of Bleeding       ____ Clothing or Blankets    │
│       ____ Temporary Splint          ____ Other                   │
│                                                                   │
│  - - - - - - - - - - - - - - - - - - - - - - - - - - - - - - -    │
│                                                                   │
│  Dispostion of Case                                               │
│       ____ Taken Home          ____ Left in Custody of Friend     │
│                                     or Relative                   │
│       ____ Removed to Hospital ____ Taken to Morgue               │
│       ____ Left at Place of    ____ Other                         │
│            Occurrence                                             │
│  - - - - - - - - - - - - - - - - - - - - - - - - - - - - - - -    │
│       Name of Officer Reporting _____          │
└─────────────────────────────────────────────────────────────────┘
```

17. Under Identification, the CORRECT entry for Place is   17._____
    A. Second Avenue, Sixth Street, SW corner
    B. Second and Seventh
    C. corner of Sixth Avenue and Second Street
    D. Second Avenue North, East Sixth Street

18. Since the man refused to give his name, Officer Firestone should check   18._____
    the space for
    A. Other, under Aid Given
    B. Unknown, under Identification
    C. Other, under Disposition of Case
    D. Unknown, under Nature of Illness

19. Under Nature of the Problem, the CORRECT space to check is   19._____
    A. Injured   B. Ill   C. Neglected   D. Destitute

20. The CORRECT spaces to check under <u>Aid Given</u> are
     A. Food or Water and Other
     B. Food or Water and Clothing or Blankets
     C. Artificial Respiration and Food or Water
     D. Artificial Respiration and Other

20._____

21. Under <u>Disposition of Case</u>, Officer Firestone should check the space for
     A. Removed to Hospital
     B. Left in Custody of Friend or Relative
     C. Other
     D. Left at Place of Occurrence

21._____

Answer questions 22 through 26 on the basis of the passage below and the Accident Report form that follows:

At approximately 5:00 p.m. on a foggy, rainy afternoon, Police Officer Ressa arrived at the scene of an accident a few minutes after it occurred. On the basis of his own observations, and from the statements of the persons involved in the accident, he decided that the accident happened this way: Mr. Goldsmith was driving his car east on Tenth Street. Tenth is a straight, one-way street that runs downhill as one goes from west to east. At the intersection of Tenth Street and Pacific Avenue, Mr. Goldsmith came to a full stop for a red light. When the light turned green, he started downhill and immediately struck Mr. Bates, a 43-year-old high school teacher who was jogging north on Pacific. Mr. Bates was not seriously injured, and admitted that he had been careless in crossing the intersection.

Police Officer Ressa filled out an <u>Accident Report</u> form, a portion of which is shown below.

```
                          ACCIDENT REPORT
Date _____  Time _____  Location of Accident _____

Vehicle in Collision With
____  Pedestrian                    ____  Motorcycle
____  Other Vehicle                 ____  Fixed Object
____  Train                         ____  Bicycle
____  Animal                        ____  Other
- - - - - - - - - - - - - - - - - - - - - - - - - - - - - - - - - -
Type of Traffic Control
____  Police Officer                ____  Stop Sign
____  Signal Light in Operation     ____  Yield Sign
____  Signal Light Not in Operation ____  Other
____  Flashing Light                ____  None
- - - - - - - - - - - - - - - - - - - - - - - - - - - - - - - - - -
Character of Road
____  Straight and Level            ____  Curve and Level
____  Straight on Hill              ____  Curve on Hill
____  Straight Approaching Hilltop  ____  Curve Approaching Hilltop
- - - - - - - - - - - - - - - - - - - - - - - - - - - - - - - - - -
Action of Pedestrian at Intersection
____  Crossing With Signal          ____  Crossing Diagonally
____  Crossing Against Signal       ____  Crossing, No Signal
- - - - - - - - - - - - - - - - - - - - - - - - - - - - - - - - - -
Action of Vehicle at Time of Accident
____  Going Straight Ahead          ____  Making U Turn
____  Overtaking                    ____  Backing Up
____  Making Right Turn             ____  Starting from Parking
____  Making Left Turn              ____  Slowing or Stopping
                                    ____  Parked
```

22. Under the section, <u>Vehicle in Collision With</u>, Officer Ressa should have checked the space for   22._____
    - A. Pedestrian
    - B. Other Vehicle
    - C. Fixed Object
    - D. Other

23. The space which he should have checked under <u>Type of Traffic Control</u> is   23._____
    - A. Flashing Light
    - B. Other
    - C. Signal Light in Operation
    - D. Stop Sign

24. Under <u>Character of Road</u>, Officer Ressa should have checked   24._____
    - A. Curve Approaching Hilltop
    - B. Straight Approaching Hilltop
    - C. Straight on Hill
    - D. Curve on Hill

25. The space which he should have checked under <u>Action of Pedestrian at Intersection</u> is   25._____
    - A. Crossing Against Signal
    - B. Crossing, No Signal
    - C. Crossing With Signal
    - D. Crossing Diagonally

26. He should have checked which space under <u>Action of Vehicle at Time of Accident</u>?   26._____
    - A. Starting from Parking
    - B. Slowing or Stopping
    - C. Going Straight Ahead
    - D. Overtaking

Answer question 27 on the basis of the information and street map below:

Below is a city street map showing an area which is divided into four
police patrol sectors as follows:

Sector Adam: bounded by Tudor, Newton, Hub, Athens and Canal
Sector Boy: bounded by Tudor, F, West 4th, Hub and Newton
Sector Charles: bounded by West 4th, F, West 2nd, C and Hub
Sector David: bounded by Athens, C, West 2nd, and Canal

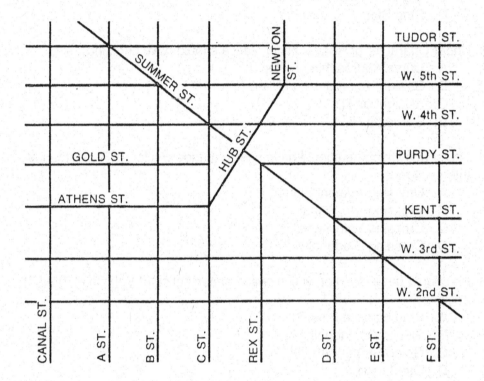

27. A bank is held up in the block bounded by West 4th, Summer and Hub   27._____
    Streets. The crime occurred in Sector
    A. David
    B. Charles
    C. Boy
    D. Adam

Answer question 28 on the basis of the information and street map below:

As indicated by arrows on the street map shown below, Adams and River Streets are one-way going north. Main is one-way going south, and Market is one-way going northwest. Oak and Ash are one-way streets going east, and Elm is one-way going west.

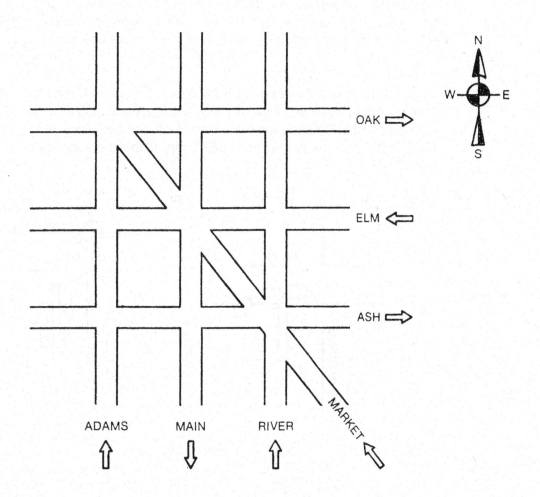

28. A patrol car heading north on River Street between Ash and Elm Streets receives a call to proceed to the intersection of Adams and Oak. In order to travel the shortest distance and not break any traffic regulations, the patrol car should turn

    A. left on Elm and right on Market
    B. left on Market and proceed directly to Oak
    C. left on Elm and right on Adams
    D. left on Oak and proceed directly to Adams

28._____

Answer questions 29 and 30 based on the corresponding information and diagrams.

Vehicles are shown by the triangular symbol (⬭) with the pointed side representing the vehicle front.

Pedestrians are represented by a circle. Solid lines show the path and direction of a vehicle or person BEFORE an accident happened. Dotted lines show the path and direction AFTER an accident happened.

29. Mrs. Wagner was walking across the intersection of Elm Street and Willow Avenue when she was struck by a car approaching from her right. After hitting Mrs. Wagner, the car swerved left and ran into a tree. Which of the four diagrams below BEST represents the accident described?

29._____

A.

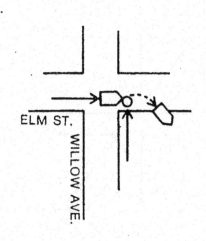

B.

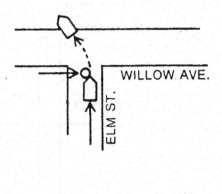

C.

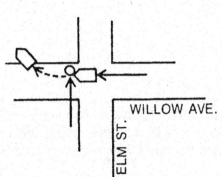

D.

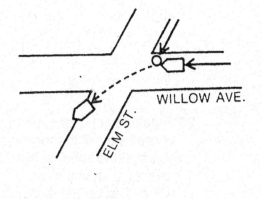

30. An automobile accident occurred at the intersection of Mill Road and Grove Street. Cars #1 and #3 were proceeding south on Mill Road and Car #2 was proceeding west on Grove Street. When Car #1 stopped quickly to avoid hitting Car #2, it was immediately struck from behind by Car #3. Car #2 continued west on Grove without stopping.
Which of the four diagrams below BEST represents the accident described?

30._____

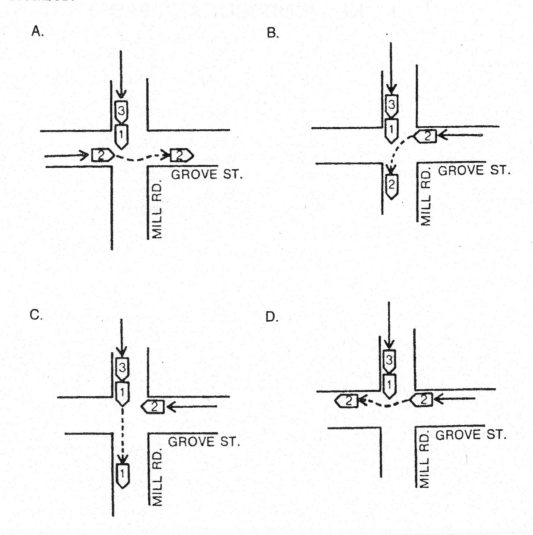

KEY (CORRECT ANSWERS)

1. D	11. D	21. C
2. B	12. B	22. A
3. A	13. A	23. C
4. C	14. C	24. C
5. A	15. A	25. A
6. A	16. D	26. C
7. A	17. A	27. D
8. D	18. B	28. A
9. B	19. B	29. B
10. A	20. C	30. D

ABILITY TO APPLY STATED LAWS, RULES AND REGULATIONS

EXAMINATION SECTION
TEST 1

DIRECTIONS: For each of the questions below, select the letter that represents the BEST of the four choices. *PRINT THE LETTER OF THE CORRECT ANSWER IN THE SPACE AT THE RIGHT.*

Questions 1-2.

DIRECTIONS: Questions 1 and 2 are to be answered on the basis of the following passage.

Effective January 1, 2017, employees who are entitled to be paid at an overtime minimum wage rate according to the terms of a state minimum wage order must be paid for overtime at a rate at least time and one-half of the appropriate regular minimum wage rate for non-overtime work. For the purpose of this policy statement, the term *appropriate regular minimum wage rate* means $10.05 per hour or a lower minimum wage rate established in accordance with the provisions of a state minimum wage order. OVERTIME MINIMUM WAGES MAY NOT BE OFFSET BY PAYMENTS IN EXCESS OF THE REGULAR MINIMUM RATE FOR NON-OVERTIME WORK.

1. A worker who ordinarily works forty hours a week at an agreed wage of $12.00 an hour is required to work ten hours in excess of forty during a payroll week and is paid for the extra ten hours at his $12.00 per hour rate.
   Using the information contained in the above passage, it is BEST to conclude

   A. this was a correct application of the regulation
   B. this was an incorrect application of the regulation
   C. the employee was not underpaid because he or she agreed upon the wage rate
   D. the employee did not perform his job well

1.____

2. According to the information in the above passage, the employee in Question 1 was MOST likely underpaid at least

   A. $180.00
   C. $60.00
   B. $30.75
   D. not underpaid at all

2.____

Question 3.

DIRECTIONS: Question 3 is to be answered on the basis of the following passage.

The following guidelines establish a range of monetary assessments for various types of child labor violations. They are general in nature and may not cover every specific situation. In determining the appropriate monetary amount within the range shown, consideration will be given to the criteria enumerated in the statute, namely *the size of the employer's business, the good faith of the employer, the gravity of the violation, the history of previous violations, and the failure to comply with record keeping or other requirements.* For example, the penalty for a larger firm (25 or more employees) would tend to be in the higher range since such firms should have knowledge of the laws. The gravity of the violation would depend on such factors as the age of the minor, whether required to be in school, and the degree of exposure to the hazards of prohibited occupations. Failure to keep records of the hours of work of the minors would also have a bearing on the size of the penalty.

1. a. No employment certificate—child of employer (Sec. 131 or 132)
    b. No posted hours of work (Sec. 178)

1. 1st violation - $ 0-$100
   2nd violation - $100-$250
   3rd violation - $250-$500

2. a. Invalid employment certificate, e.g., *student non-factory* rather than *general* for a 16 year old in non-factory work (Sec. 132)
    b. Maximum or prohibited hours – less than one half hour beyond limit on any day, occasional, no pattern. (Sec. 130. 2e, 131.3f, 170.1, 171.1, 170.2, 172.1, 173.1; Ed. L. 3227, 3228)

2. 1st violation - $ 0-$100
   2nd violation - $150-$250
   3rd violation - $250-$500

3. a. No employment certificate. (Sec. 130. 2e, 131. 3f, 131, 132, 138; Ed. L. 3227, 3228; ACAL 35.01, 35.05)
    b. Maximum or prohibited hours – (1) less than one half hour beyond limit on regular basis, (2) more than one half hour beyond limit either occasional or on a regular basis (Sec. 130. 2e, 131. 3f, 170.1, 171.1, 170.2, 172.1, 173.1; Ed. L. 3227, 3228)

3. 1st violation - $100-$250
   2nd violation - $250-$500
   3rd violation - $400-$500

4. Prohibited Occupations -Hazardous Employment (Sec. 130.1, 131.3f, 131.2, 133)

4. 1st violation - $300-$500
   2nd violation - $400-$500
   3rd violation - $400-$500

COMPLIANCE CONFERENCE PRIOR TO ASSESSMENT OF PENALTY.

After a child labor violation is reported, a compliance conference will be scheduled affording the employer the opportunity to be heard on the reported violation. A determination regarding the assessment of a civil penalty will be made following the conference.

RIGHT TO APPEAL

If the employer is aggrieved by the determination following such conference, the employer has the right to appeal such determination within 60 days of the date of issuance to the Industrial Board of Appeals, 194 Washington Avenue, Albany, New York 12210 as prescribed by its Rules of Procedure.

3. According to the above passage, a firm with its third violation of child labor laws regarding no posted hours of work (Sec. 178) and prohibited occupations-hazardous employment would be fined

    A. $600-$1,000
    B. $650
    C. $1,000
    D. cannot be determined from the information given

3.____

Question 4.

DIRECTIONS: Question 4 is to be answered on the basis of the following passage.

Section 198c.   <u>Benefits or Wage Supplements</u>.

    1.   In addition to any other penalty or punishment otherwise prescribed by law, any employer who is party to an agreement to pay or provide benefits or wage supplements to employees or to a third party or fund for the benefit of employees and who fails, neglects, or refuses to pay the amount or amounts necessary to provide such benefits or furnish such supplements within thirty days after such payments are required to be made, shall be guilty of a misdemeanor, and upon conviction shall be punished as provided in Section One Hundred Ninety-Eight-a of this article. Where such employer is a corporation, the president, secretary, treasurer, or officers exercising corresponding functions shall each be guilty of a misdemeanor.

    2.   As used in this section, the term *benefits or wage supplements* includes, but is not limited to, reimbursement for expenses; health, welfare, and retirement benefits; and vacation, separation or holiday pay.

4. According to the above passage, an employer who had agreed to furnish an employee with a car and then failed to provide a car is

4.____

    A. not guilty of a misdemeanor
    B. most likely guilty of a misdemeanor
    C. not affected by the above regulation
    D. guilty of a felony

Question 5.

DIRECTIONS: Question 5 is to be answered on the basis of the following passage.

    Manual workers must be paid weekly and not later than seven calendar days after the end of the week in which the wages are earned. However, a manual worker employed by a non-profitmaking organization must be paid in accordance with the agreed terms of employment, but not less frequently than semi-monthly. A manual worker means a mechanic, workingman, or laborer. Railroad workers, other than executives, must be paid on or before Thursday of each week the wages earned during the seven day period ending on Tuesday of the preceding week. Commission sales personnel must be paid in accordance with the agreed terms of employment but not less frequently than once in each month and not later than the last day of the month following the month in which the money is earned. If the monthly payment of wages, salary, drawing account or commissions is substantial, then additional compensation such as incentive earnings may be paid less frequently than once in each month, but in no event later than the time provided in the employment agreement.

5. A non-executive railroad worker has not been paid for the previous week's work. It is Wednesday.
   According to the above passage, which of the following is TRUE?
   The above regulation

   A. was not violated since the ending period is the following Tuesday
   B. was violated
   C. was not violated since the employee could be paid on Thursday
   D. does not apply in this case

5._____

Question 6.

DIRECTIONS: Question 6 is to be answered on the basis of the following passage.

No deductions may be made from wages except deductions authorized by law, or which are authorized in writing by the employee and are for the employee's benefit. Authorized deductions include payments for insurance premiums, pensions, U.S. bonds, and union dues, as well as similar payments for the benefit of the employee. An employer may not make any payment by separate transaction unless such charge or payment is permitted as a deduction from wages. Examples of illegal deductions or charges include payments by the employee for spoilage, breakage, cash shortages or losses, and cost and maintenance of required uniforms.

6. An employee working on a cash register is short $40 at the end of his shift. The $40 is deducted from his wages.
   According to the above passage, the deduction is

   A. legal because it is legal to deduct cash losses
   B. legal because the employee is at fault
   C. illegal because the employee was not told of the deduction in advance
   D. illegal

6._____

Questions 7-8.

DIRECTIONS: Questions 7 and 8 are to be answered on the basis of the following passage.

No employee shall be paid a wage at a rate less than the rate at which an employee of the opposite sex in the same establishment is paid for equal work on a job, the performance of which requires equal skill, effort, and responsibility, and which is performed under similar working conditions, except where payment is made pursuant to a differential based on:
   a. A system which measures earnings by quantity or quality of production
   b. A merit system
   c. A seniority system; or
   d. Any other factor other than sex.

Any violation of the above is illegal.

7. A woman working in a factory on a piece-rate system as a sewing machine operator   7.____
   received less pay than a male sewing machine operator who finished more items.
   According to the above regulation, this is

   A. legal
   B. illegal
   C. legal, but not ethical
   D. no conclusion can be made from the information given.

8. A male worker is in the same job title as a female worker. The male worker has been   8.____
   employed by the firm for three years, the female for two.
   Using the regulation stated above, if the male worker is paid more than the female
   worker, the action is

   A. legal
   B. illegal
   C. legal, but not ethical
   D. no conclusion can be made from the information given

Question 9.

DIRECTIONS: Question 9 is to be answered on the basis of the following passage.

Section 162. Time Allowed for Meals.

   1. Every person employed in or in connection with a factory shall be allowed at least
      sixty minutes for the noon day meal.
   2. Every person employed in or in connection with a mercantile or other establish-
      ment or occupation coming under the provisions of this chapter shall be allowed at
      least forty-five minutes for the noon day meal, except as in this chapter otherwise
      provided.
   3. Every person employed for a period or shift starting before noon and continuing
      later than seven o'clock in the evening shall be allowed an additional meal period of
      at least twenty minutes between five and seven o'clock in the evening.
   4. Every person employed for a period or shift of more than six hours starting
      between the hours of one o'clock in the afternoon and six o'clock in the morning,
      shall be allowed at least sixty minutes for a meal period when employed in or in
      connection with a factory, and forty-five minutes for a meal period when employed
      in or in connection with a mercantile or other establishment or occupation coming
      under the provision of this chapter, at a time midway between the beginning and
      end of such employment.
   5. The commissioner may permit a shorter time to be fixed for meal periods than
      hereinbefore provided. The permit therefore shall be in writing and shall be kept
      conspicuously posted in the main entrance of the establishment. Such permit may
      be revoked at any time.

   In administering this statute, the Department applies the following interpretations and
guidelines:

Employee Coverage. Section 162 applies to every person in any establishment or occupation
covered by the Labor Law. Accordingly, all categories of workers are covered, including white

collar management staff.

<u>Shorter Meal Periods</u>. The Department will permit a shorter meal period of not less than 30 minutes as a matter of course, without application by the employer, so long as there is no indication of hardship to employees. A meal period of not less than 20 minutes will be permitted only in special or unusual cases after investigation and issuance of a special permit.

9. An employee is given twenty minutes for lunch.
    According to the information given in the above passage, the employer

    A. is in violation
    B. is not in violation
    C. should be fined $250
    D. no conclusion can be made from the information given

9._____

Question 10.

DIRECTIONS: Question 10 is to be answered on the basis of the following passage.

An employee shall not be obliged to incur expenses in the arrangement whereby the employee's wages or salary are directly deposited in a bank or financial institution or in the withdrawal of such wages or salary from the bank or financial institution. Some examples of expenses are as follows:

    1. A service charge, *per check* charge, or administrative or processing charge
    2. Carfare in order to get to the bank or financial institution to withdraw wages

An employee shall not be obliged to lose a substantial amount of uncompensated time in order to withdraw wages from a bank or financial institution. Although the employer is not required to provide employees with paid time in which to withdraw such monies, the Department has held that the employer should provide for the loss of time when the employee requires more than 15 minutes to withdraw wages. Such time includes travel time to and from, as well as actual time spent at the bank or financial institution in withdrawing such monies. The loss of such time without compensation constitutes a difficulty.

The withdrawal of wages may not interfere with an employee's meal period to the extent that it decreases the meal period to less than 30 minutes. Thus, although the time required for withdrawal of wages may be 15 minutes or less, the loss of even 8 or 9 minutes from a thirty minute meal period creates a difficulty.

10. An employee is unable to withdraw wages at any time other than her lunch break. She needs twenty minutes to withdraw wages and has a forty-five minute lunch break. According to the information contained in the above passage, the employer

    A. is in violation
    B. is not in violation
    C. should be fined $250
    D. no conclusion can be made from the information given

10._____

KEY (CORRECT ANSWERS)

1.	B	6.	D
2.	B	7.	A
3.	D	8.	A
4.	B	9.	D
5.	C	10.	A

———

SOLUTIONS

1. The answer is choice B. According to the passage, the employee should have been paid "at a rate at least time and one half of the appropriate regular <u>minimum wage rate</u> for non-overtime work." Remember, it's important to consider only what has been given in the reading passage. Choice c is incorrect because it is illegal in this case to agree on something other than the law. Minimum standards are set by law so that employers cannot coerce, or otherwise persuade, employees to work at less than what is deemed fair. It could be argued that this is outside knowledge, but if you think about it, it's only common sense. Why bother having a minimum wage law, or minimum rates for overtime, or child labor laws if someone can just sign away his or her rights when an employer asks him or her to? If you didn't know this, you could still have eliminated this choice because the passage says, "ordinarily works 40 hours at an agreed wage of $12.00 per hour." The wording implies that this was agreed on for the <u>normal</u> work week.

2. The answer is choice B. The employee needs to be paid at a rate of time and a half. The employee has worked an extra ten hours at the hourly rate of $12.00 an hour. The passage states that the employee must be paid "at least time and one half of the appropriate regular minimum wage rate for non-overtime work." Minimum wage is given as $10.05 per hour. Time and a half of that would be $10.05 times 1.5, or $15.075 per hour. This employee is paid only $12.00 per hour for each hour of overtime. That's $3.075 less for each of the ten hours over forty hours, or a total of $30.75 less than he should have been paid. (10 x $3.075 = $30.75) You may have read the passage incorrectly, and thought the employee should have been paid time and a half on the $12.00 wage, but the passage does not state this. It states that the minimum payment is time and a half on <u>minimum hourly wage</u>, not on the employee's current wage rate. If you assumed the employee should have been paid $18.00 an hour, you probably would have picked choice c. Very tricky question. NOTE: The employee could have been paid less than half the minimum wage under special circumstances. Since there is nothing to indicate that the special circumstances apply, and since the question stem says "most likely," choice b is still considered the best choice.

3. The answer is choice B. This is another tricky question. The passage states, "The following guidelines establish a range of monetary assessments for various types of violations. They are general in nature and <u>may not cover every specific situation</u>. In determining the appropriate monetary amount within the range shown, consideration will be given to the criteria enumerated in the statute . . . ." The passage then goes on to list all of, the various possibilities. We don't know the circumstances, so choice d is the safest choice. If the question stem had been phrased "would most likely be fined," a case might possibly have been made for a different answer. The way it stands, choice d is the best choice because we can't say what, the fine <u>definitely</u> <u>would be</u>.

4. The answer is choice B. The last sentence states that "the term benefits or wage supplements includes <u>but is not limited to</u> . . . ." This, coupled with the wording of the first paragraph, would mean that there is a good possibility the broken agreement would be judged a misdemeanor,

5. The answer is choice C. This is directly supported by the fourth sentence.

6. The answer is choice D. The last sentence states that "examples of <u>illegal deductions</u> or charges include payments by the employee for spoilage, breakage, <u>cash shortages</u> or losses . . . ."

7. The answer is choice A. The key here is the phrase <u>piece-rate system</u>. The passage states that one of the exceptions is "a system which measures earnings by quantity or quality of production." That's piecework, where extra pay may be given for extra production or effort. It's logical -- and not too much -- to assume that the man was paid more because he finished more items.

8. The answer is choice A. The passage states that one of the exceptions is a seniority system. The question stem says that the man had worked there for three years while the woman had only worked there for two years.

9. The answer is choice D. The last sentence of the passage states that "a meal period of not less than twenty minutes will be permitted only in special or unusual cases after investigation and issuance of the special permit." Since we don't know the circumstances, we can't <u>definitely</u> say the employer is or is not in violation.

10. The answer is choice A. The next to last sentence of the passage states that "the withdrawal of wages may not interfere with an employee's meal period to the extent that it decreases the meal period to less than twenty minutes." The employee can only withdraw wages during her meal period. If the employee has a forty-five minute lunch break, and needs twenty minutes to withdraw funds, then she only has twenty-five minutes for lunch, which the passage states is not sufficient.

READING COMPREHENSION
UNDERSTANDING AND INTERPRETING WRITTEN MATERIAL
EXAMINATION SECTION
TEST 1

DIRECTIONS: Each question or incomplete statement is followed by several suggested answers or completions. Select the one that BEST answers the question or completes the statement. *PRINT THE LETTER OF THE CORRECT ANSWER IN THE SPACE AT THE RIGHT.*

Questions 1-3.

DIRECTIONS: Questions 1 through 3 are to be answered SOLELY on the basis of the following passage.

Foot patrol has some advantages over all other methods of patrol. Maximum opportunity is provided for observation within range of the senses and for close contact with people and things that enable the patrolman to provide a maximum service as an information source and counselor to the public and as the eyes and ears of the police department. A foot patrolman loses no time in alighting from a vehicle, and the performance of police tasks is not hampered by responsibility for his vehicle while afoot. Foot patrol, however, does not have many of the advantages of a patrol car. Lack of both mobility and immediate communication with headquarters lessens the officer's value in an emergency. The area that he can cover effectively is limited and, therefore, this method of patrol is costly.

1. According to the above passage, the foot patrolman is the eyes and ears of the police department because he is

   A. in direct contact with the station house
   B. not responsible for a patrol vehicle
   C. able to observe closely conditions on his patrol post
   D. a readily available information source to the public

1.____

2. The MOST accurate of the following statements concerning the various methods of patrol, according to the above passage, is that

   A. foot patrol should sometimes be combined with a motor patrol
   B. foot patrol is better than motor patrol
   C. helicopter patrol has the same advantages as motor patrol
   D. motor patrol is more readily able to communicate with superior officers in an emergency

2.____

3. According to the above passage, it is CORRECT to state that foot patrol is

   A. economical since increased mobility makes more rapid action possible
   B. expensive since the area that can be patrolled is relatively small
   C. economical since vehicle costs need not be considered
   D. expensive since giving information to the public is time consuming

3.____

Questions 4-6.

DIRECTIONS: Questions 4 through 6 are to be answered SOLELY on the basis of the following passage.

All applicants for an original license to operate a catering establishment shall be fingerprinted. This shall include the officers, employees, and stockholders of the company and the
members of a partnership. In case of a change, by addition or substitution, occurring during
the existence of a license, the person added or substituted shall be fingerprinted. However, in
the case of a hotel containing more than 200 rooms, only the officer or manager filing the
application is required to be fingerprinted. The police commissioner may also at his discretion
exempt the employees and stockholders of any company. The fingerprints shall be taken on
one copy of form C.E. 20 and on two copies of C.E. 21. One copy of form C.E. 21 shall
accompany the application. Fingerprints are not required with a renewal application.

4.   According to the above passage, an employee added to the payroll of a licensed catering   4.____
establishment which is not in a hotel must

   A.   always be fingerprinted
   B.   be fingerprinted unless he has been previously fingerprinted for another license
   C.   be fingerprinted unless exempted by the police commissioner
   D.   be fingerprinted only if he is the manager or an officer of the company

5.   According to the above passage, it would be MOST accurate to state that   5.____

   A.   form C.E. 20 must accompany a renewal application
   B.   form C.E. 21 must accompany all applications
   C.   form C.E. 21 must accompany an original application
   D.   both forms C.E. 20 and C.E. 21 must accompany all applications

6.   A hotel of 270 rooms has applied for a license to operate a catering establishment on the   6.____
premises.
According to the instructions for fingerprinting given in the above passage, the _____
shall be fingerprinted.

   A.   officers, employees, and stockholders
   B.   officers and the manager
   C.   employees
   D.   officer filing the application

Questions 7-9.

DIRECTIONS: Questions 7 through 9 are to be answered SOLELY on the basis of the following passage.

It is difficult to instill in young people inner controls on aggressive behavior in a world
marked by aggression. The slum child's environment, full of hostility, stimulates him to delinquency; he does that which he sees about him. The time to act against delinquency is before
it is committed. It is clear that juvenile delinquency, especially when it is committed in groups
or gangs, leads almost inevitably to an adult criminal life unless it is checked at once. The first
signs of vandalism and disregard for the comfort, health, and property of the community

should be considered as storm warnings which cannot be ignored. The delinquent's first crime has the underlying element of testing the law and its ability to hit back.

7. A SUITABLE title for this entire paragraph based on the material it contains is　　　　　7.____

    A. The Need for Early Prevention of Juvenile Delinquency
    B. Juvenile Delinquency as a Cause of Slums
    C. How Aggressive Behavior Prevents Juvenile Delinquency
    D. The Role of Gangs in Crime

8. According to the above passage, an initial act of juvenile crime USUALLY involves a(n)　　8.____

    A. group or gang activity
    B. theft of valuable property
    C. test of the strength of legal authority
    D. act of physical violence

9. According to the above passage, acts of juvenile delinquency are MOST likely to lead to　　9.____
a criminal career when they are

    A. acts of vandalism
    B. carried out by groups or gangs
    C. committed in a slum environment
    D. such as to impair the health of the neighborhood

Questions 10-12.

DIRECTIONS: Questions 10 through 12 are to be answered SOLELY on the basis of the following passage.

The police laboratory performs a valuable service in crime investigation by assisting in the reconstruction of criminal action and by aiding in the identification of persons and things. When studied by a technician, physical things found at crime scenes often reveal facts useful in identifying the criminal and in determining what has occurred. The nature of substances to be examined and the character of the examinations to be made vary so widely that the services of a large variety of skilled scientific persons are needed in crime investigations. To employ such a complete staff and to provide them with equipment and standards needed for all possible analyses and comparisons is beyond the means and the needs of any but the largest police departments. The search of crime scenes for physical evidence also calls for the services of specialists supplied with essential equipment and assigned to each tour of duty so as to provide service at any hour.

10. If a police department employs a large staff of technicians of various types in its labora-　　10.____
tory, it will affect crime investigation to the extent that

    A. most crimes will be speedily solved
    B. identification of criminals will be aided
    C. search of crime scenes for physical evidence will become of less importance
    D. investigation by police officers will not usually be required

11. According to the above passage, the MOST complete study of objects found at the scenes of crimes is   11.____

    A. always done in all large police departments
    B. based on assigning one technician to each tour of duty
    C. probably done only in large police departments
    D. probably done in police departments of communities with low crime rates

12. According to the above passage, a large variety of skilled technicians is useful in criminal investigations because   12.____

    A. crimes cannot be solved without their assistance as a part of the police team
    B. large police departments need large staffs
    C. many different kinds of tests on various substances can be made
    D. the police cannot predict what methods may be tried by wily criminals

Questions 13-14.

DIRECTIONS: Questions 13 and 14 are to be answered SOLELY on the basis of the following passage.

The emotionally unstable person is always potentially a dangerous criminal, who causes untold misery to other persons and is a source of considerable trouble and annoyance to law enforcement officials. Like his fellow criminals, he will be a menace to society as long as he is permitted to be at large. Police activities against him serve to sharpen his wits and imprisonment gives him the opportunity to learn from others how to commit more serious crimes when he is released. This criminal's mental structure makes it impossible for him to profit by his experience with the police officials, by punishment of any kind or by sympathetic understanding and treatment by well-intentioned persons, professional and otherwise.

13. According to the above passage, the MOST accurate of the following statements concerning the relationship between emotional instability and crime is that   13.____

    A. emotional instability is proof of criminal activities
    B. the emotionally unstable person can become a criminal
    C. all dangerous criminals are emotionally unstable
    D. sympathetic understanding will prevent the emotionally unstable person from becoming a criminal

14. According to the above passage, the effect of police activities on the emotionally unstable criminal is that   14.____

    A. police activities aid this type of criminal to reform
    B. imprisonment tends to deter this type of criminal from committing future crimes
    C. contact with the police serves to assist sympathetic understanding and medical treatment
    D. police methods against this type of criminal develop him for further unlawful acts

Questions 15-17.

DIRECTIONS: Questions 15 through 17 are to be answered SOLELY on the basis of the following passage.

Proposals to license gambling operations are based on the belief that the human desire to gamble cannot be suppressed and, therefore, it should be licensed and legalized with the people sharing in the profits, instead of allowing the underworld to benefit. If these proposals are sincere, then it is clear that only one is worthwhile at all. Legalized gambling should be completely controlled and operated by the state with all the profits used for its citizens. A state agency should be set up to operate and control the gambling business. It should be as completely removed from politics as possible. In view of the inherent nature of the gambling business, with its close relationship to lawlessness and crime, only a man of the highest integrity should be eligible to become head of this agency. However, state gambling would encourage mass gambling with its attending social and economic evils in the same manner as other forms of legal gambling; but there is no justification whatever for the business of gambling to be legalized and then permitted to operate for private profit or for the benefit of any political organization.

15. The central thought of this passage may be CORRECTLY expressed as the   15._____

    A. need to legalize gambling in the state
    B. state operation of gambling for the benefit of the people
    C. need to license private gambling establishments
    D. evils of gambling

16. According to the above passage, a problem of legalized gambling which will still occur if   16._____
    the state operates the gambling business is

    A. the diversion of profits from gambling to private use
    B. that the amount of gambling will tend to diminish
    C. the evil effects of any form of mass gambling
    D. the use of gambling revenues for illegal purposes

17. According to the above passage, to legalize the business of gambling would be   17._____

    A. *justified* because gambling would be operated only by a man of the highest integrity
    B. *justified* because this would eliminate politics
    C. *unjustified* under any conditions because the human desire to gamble cannot be suppressed
    D. *unjustified* if operated for private or political profit

Questions 18-19.

DIRECTIONS: Questions 18 and 19 are to be answered SOLELY on the basis of the following passage.

For many years, slums had been recognized as breeding disease, juvenile delinquency, and crime which not only threatened the health and welfare of the people who lived there, but also weakened the structure of society as a whole. As far back as 1834, a sanitary inspection report in New York City pointed out the connection between unsanitary, overcrowded housing and the spread of epidemics. Down through the years, evidence of slum-produced evils accumulated as the slums themselves continued to spread. This spread of slums was nationwide. Its symptoms and its ill effects were peculiar to no locality, but were characteristic of the country as a whole and imperiled the national welfare.

18. According to the above passage, people who live in slum dwellings

    A. cause slums to become worse
    B. are threatened by disease and crime
    C. create bad housing
    D. are the chief source of crime in the country

18.____

19. According to the above passage, the effects of juvenile delinquency and crime in slum areas were

    A. to destroy the structure of society
    B. noticeable in all parts of the country
    C. a chief cause of the spread of slums
    D. to spread unsanitary conditions in New York City

19.____

Questions 20-22.

DIRECTIONS: Questions 20 through 22 are to be answered SOLELY on the basis of the following passage.

    Whenever, in the course of the performance of their duties in an emergency, members of the force operate the emergency power switch at any location on the transit system and thereby remove power from portions of the track, or they are on the scene where this has been done, they will bear in mind that, although power is removed, further dangers exist; namely, that a train may coast into the area even though the power is off, or that the rails may be energized by a train which may be in a position to transfer electricity from a live portion of the third rail through its shoe beams. Employees must look in each direction before stepping upon, crossing, or standing close to tracks, being particularly careful not to come into contact with the third rail.

20. According to the above passage, whenever an emergency occurs which has resulted in operating the emergency power switch, it is MOST accurate to state that

    A. power is shut off and employees may perform their duties in complete safety
    B. there may still be power in a portion of the third rail
    C. the switch will not operate if a portion of the track has been broken
    D. trains are not permitted to stop in the area of the emergency

20.____

21. An IMPORTANT precaution which this passage urges employees to follow after operating the emergency power switch is to

    A. look carefully in both directions before stepping near the rails
    B. inspect the nearest train which has stopped to see if the power is on
    C. examine the third rail to see if the power is on
    D. check the emergency power switch to make sure it has operated properly

21.____

22. A trackman reports to you, the patrolman, that a dead body is lying on the road bed. You operate the emergency power switch. A train which has been approaching comes to a stop near the scene.
In order to act in accordance with the instructions in the above passage, you should

22.____

A. climb down to the road bed and remove the body
B. direct the train motorman to back up to the point where his train will not be in position to transfer electricity through its shoe beams
C. carefully cross over the road bed to the body, avoiding the third rail and watching for train movements
D. have the train motorman check to see if power is on before crossing to the tracks

Questions 23-25.

DIRECTIONS: Questions 23 through 25 are to be answered SOLELY on the basis of the following passage.

Pickpockets operate most effectively when there are prospective victims in either heavily congested areas or in lonely places. In heavily populated areas, the large number of people about them covers the activities of these thieves. In lonely spots, they have the advantage of working unobserved. The main factor in the pickpocket's success is the selection of the *right* victim. A pickpocket's victim must, at the time of the crime, be inattentive, distracted, or unconscious. If any of these conditions exist, and if the pickpocket is skilled in his operations, the stage is set for a successful larceny. With the coming of winter, the crowds move southward-- and so do most of the pickpockets. However, some pickpockets will remain in certain areas all year around. They will concentrate on theater districts, bus and railroad terminals, hotels or large shopping centers. A complete knowledge of the methods of this type of criminal and the ability to recognize them come only from long years of experience in performing patient surveillance and trailing of them. This knowledge is essential for the effective control and apprehension of this type of thief.

23. According to the above passage, the pickpocket is LEAST likely to operate in a   23._____

    A. baseball park with a full capacity attendance
    B. subway station in an outlying area late at night
    C. moderately crowded dance hall
    D. overcrowded department store

24. According to the above passage, the one of the following factors which is NOT necessary   24._____
for the successful operation of the pickpocket is that

    A. he be proficient in the operations required to pick pockets
    B. the *right* potential victims be those who have been the subject of such a theft previously
    C. his operations be hidden from the view of others
    D. the potential victim be unaware of the actions of the pickpocket

25. According to the above passage, it would be MOST correct to conclude that police offic-   25._____
ers who are successful in apprehending pickpockets

    A. are generally those who have had lengthy experience in recognizing all types of criminals
    B. must, by intuition, be able to recognize potential *right* victims
    C. must follow the pickpockets in their southward movement
    D. must have acquired specific knowledge and skills in this field

KEY (CORRECT ANSWERS)

1.	C		11.	C
2.	D		12.	C
3.	B		13.	B
4.	C		14.	D
5.	C		15.	B
6.	B		16.	C
7.	A		17.	D
8.	C		18.	D
9.	B		19.	B
10.	B		20.	B

21. A
22. C
23. C
24. B
25. D

———

TEST 2

DIRECTIONS: Each question or incomplete statement is followed by several suggested answers or completions. Select the one that BEST answers the question or completes the statement. *PRINT THE LETTER OF THE CORRECT ANSWER IN THE SPACE AT THE RIGHT.*

Questions 1-2.

DIRECTIONS: Questions 1 and 2 are to be answered SOLELY on the basis of the following passage.

The medical examiner may contribute valuable data to the investigator of fires which cause fatalities. By careful examination of the bodies of any victims, he not only establishes cause of death, but may also furnish, in many instances, answers to questions relating to the identity of the victim and the source and origin of the fire. The medical examiner is of greatest value to law enforcement agencies because he is able to determine the exact cause of death through an examination of tissue of apparent arson victims. Thorough study of a burned body or even of parts of a burned body will frequently yield information which illuminates the problems confronting the arson investigator and the police.

1. According to the above passage, the MOST important task of the medical examiner in the investigation of arson is to obtain information concerning the

    A. identity of arsonists
    B. cause of death
    C. identity of victims
    D. source and origin of fires

1.____

2. The central thought of the above passage is that the medical examiner aids in the solution of crimes of arson when

    A. a person is burnt to death
    B. identity of the arsonist is unknown
    C. the cause of the fire is known
    D. trained investigators are not available

2.____

Questions 3-6.

DIRECTIONS: Questions 3 through 6 are to be answered SOLELY on the basis of the following passage.

A foundling is an abandoned child whose identity is unknown. Desk officers shall direct the delivery, by a policewoman if available, of foundlings actually or apparently under two years of age to the American Foundling Hospital, or if actually or apparently two years of age or over to the Children's Center. In all other cases of dependent or neglected children, other than foundlings, requiring shelter, desk officers shall provide for obtaining such shelter as follows: between 9 A.M. and 5 P.M., Monday through Friday, by telephone direct to the Bureau of Child Welfare, in order to ascertain the shelter to which the child shall be sent; at all other times, direct the delivery of a child actually or apparently under two years of age to the American Foundling Hospital, or if the child is actually or apparently two years of age or over to the Children's Center.

3.	According to the above passage, it would be MOST correct to state that	3._____

A.	a foundling as well as a neglected child may be delivered to the American Found-ling Hospital
B.	a foundling but not a neglected child may be delivered to the Children's Center
C.	a neglected child requiring shelter, regardless of age, may be delivered to the Bureau of Child Welfare
D.	the Bureau of Child Welfare may determine the shelter to which a foundling may be delivered

4.	According to the above passage, the desk officer shall provide for obtaining shelter for a neglected child apparently under two years of age by	4._____

A.	directing its delivery to Children's Center if occurrence is on a Monday between 9 A.M. and 5 P.M.
B.	telephoning the Bureau of Child Welfare if occurrence is on a Sunday
C.	directing its delivery to the American Foundling Hospital if occurrence is on a Wednesday at 4 P.M.
D.	telephoning the Bureau of Child Welfare if occurrence is at 10 A.M. on a Friday

5.	According to the above passage, the desk officer should direct delivery to the American Foundling Hospital of any child who is	5._____

A.	actually under 2 years of age and requires shelter
B.	apparently under 2 years of age and is neglected or dependent
C.	actually 2 years of age and is a foundling
D.	apparently under 2 years of age and has been abandoned

6.	A 12-year-old neglected child requiring shelter is brought to a police station on Thursday at 2 P.M.	6._____
	Such a child should be sent to

A.	a shelter selected by the Bureau of Child Welfare
B.	a shelter selected by the desk officer
C.	the Children's Center
D.	the American Foundling Hospital when a brother or sister under 2 years of age also requires shelter

Questions 7-10.

DIRECTIONS:	Questions 7 through 10 are to be answered SOLELY on the basis of the follow-ing passage.

In addition to making the preliminary investigation of crimes, patrolmen should serve as eyes, ears, and legs for the detective division. The patrol division may be used for surveil-lance, to serve warrants and bring in suspects and witnesses, and to perform a number of routine tasks for the detectives which will increase the time available for tasks that require their special skills and facilities. It is to the advantage of individual detectives, as well as of the detective division, to have patrolmen working in this manner; more cases are cleared by arrest and a greater proportion of stolen property is recovered when, in addition to the detec-tive regularly assigned, a number of patrolmen also work on the case. Detectives may stimu-late the interest and participation of patrolmen by keeping them currently informed of the presence, identity or description, hangouts, associates, vehicles, and method of operation of each criminal known to be in the community.

7. According to the above passage, a patrolman should

7.____

    A. assist the detective in certain of his routine functions
    B. be considered for assignment as a detective on the basis of his patrol performance
    C. leave the scene once a detective arrives
    D. perform as much of the detective's duties as time permits

8. According to the above passage, patrolmen should aid detectives by

8.____

    A. accepting assignments from detectives which give promise of recovering stolen property
    B. making arrests of witnesses for the detective's interrogation
    C. performing all special investigative work for detectives
    D. producing for questioning individuals who may aid the detective in his investigation

9. According to the above passage, detectives can keep patrolmen interested by

9.____

    A. ascertaining that patrolmen are doing investigative work properly
    B. having patrolmen directly under his supervision during an investigation
    C. informing patrolmen of the value of their efforts in crime prevention
    D. supplying the patrolmen with information regarding known criminals in the community

10. Which of the following is NOT a result of cooperation between detectives and patrolmen?

10.____

    A. A greater proportion of stolen property is recovered.
    B. Detectives have more time to make preliminary investigations.
    C. Detectives have more time to finish tasks requiring their special skills.
    D. Patrolmen may become more interested and participate more in solving the case.

Questions 11-12.

DIRECTIONS: Questions 11 and 12 are to be answered SOLELY on the basis of the following passage.

    State motor vehicle registration departments should and do play a vital role in the prevention and detection of automobile thefts. The combatting of theft is, in fact, one of the primary purposes of the registration of motor vehicles. In 1983 there were approximately 61,309,000 motor vehicles registered in the United States. That same year some 200,000 of them were stolen. All but 6 percent have been or will be recovered. This is a very high recovery ratio compared to the percentage of recovery of other stolen personal property. The reason for this is that automobiles are carefully identified by the manufacturers and carefully registered by many of the states.

11. The central thought of this passage is that there is a close relationship between the

11.____

    A. number of automobiles registered in the United States and the number stolen
    B. prevention of automobile thefts and the effectiveness of police departments in the United States

C. recovery of stolen automobiles and automobile registration
D. recovery of stolen automobiles and of other stolen property

12. According to the above passage, the high recovery ratio for stolen automobiles is due to   12._____

   A. state registration and manufacturer identification of motor vehicles
   B. successful prevention of automobile thefts by state motor vehicle departments
   C. the fact that only 6% of stolen vehicles are not properly registered
   D. the high number of motor vehicles registered in the United States

Questions 13-16.

DIRECTIONS: Questions 13 through 16 are to be answered SOLELY on the basis of the following passage.

It is not always understood that the term *physical evidence* embraces any and all objects, living or inanimate. A knife, gun, signature, or burglar tool is immediately recognized as physical evidence. Less often is it considered that dust, microscopic fragments of all types, even an odor, may equally be physical evidence and often the most important of all. It is well established that the most useful types of physical evidence are generally microscopic in dimensions, that is, not noticeable by the eye and, therefore, most likely to be overlooked by the criminal and by the investigator. For this reason, microscopic evidence persists for months or years after all other evidence has been removed and found inconclusive. Naturally, there are limitations to the time of collecting microscopic evidence as it may be lost or decayed. The exercise of judgment as to the possibility or profit of delayed action in collecting the evidence is a field in which the expert investigator should judge.

13. The one of the following which the above passage does NOT consider to be physical evidence is a   13._____

   A. criminal thought   B. minute speck of dust
   C. raw onion smell   D. typewritten note

14. According to the above passage, the rechecking of the scene of a crime   14._____

   A. is useless when performed years after the occurrence of the crime
   B. is advisable chiefly in crimes involving physical violence
   C. may turn up microscopic evidence of value
   D. should be delayed if the microscopic evidence is not subject to decay or loss

15. According to the above passage, the criminal investigator should   15._____

   A. give most of his attention to weapons used in the commission of the crime
   B. ignore microscopic evidence until a request is received from the laboratory
   C. immediately search for microscopic evidence and ignore the more visible objects
   D. realize that microscopic evidence can be easily overlooked

16. According to the above passage,   16._____

   A. a delay in collecting evidence must definitely diminish its value to the investigator
   B. microscopic evidence exists for longer periods of time than other physical evidence
   C. microscopic evidence is generally the most useful type of physical evidence
   D. physical evidence is likely to be overlooked by the criminal and by the investigator

Questions 17-20.

DIRECTIONS: Questions 17 through 20 are to be answered SOLELY on the basis of the following passage.

Sometimes, but not always, firing a gun leaves a residue of nitrate particles on the hands. This fact is utilized in the paraffin test which consists of applying melted paraffin and gauze to the fingers, hands, and wrists of a suspect until a cast of approximately 1/8 of an inch is built up. The heat of the paraffin causes the pores of the skin to open and release any particles embedded in them. The paraffin cast is then removed and tested chemically for nitrate particles. In addition to gunpowder, fertilizers, tobacco ashes, matches, and soot are also common sources of nitrates on the hands.

17. Assume that the paraffin test has been given to a person suspected of firing a gun and that nitrate particles have been found.
It would be CORRECT to conclude that the suspect

    A. is guilty
    B. is innocent
    C. may be guilty or innocent
    D. is probably guilty

17.____

18. In testing for the presence of gunpowder particles on human hands, the characteristic of paraffin which makes it MOST serviceable is that it

    A. causes the nitrate residue left by a fired gun to adhere to the gauze
    B. is waterproof
    C. melts at a high temperature
    D. helps to distinguish between gunpowder nitrates and other types

18.____

19. According to the above passage, in the paraffin test the nitrate particles are removed from the pores because the paraffin

    A. enlarges the pores
    B. contracts the pores
    C. reacts chemically with nitrates
    D. dissolves the particles

19.____

20. The presence of a residue of nitrate particles on the hands is a COMMON result of

    A. the paraffin test
    B. handling fertilizer
    C. a bullet wound
    D. enlarged pores

20.____

KEY (CORRECT ANSWERS)

1.	B		11.	C
2.	A		12.	A
3.	A		13.	A
4.	D		14.	C
5.	D		15.	D
6.	A		16.	C
7.	A		17.	C
8.	D		18.	A
9.	D		19.	A
10.	B		20.	B

———

REPORT WRITING

EXAMINATION SECTION
TEST 1

DIRECTIONS: Each question or incomplete statement is followed by several suggested answers or completions. Select the one that BEST answers the question or completes the statement. *PRINT THE LETTER OF THE CORRECT ANSWER IN THE SPACE AT THE RIGHT.*

Questions 1-5.

DIRECTIONS: Questions 1 through 5 are to be answered on the basis of the following sample of a report relating to a civilian complaint against a member of the force. The sample report consists of fourteen numbered sentences, some of which may not be consistent with the principles of good police report writing.

1. The undersigned responded to the resident apartment of the complainant, Mrs. Eve Black, a female, 30 years of age, of 286 6th Avenue, apartment 4D. 2. Mrs. Black alleged that Police Officer M, shield #728, used abusive language to her while she was interceding on behalf of her son, Matt Black, M/W/10, same address, who was being reprimanded by the police officer for playing on the grass in front of 286 6th Avenue. 3. Response to this incident by the undersigned was as a result of a notification received from the Desk Officer, Lieutenant A. 4. Mrs. Black went on to say that the police officer stated to her, "Mind your own damn business, or I'll lock you up." 5. Complainant advised that there were three witnesses to the alleged remark - her son and two adult females, identities and addresses unknown. 6. The undersigned was unable to find and interview the alleged female witnesses. 7. Matt Black, when interviewed, corroborated his aunt's version of the incident. 8. Interviewed Police Officer M, who stated that he was in fact involved in an incident with the complainant, and he prepared a memorandum book entry in connection therewith. 9. The undersigned reviewed the entry concerned. 10. Police Officer M stated that, at the time and place of occurrence, while reprimanding a youth, then the youth's mother became enraged and threatened to "get the officer's job." 11. The officer denied the allegation of use of abusive language and further advised that there were no witnesses present. 12. He stated that at the time in question his radio was not operating properly. 13. It is apparent from the information obtained during this investigation that Mrs. Black's allegation is without substance, and that she dislikes Police Officer M as a result of previous contacts with him. 14. It is recommended that this matter be filed without prejudice to the officer concerned.

1. Which of the following sentences does NOT appear in its proper sequence in the report?   1.____

    A. 3   B. 5   C. 9   D. 11

2. Which one of the following sentences contains material which is LEAST relevant to this report?   2.____

    A. 2   B. 4   C. 10   D. 12

3. Which one of the following important aspects of report writing was omitted from this report?   3.____

    A. Where   B. What   C. Who   D. When

4. Which one of the following sentences from the report contains material which apparently   4._____
    CONTRADICTS other information given in the report?

    A. 7   B. 8   C. 9   D. 10

5. Which one of the following sentences from the sample report contains a conclusion   5._____
    which is NOT based on facts provided in the report?

    A. 1   B. 3   C. 4   D. 13

Questions 6-8.

DIRECTIONS: Questions 6 through 8 are to be answered on the basis of the following report
               relating to a community relations police officer under your command. The
               report consists of ten numbered sentences which may or may not be correct or
               consistent with principles of good report writing.

1. Mrs. Dorothy Lew of 7686 E. Elm Street started the meeting by complaining that neighborhood children continually loiter on the sidewalk in front of her residence, annoying residents of
her building. 2. The undersigned was directed to attend a meeting of community residents by
the Captain. 3. The meeting, scheduled to start at 1830 hours, actually began at 1915 hours. 4.
Present at the meeting were Sergeant Joseph Patt of the Youth Division, Mr. Fred Price, head of
a local merchant's group, Ms. Susan May, president of the community group, several residents
of the neighborhood, and the undersigned. 5. Mr. Jeffrey Brown, of 7688 E. Elm Street, stated
that conditions in front of the building at which he resides had improved since the last meeting.
6. Mrs. Mary Pence, of 7690 E. Elm Street, complained that vandalism in her building was still a
serious problem. 7. Mrs. Pence added that the County had not yet lived up to the promises
made to the tenants. 8. Mrs. Maria Garcia stated that mailbox tampering and vandalism continued to be a problem in her building, 7692 E. Elm Street. 9. The undersigned, when called upon
to speak, told the group that special attention would be given to premises 7688, 7690, and 7692
E. Elm Street in an effort to alleviate the conditions reported. 10. The meeting concluded at
2100 hours.

6. Of the following, the MOST logical sequence for the first four sentences of the report is   6._____

    A. 3, 2, 4, 1   B. 3, 1, 4, 2
    C. 2, 3, 4, 1   D. 4, 1, 3, 2

7. Which one of the following sentences contains material which is LEAST relevant to the   7._____
    report?

    A. 1   B. 2   C. 5   D. 7

8. Based on the report, the police officer concerned FAILED to respond to the complaint   8._____
    made by

    A. Lew   B. Brown   C. Pence   D. Garcia

Questions 9-11.

DIRECTIONS: Questions 9 through 11 are to be answered on the basis of the following portion of an Unusual Occurrence Report consisting of sixteen numbered sentences, some of which may not follow the principles of good report writing.
Assume that one of your subordinates has submitted this report to you for your
review, and that all necessary control numbers have been properly assigned
and included.

1. On June 17, at about 1520 hours, Officer Chou, while on routine patrol, was approached by
an apparently distraught female who stated to the officer that a male presently on the street had
raped her on a previous occasion. 2. The officer, accompanied by the female, responded to the
location where she pointed to a male as the perpetrator. 3. The officer noted that the male was
wearing a dark jacket. 4. As the officer approached, the rapist turned and fled. 5. As the officer
gave pursuit, he notified his command via radio, requesting that other units be notified of the
pursuit in progress. 6. The officer was joined by two other officers in their pursuit. 7. Approximately 300 feet into the chase, the suspect fled into a building through an emergency exit and
was apprehended by an officer inside. 8. The male was removed to the station house by officers. 9. A search of the street for the complainant proved fruitless. 10. At 510 hours, the male
was taken to the Detective Office for further investigation. 11. At the Detective Office, the male
was questioned by two detectives. 12. Determination as to the conclusion of the matter was
made by the desk officer. 13. Further efforts by the desk officer to locate the complainant were
negative. 14. Officer Chou was directed by the desk officer to prepare a Stop and Frisk report,
15. Officer Chou and the desk officer conferred as to the determination and he went to meal. 16.
Necessary forms were prepared and forwarded as per departmental policy.

9.   Which of the following sentences contains material which is CONTRADICTED by other   9.____
     information given in the report?

         A.   5   B.   6   C.   9   D.   10

10.   Which one of the following sentences contains a conclusion which may NOT be justified?   10.____

         A.   4   B.   8   C.   11   D.   14

11.   Which one of the following sentences is AMBIGUOUS?   11.____

         A.   9   B.   14   C.   15   D.   16

Questions 12-14.

DIRECTIONS: Questions 12 through 14 are to be answered on the basis of the following
example of a police report. The report consists of nine numbered sentences,
some of which are not consistent with the principles of good police report writing.

1. At 10:30 P.M., May 23, I received a radio message from Sergeant William Smith, who directed me to report to the Tremont Motel, 10 Wilson Avenue, to investigate an attempted burglary. 2. When I arrived at the motel at 10:45 P.M., John Jones told me that he had seen a blue sedan park across the street earlier in the evening. 3. A few minutes later, Jones heard a noise at the far end of the motel. 4. Noticing that the door to one of the motel units was open, Jones walked in and saw a man about six feet tall and 25-30 years old. 5. When he saw Jones, the man ran into the next room and escaped through a window. 6. While returning to the motel office, Jones passed several cars parked in front of other units. 7. He then saw the man run across the street and get into the blue sedan, which immediately sped away. 8. No evidence was obtained at the scene of the attempted burglary. 9. Jones could not remember the license number of the car, but he thought that it was an out-of-state license plate.

12. A good police report should be arranged in logical order. Which of the following sentences from the report does NOT appear in its proper sequence in the report?　　　　　12.____

    A. 3　　　　　B. 5　　　　　C. 7　　　　　D. 9

13. Only material that is relevant to the main thought of a report should be included. Which of the following sentences from the report contains material which is LEAST relevant to this report?　　　　　13.____

    A. 2　　　　　B. 3　　　　　C. 6　　　　　D. 8

14. Police reports should include all essential information. Which of the following sentences from the report is LEAST complete in terms of providing necessary information?　　　　　14.____

    A. 2　　　　　B. 4　　　　　C. 5　　　　　D. 9

15. Suppose you have to write a report on a serious infraction of rules by one of the men you supervise. The circumstances in which the infraction occurred are quite complicated. The BEST way to organize this report would be to　　　　　15.____

    A. give all points equal emphasis throughout the report
    B. include more than one point in a paragraph only if necessary to equalize the size of paragraphs
    C. place the least important points before the most important points
    D. present each significant point in a separate paragraph

KEY (CORRECT ANSWERS)

1. A	6. C
2. D	7. D
3. D	8. A
4. A	9. D
5. D	10. A

11. C
12. D
13. C
14. A
15. D

TEST 2

DIRECTIONS: Each question or incomplete statement is followed by several suggested answers or completions. Select the one that BEST answers the question or completes the statement. *PRINT THE LETTER OF THE CORRECT ANSWER IN THE SPACE AT THE RIGHT.*

1. All police officers wish to achieve higher rank.   1.____
   Most police officers who achieve higher rank have studied diligently.
   Some police officers who achieve higher rank have not studied at all.
   Which of the following BEST presents the above information?

   A. Diligent study by most police officers permits them to achieve higher rank but some
      do not study.
   B. While all police officers wish to achieve higher rank, most, but not all, study dili-
      gently to do so.
   C. Diligent study is required for most police officers who wish to achieve higher rank.
   D. In order for all police officers to achieve their wish for higher rank, most, but not all,
      must study to achieve it.

2. In order to properly prepare a budget, facts are needed. These facts must be current and   2.____
   accurate.
   Without such facts, no budget can be prepared.
   Which of the following BEST presents the above information?

   A. Without facts which are up to date and accurate, a budget cannot be prepared.
   B. Because facts are needed to prepare a budget, they must be current and accurate.
   C. Without facts, which are needed to properly prepare a budget, no budget can be
      prepared.
   D. Facts are the sine qua non of budget preparation.

Questions 3-7.

DIRECTIONS: Questions 3 through 7 are to be answered on the basis of the information given below.

   Assume that you and your partner, Police Officer Sam, have investigated the report of a
terrorist threat to derail a passenger train on the Amtrak line passing through your command.
Assume further that you will have to prepare a report based on the following notes:

   - Station Master, Joe Jackson, received a threat by telephone.
   - I searched the train station and tracks with Sam and Jackson; found no bomb.
   - Jackson said the caller sounded like a Japanese immigrant.
   - He reported that the caller said, *A bomb will go off in 1/2 hour on the tracks just out-
     side the station platform,* and then hung up.
   - Jackson said that a man entered the station about a half hour before the call; he stud-
     ied several booklets of train schedules.
   - He said that he asked the man where he wanted to go, and the man replied, *I want
     free passage to New York City.*
   - Mr. Jackson said that he replied, *There are no free passages. If you want a ticket you
     must pay. If you won't pay, please leave the station.*

- A bystander heard the commotion, saw the man leave, and recognized him as a chauffeur for a foreign ambassador who lives at 969 Book Street.
- We went to the address and spoke with a man who said his name was Wang Chung, and that he was a chauffeur for the Chinese Embassy.
- Mr. Chung said he had been home all day and had not been at the train station.

In each of the following questions, select the choice which MOST clearly and accurately restates the relevant information from the notes. Grammar and style are only important if they affect clarity and accuracy.

3.   A.   Sam, Jackson, and I searched the station and tracks, but there was no bomb.   3.____
        B.   By searching the station and tracks, Sam, Jackson, and I found there was no bomb.
        C.   Sam, Jackson, and I searched the station and tracks and found no bomb.
        D.   After a search of the station and tracks, Sam, Jackson, and I found no bomb.

4.   A.   Jackson reported that the caller, a Japanese immigrant, said, *A bomb will go off in*   4.____
           1/2 hour on the tracks just outside the station platform.
        B.   According to Jackson, the caller sounded like a Japanese immigrant and said, *A bomb will go off in 1/2 hour on the tracks just outside the station platform.*
        C.   Jackson reported that a Japanese immigrant caller had said, *A bomb will go off in 1/2 hour on the tracks just outside the station platform.*
        D.   A person who sounded like a Japanese immigrant called and said, *A bomb will go off in 1/2 hour on the tracks just outside the station platform.*

5.   A.   According to Jackson, he asked the man to leave the station after telling him that if   5.____
           the man would not pay he would have to leave.
        B.   According to Jackson, the man didn't have the money to buy a ticket so he asked him to leave the station.
        C.   Jackson said that the man refused to buy a ticket when he told him he would have to leave the station.
        D.   Jackson said that the man was asked to leave the station because he could not buy a ticket.

6.   A.   One half hour before the call, Jackson said, a man entered the station; he said that   6.____
           the man studied several booklets of train schedules.
        B.   One half hour before the call, Jackson said that a man entered the station and studied several booklets of train schedules.
        C.   One half hour before police arrived, Jackson said, he received a telephone threat about a bomb.
        D.   Jackson stated that 1/2 hour before he received a telephone bomb threat, a Japanese immigrant was at the station studying train schedules.

7.   A.   The chauffeur for the Chinese Embassy said he had been home all day.   7.____
        B.   The chauffeur who lived at 969 Book Street worked for the Chinese Embassy and was at home all day.
        C.   Mr. Chung, who said he was a chauffeur for the Chinese Embassy was at home all day and had not been at the train station.
        D.   A man who identified himself as Wang Chung and a chauffeur for the Chinese Embassy said that he had been home all day and had not been at the station.

Questions 8-12.

DIRECTIONS: Questions 8 through 12 are to be answered on the basis of the information
                below.

Assume that you and your partner, Police Officer Smith, have investigated a report of an
arson threat at Public School 276. You must also assume that you will be expected to prepare
a report based solely on the following notes:

- The school principal, Frank Adams, received threat by telephone.
- I searched school with Smith and Adams; found no incendiary device.
- Adams said the caller sounded like a young boy.
- He reported that the caller stated, *A fire will start in the school in an hour or two.*
- Adams said that two young boys entered the school about an hour before the call;
  asked if the gymnasium was available to non-students on Saturdays.
- One of the boys identified himself as Jason Mason, 86 Front Street.
- We went to that location.
- Spoke with Grayson Mason, his son, Jason, son's friend, Paul Mall.
- The boys confirmed Adams' story.
- The boys also said they did not call the school.
- Grayson Mason said boys had been in his yard playing touch football; he had not
  heard the boys enter the house; no phone calls being made.
- There is a phone extension in Jason's room.

In each of the following questions, choose the choice which MOST clearly and accurately
states the relevant information from the notes. Grammar and style are important ONLY when
they impact on clarity and accuracy.

8.   A.   Smith and I searched the school with Mr. Adams, but there was no incendiary   8._____
           device.
      B.   After Smith, Adams, and I searched the school, no incendiary device was found.
      C.   Smith, Adams, and I searched the school, but there was no incendiary device.
      D.   Neither Smith, Adams, nor I found an incendiary device when we searched the
           school.

9.   A.   Adams stated that the caller, a young boy, had said, *A fire will start in the school in*   9._____
           an hour or two.
      B.   According to Adams, the caller sounded like a young boy and had said, *A bomb*
           will go off in the school in an hour or two.
      C.   Adams said that the caller, who sounded like a young boy had said, *A fire will*
           start in the school in an hour or two.
      D.   Smith said that a caller, who sounded like a young boy, had stated that, *A fire will*
           start in the school in an hour or two.

10.
   A. An hour before the call Adams stated that two young boys entered the school and asked if the gymnasium was available to non-students on Saturdays.
   B. Adams said that the two teenaged boys who had entered the school had asked if the gymnasium was available to non-students on Saturdays.
   C. Adams said that two young boys entered the school about an hour before the phone call was received and asked if the gymnasium was available to non-students on Saturdays.
   D. Two teenaged boys entered the school about an hour before the phone call was received and asked if the gymnasium was available to non-students on Saturdays.

10._____

11.
   A. The officers spoke with Jason Mason, his son, Grayson, and Paul Mall.
   B. The boys confirmed Adams' story, but denied making the call.
   C. Grayson Mason said that the boys did not make any phone calls.
   D. Grayson Mason stated that the boys were wrestling in the yard at the time of the phone call.

11._____

12.
   A. Grayson Mason said that he did not hear a phone call being made because there is a phone extension in Jason's room.
   B. Because there is a phone extension in Jason's room, Grayson Mason did not hear the phone call being made.
   C. There is a phone extension in Jason's room. Grayson Mason stated that he heard no phone calls being made.
   D. The boys confirmed everything that Mr. Adams reported.

12._____

13. Sam was clearing his driveway after a heavy snowstorm. He was clearing it in order to get to work on time.
He suffered a heart attack and died before he finished the job.
Which one of the following BEST presents the information given above?

   A. Because he was in a hurry to get to work, Sam suffered a fatal heart attack while clearing his driveway after a heavy snowstorm.
   B. Because of a heavy snowstorm, Sam suffered a heart attack in order to get to work after it.
   C. Sam, while clearing his driveway in order to get to work after a heavy snowstorm, suffered a fatal heart attack before finishing the job.
   D. Before he could finish shoveling his driveway in order to get to work after a heavy snowstorm, Sam suffered a fatal heart attack and died.

13._____

14. An auxiliary police officer named Sue was patrolling her post.
She surprised a woman trying to break into a closed liquor store.
The woman tried to hit Sue with a pinch bar.
Which of the following BEST presents the information given above?

   A. While Auxiliary Police Officer Sue was patrolling her post, she surprised a woman trying to break into a closed liquor store. The woman tried to hit her with a pinch bar.
   B. While she was patrolling her post, Auxiliary Police Officer Sue surprised a woman trying to break into a closed liquor store and she tried to hit her with a pinch bar.

14._____

C. The woman trying to break into a closed liquor store was surprised by Auxiliary Police Officer Sue who was patrolling her post and tried to hit her with a pinch bar.

D. The woman tried to hit Auxiliary Police Officer Sue, who was patrolling her area, and surprised her while she was trying to break into a closed liquor store.

15. The assigned detective returned from investigating the crime.
When he returned he gave some details to his supervisor.
The supervisor included these details in a written report.
Which of the following BEST presents the information given above?

15.____

A. When he returned from investigating the crime, the detective gave some details to his supervisor, and he included this information in a written report.

B. Upon returning from investigating the crime, the supervisor included the details the detective gave him in a written report.

C. Upon his return from investigating the crime, the detective gave some details to his supervisor and then included them in a written report.

D. When he returned from investigating the crime the detective gave some details to his supervisor, who then included the details in a written report.

KEY (CORRECT ANSWERS)

1.	B		6.	A
2.	A		7.	D
3.	C		8.	D
4.	B		9.	C
5.	A		10.	C

11.	B
12.	C
13.	C
14.	A
15.	D

PREPARING WRITTEN MATERIAL

EXAMINATION SECTION
TEST 1

DIRECTIONS: Each question or incomplete statement is followed by several suggested answers or completions. Select the one that BEST answers the question or completes the statement. *PRINT THE LETTER OF THE CORRECT ANSWER IN THE SPACE AT THE RIGHT.*

1. The one of the following sentences which is LEAST acceptable from the viewpoint of correct usage is:

    A. The police thought the fugitive to be him.
    B. The criminals set a trap for whoever would fall into it.
    C. It is ten years ago since the fugitive fled from the city.
    D. The lecturer argued that criminals are usually cowards.
    E. The police removed four bucketfuls of earth from the scene of the crime.

1.____

2. The one of the following sentences which is LEAST acceptable from the viewpoint of correct usage is:

    A. The patrolman scrutinized the report with great care.
    B. Approaching the victim of the assault, two bruises were noticed by the patrolman.
    C. As soon as I had broken down the door, I stepped into the room.
    D. I observed the accused loitering near the building, which was closed at the time.
    E. The storekeeper complained that his neighbor was guilty of violating a local ordinance.

2.____

3. The one of the following sentences which is LEAST acceptable from the viewpoint of correct usage is:

    A. I realized immediately that he intended to assault the woman, so I disarmed him.
    B. It was apparent that Mr. Smith's explanation contained many inconsistencies.
    C. Despite the slippery condition of the street, he managed to stop the vehicle before injuring the child.
    D. Not a single one of them wish, despite the damage to property, to make a formal complaint.
    E. The body was found lying on the floor.

3.____

4. The one of the following sentences which contains NO error in usage is:

    A. After the robbers left, the proprietor stood tied in his chair for about two hours before help arrived.
    B. In the cellar I found the watchmans' hat and coat.
    C. The persons living in adjacent apartments stated that they had heard no unusual noises.
    D. Neither a knife or any firearms were found in the room.
    E. Walking down the street, the shouting of the crowd indicated that something was wrong.

4.____

5. The one of the following sentences which contains NO error in usage is:

    5.____

    A. The policeman lay a firm hand on the suspect's shoulder.
    B. It is true that neither strength nor agility are the most important requirement for a good patrolman.
    C. Good citizens constantly strive to do more than merely comply the restraints imposed by society.
    D. No decision was made as to whom the prize should be awarded.
    E. Twenty years is considered a severe sentence for a felony.

6. Which of the following is NOT expressed in standard English usage?

    6.____

    A. The victim reached a pay-phone booth and manages to call police headquarters.
    B. By the time the call was received, the assailant had left the scene.
    C. The victim has been a respected member of the community for the past eleven years.
    D. Although the lighting was bad and the shadows were deep, the storekeeper caught sight of the attacker.
    E. Additional street lights have since been installed, and the patrols have been strengthened.

7. Which of the following is NOT expressed in standard English usage?

    7.____

    A. The judge upheld the attorney's right to question the witness about the missing glove.
    B. To be absolutely fair to all parties is the jury's chief responsibility.
    C. Having finished the report, a loud noise in the next room startled the sergeant.
    D. The witness obviously enjoyed having played a part in the proceedings.
    E. The sergeant planned to assign the case to whoever arrived first.

8. In which of the following is a word misused?

    8.____

    A. As a matter of principle, the captain insisted that the suspect's partner be brought for questioning.
    B. The principle suspect had been detained at the station house for most of the day.
    C. The principal in the crime had no previous criminal record, but his closest associate had been convicted of felonies on two occasions.
    D. The interest payments had been made promptly, but the firm had been drawing upon the principal for these payments.
    E. The accused insisted that his high school principal would furnish him a character reference.

9. Which of the following statements is ambiguous?

    9.____

    A. Mr. Sullivan explained why Mr. Johnson had been dismissed from his job.
    B. The storekeeper told the patrolman he had made a mistake.
    C. After waiting three hours, the patients in the doctor's office were sent home.
    D. The janitor's duties were to maintain the building in good shape and to answer tenants' complaints.
    E. The speed limit should, in my opinion, be raised to sixty miles an hour on that stretch of road.

10. In which of the following is the punctuation or capitalization faulty?   10._____

    A. The accident occurred at an intersection in the Kew Gardens section of Queens, near the bus stop.

    B. The sedan, not the convertible, was struck in the side.

    C. Before any of the patrolmen had left the police car received an important message from headquarters.

    D. The dog that had been stolen was returned to his master, John Dempsey, who lived in East Village.

    E. The letter had been sent to 12 Hillside Terrace, Rutland, Vermont 05701.

Questions 11-25.

DIRECTIONS: Questions 11 through 25 are to be answered in accordance with correct English usage; that is, standard English rather than nonstandard or substandard. Nonstandard and substandard English includes words or expressions usually classified as slang, dialect, illiterate, etc., which are not generally accepted as correct in current written communication. Standard English also requires clarity, proper punctuation and capitalization and appropriate use of words. Write the letter of the sentence NOT expressed in standard English usage in the space at the right.

11.   A. There were three witnesses to the accident.   11._____
    B. At least three witnesses were found to testify for the plaintiff.
    C. Three of the witnesses who took the stand was uncertain about the defendant's competence to drive.
    D. Only three witnesses came forward to testify for the plaintiff.
    E. The three witnesses to the accident were pedestrians.

12.   A. The driver had obviously drunk too many martinis before leaving for home.   12._____
    B. The boy who drowned had swum in these same waters many times before.
    C. The petty thief had stolen a bicycle from a private driveway before he was apprehended.
    D. The detectives had brung in the heroin shipment they intercepted.
    E. The passengers had never ridden in a converted bus before.

13.   A. Between you and me, the new platoon plan sounds like a good idea.   13._____
    B. Money from an aunt's estate was left to his wife and he.
    C. He and I were assigned to the same patrol for the first time in two months.
    D. Either you or he should check the front door of that store.
    E. The captain himself was not sure of the witness's reliability.

14.   A. The alarm had scarcely begun to ring when the explosion occurred.   14._____
    B. Before the firemen arrived on the scene, the second story had been destroyed.
    C. Because of the dense smoke and heat, the firemen could hardly approach the now-blazing structure.
    D. According to the patrolman's report, there wasn't nobody in the store when the explosion occurred.
    E. The sergeant's suggestion was not at all unsound, but no one agreed with him.

15. A. The driver and the passenger they were both found to be intoxicated.   15.____
     B. The driver and the passenger talked slowly and not too clearly.
     C. Neither the driver nor his passengers were able to give a coherent account of the accident.
     D. In a corner of the room sat the passenger, quietly dozing.
     E. The driver finally told a strange and unbelievable story, which the passenger contradicted.

16. A. Under the circumstances I decided not to continue my examination of the premises.   16.____
     B. There are many difficulties now not comparable with those existing in 1960.
     C. Friends of the accused were heard to announce that the witness had better been away on the day of the trial.
     D. The two criminals escaped in the confusion that followed the explosion.
     E. The aged man was struck by the considerateness of the patrolman's offer.

17. A. An assemblage of miscellaneous weapons lay on the table.   17.____
     B. Ample opportunities were given to the defendant to obtain counsel.
     C. The speaker often alluded to his past experience with youthful offenders in the armed forces.
     D. The sudden appearance of the truck aroused my suspicions.
     E. Her studying had a good affect on her grades in high school.

18. A. He sat down in the theater and began to watch the movie.   18.____
     B. The girl had ridden horses since she was four years old.
     C. Application was made on behalf of the prosecutor to cite the witness for contempt.
     D. The bank robber, with his two accomplices, were caught in the act.
     E. His story is simply not credible.

19. A. The angry boy said that he did not like those kind of friends.   19.____
     B. The merchant's financial condition was so precarious that he felt he must avail himself of any offer of assistance.
     C. He is apt to promise more than he can perform.
     D. Looking at the messy kitchen, the housewife felt like crying.
     E. A clerk was left in charge of the stolen property.

20. A. His wounds were aggravated by prolonged exposure to sub-freezing temperatures.   20.____
     B. The prosecutor remarked that the witness was not averse to changing his story each time he was interviewed.
     C. The crime pattern indicated that the burglars were adapt in the handling of explosives.
     D. His rigid adherence to a fixed plan brought him into renewed conflict with his subordinates.
     E. He had anticipated that the sentence would be delivered by noon.

21.
   A. The whole arraignment procedure is badly in need of revision.
   B. After his glasses were broken in the fight, he would of gone to the optometrist if he could.
   C. Neither Tom nor Jack brought his lunch to work.
   D. He stood aside until the quarrel was over.
   E. A statement in the psychiatrist's report disclosed that the probationer vowed to have his revenge.

   21.____

22.
   A. His fiery and intemperate speech to the striking employees fatally affected any chance of a future reconciliation.
   B. The wording of the statute has been variously construed.
   C. The defendant's attorney, speaking in the courtroom, called the official a demagogue who contempuously disregarded the judge's orders.
   D. The baseball game is likely to be the most exciting one this year.
   E. The mother divided the cookies among her two children.

   22.____

23.
   A. There was only a bed and a dresser in the dingy room.
   B. John is one of the few students that have protested the new rule.
   C. It cannot be argued that the child's testimony is negligible; it is, on the contrary, of the greatest importance.
   D. The basic criterion for clearance was so general that officials resolved any doubts in favor of dismissal.
   E. Having just returned from a long vacation, the officer found the city unbearably hot.

   23.____

24.
   A. The librarian ought to give more help to small children.
   B. The small boy was criticized by the teacher because he often wrote careless.
   C. It was generally doubted whether the women would permit the use of her apartment for intelligence operations.
   D. The probationer acts differently every time the officer visits him.
   E. Each of the newly appointed officers has 12 years of service.

   24.____

25.
   A. The North is the most industrialized region in the country.
   B. L. Patrick Gray 3d, the bureau's acting director, stated that, while "rehabilitation is fine" for some convicted criminals, "it is a useless gesture for those who resist every such effort."
   C. Careless driving, faulty mechanism, narrow or badly kept roads all play their part in causing accidents.
   D. The childrens' books were left in the bus.
   E. It was a matter of internal security; consequently, he felt no inclination to rescind his previous order.

   25.____

KEY (CORRECT ANSWERS)

1.	C	11.	C
2.	B	12.	D
3.	D	13.	B
4.	C	14.	D
5.	E	15.	A
6.	A	16.	C
7.	C	17.	E
8.	B	18.	D
9.	B	19.	A
10.	C	20.	C

21.	B
22.	E
23.	B
24.	B
25.	D

TEST 2

DIRECTIONS: Each question or incomplete statement is followed by several suggested answers or completions. Select the one that BEST answers the question or completes the statement. *PRINT THE LETTER OF THE CORRECT ANSWER IN THE SPACE AT THE RIGHT.*

Questions 1-6.

DIRECTIONS: Each of Questions 1 through 6 consists of a statement which contains a word (one of those underlined) that is either incorrectly used because it is not in keeping with the meaning the quotation is evidently intended to convey, or is misspelled. There is only one INCORRECT word in each quotation. Of the four underlined words, determine if the first one should be replaced by the word lettered A, the second replaced by the word lettered B, the third replaced by the word lettered C, or the fourth replaced by the word lettered D. *PRINT THE LETTER OF THE REPLACEMENT WORD YOU HAVE SELECTED IN THE SPACE AT THE RIGHT.*

1. Whether one depends on <u>fluorescent</u> or artificial light or both, adequate <u>standards</u> should be <u>maintained</u> by means of <u>systematic</u> tests.   1.____

    A. natural   B. safeguards
    C. established   D. routine

2. A police officer has to be <u>prepared</u> to assume his <u>knowledge</u> as a social <u>scientist</u> in the <u>community</u>.   2.____

    A. forced   B. role
    C. philosopher   D. street

3. It is <u>practically</u> impossible to <u>indicate</u> whether a sentence is <u>too</u> long simply by <u>measuring</u> its length.   3.____

    A. almost   B. tell   C. very   D. guessing

4. Strong <u>leaders</u> are <u>required</u> to organize a community for delinquency prevention and for <u>dissemination</u> of organized <u>crime</u> and drug addiction.   4.____

    A. tactics   B. important   C. control   D. meetings

5. The <u>demonstrators</u> who were taken to the Criminal Courts building in <u>Manhattan</u> (because it was large enough to <u>accommodate</u> them), contended that the arrests were <u>unwarrented.</u>   5.____

    A. demonstraters   B. Manhatten
    C. accomodate   D. unwarranted

6. They were <u>guaranteed</u> a calm <u>atmosphere</u>, free from <u>harrassment</u>, which would be conducive to quiet consideration of the <u>indictments</u>.   6.____

    A. guarenteed   B. atmospher
    C. harassment   D. inditements

Questions 7-11.

DIRECTIONS: Each of Questions 7 through 11 consists of a statement containing four words
in capital letters. One of these words in capital letters is not in keeping with the
meaning which the statement is evidently intended to carry. The four words in
capital letters in each statement are reprinted after the statement. Print the
capital letter preceding the one of the four words which does MOST to spoil
the true meaning of the statement in the space at the right.

7. Retirement and pension systems are essential not only to provide employees with a   7.____
means of support in the future, but also to prevent longevity and CHARITABLE consider-
ations from UPSETTING the PROMOTIONAL opportunities for RETIRED members of
the career service.

   A. charitable   B. upsetting
   C. promotional   D. retired

8. Within each major DIVISION in a properly set up public or private organization, provision   8.____
is made so that each NECESSARY activity is CARED for and lines of authority and
responsibility are clear-cut and INFINITE.

   A. division   B. necessary   C. cared   D. infinite

9. In public service, the scale of salaries paid must be INCIDENTAL to the services ren-   9.____
dered, with due CONSIDERATION for the attraction of the desired MANPOWER and for
the maintenance of a standard of living COMMENSURATE with the work to be performed.

   A. incidental   B. consideration
   C. manpower   D. commensurate

10. An understanding of the AIMS of an organization by the staff will AID greatly in increas-   10.____
ing the DEMAND of the correspondence work of the office, and will to a large extent
DETERMINE the nature of the correspondence.

   A. aims   B. aid   C. demand   D. determine

11. BECAUSE the Civil Service Commission strongly feels that the MERIT system is a key   11.____
factor in the MAINTENANCE of democratic government, it has adopted as one of its
major DEFENSES the progressive democratization of its own procedures in dealing with
candidates for positions in the public service.

   A. Because   B. merit
   C. maintenance   D. defenses

Questions 12-14.

DIRECTIONS: Questions 12 through 14 consist of one sentence each. Each sentence contains an incorrectly used word. First, decide which is the incorrectly used word.
Then, from among the options given, decide which word, when substituted for
the incorrectly used word, makes the meaning of the sentence clear.

EXAMPLE:
The U.S. national income exhibits a pattern of long term deflection.
A. reflection
B. subjection
C. rejoicing
D. growth

The word *deflection* in the sentence does not convey the meaning the sentence evidently intended to convey. The word *growth* (Answer D), when substituted for the word *deflection,* makes the meaning of the sentence clear. Accordingly, the answer to the question is D.

12. The study commissioned by the joint committee fell compassionately short of the mark and would have to be redone.

    A. successfully
    C. experimentally
    B. insignificantly
    D. woefully

12.____

13. He will not idly exploit any violation of the provisions of the order.

    A. tolerate   B. refuse   C. construe   D. guard

13.____

14. The defendant refused to be virile and bitterly protested service.

    A. irked   B. feasible   C. docile   D. credible

14.____

Questions 15-25.

DIRECTIONS: Questions 15 through 25 consist of short paragraphs. Each paragraph contains one word which is INCORRECTLY used because it is NOT in keeping with the meaning of the paragraph. Find the word in each paragraph which is INCORRECTLY used and then select as the answer the suggested word which should be substituted for the incorrectly used word.

SAMPLE QUESTION:
In determining who is to do the work in your unit, you will have to decide just who does what from day to day. One of your lowest responsibilities is to assign work so that everybody gets a fair share and that everyone can do his part well.
A. new   B. old   C. important   D. performance

EXPLANATION:
The word which is NOT in keeping with the meaning of the paragraph is *lowest.* This is the INCORRECTLY used word. The suggested word *important* would be in keeping with the meaning of the paragraph and should be substituted for *lowest.* Therefore, the CORRECT answer is choice C.

15. If really good practice in the elimination of preventable injuries is to be achieved and held in any establishment, top management must refuse full and definite responsibility and must apply a good share of its attention to the task.

    A. accept   B. avoidable   C. duties   D. problem

15.____

16. Recording the human face for identification is by no means the only service performed by the camera in the field of investigation. When the trial of any issue takes place, a word picture is sought to be distorted to the court of incidents, occurrences, or events which are in dispute.

16.____

A. appeals   B. description
C. portrayed   D. deranged

17. In the collection of physical evidence, it cannot be emphasized too strongly that a hap-   17.____
hazard systematic search at the scene of the crime is vital. Nothing must be overlooked.
Often the only leads in a case will come from the results of this search.

     A. important   B. investigation
     C. proof   D. thorough

18. If an investigator has reason to suspect that the witness is mentally stable, or a habitual   18.____
drunkard, he should leave no stone unturned in his investigation to determine if the witness was under the influence of liquor or drugs, or was mentally unbalanced either at the
time of the occurrence to which he testified or at the time of the trial.

     A. accused   B. clue   C. deranged   D. question

19. The use of records is a valuable step in crime investigation and is the main reason every   19.____
department should maintain accurate reports. Crimes are not committed through the use
of departmental records alone but from the use of all records, of almost every type, wherever they may be found and whenever they give any incidental information regarding the
criminal.

     A. accidental   B. necessary
     C. reported   D. solved

20. In the years since passage of the Harrison Narcotic Act of 1914, making the possession   20.____
of opium amphetamines illegal in most circumstances, drug use has become a subject of
considerable scientific interest and investigation. There is at present a voluminous litera-
ture on drug use of various kinds.

     A. ingestion   B. derivatives
     C. addiction   D. opiates

21. Of course, the fact that criminal laws are extremely patterned in definition does not mean   21.____
that the majority of persons who violate them are dealt with as criminals. Quite the contrary, for a great many forbidden acts are voluntarily engaged in within situations of privacy and go unobserved and unreported.

     A. symbolic   B. casual
     C. scientific   D. broad-gauged

22. The most punitive way to study punishment is to focus attention on the pattern of punitive   22.____
action: to study how a penalty is applied, to study what is done to or taken from an
offender.

     A. characteristic   B. degrading
     C. objective   D. distinguished

23. The most common forms of punishment in times past have been death, physical torture,   23.____
mutilation, branding, public humiliation, fines, forfeits of property, banishment, transportation, and imprisonment. Although this list is by no means differentiated, practically every
form of punishment has had several variations and applications.

     A. specific   B. simple
     C. exhaustive   D. characteristic

24. There is another important line of inference between ordinary and professional criminals, and that is the source from which they are recruited. The professional criminal seems to be drawn from legitimate employment and, in many instances, from parallel vocations or pursuits.

24.____

    A. demarcation   B. justification
    C. superiority   D. reference

25. He took the position that the success of the program was insidious on getting additional revenue.

25.____

    A. reputed   B. contingent
    C. failure   D. indeterminate

KEY (CORRECT ANSWERS)

1.	A	11.	D
2.	B	12.	D
3.	B	13.	A
4.	C	14.	C
5.	D	15.	A
6.	C	16.	C
7.	D	17.	D
8.	D	18.	C
9.	A	19.	D
10.	C	20.	B

21.	D
22.	C
23.	C
24.	A
25.	B

TEST 3

DIRECTIONS: Each question or incomplete statement is followed by several suggested answers or completions. Select the one that BEST answers the question or completes the statement. *PRINT THE LETTER OF THE CORRECT ANSWER IN THE SPACE AT THE RIGHT.*

Questions 1-5.

DIRECTIONS: Question 1 through 5 are to be answered on the basis of the following:

You are a supervising officer in an investigative unit. Earlier in the day, you directed Detectives Tom Dixon and Sal Mayo to investigate a reported assault and robbery in a liquor store within your area of jurisdiction.

Detective Dixon has submitted to you a preliminary investigative report containing the following information:

- At 1630 hours on 2/20, arrived at Joe's Liquor Store at 350 SW Avenue with Detective Mayo to investigate A & R.
- At store interviewed Rob Ladd, store manager, who stated that he and Joe Brown (store owner) had been stuck up about ten minutes prior to our arrival.
- Ladd described the robbers as male whites in their late teens or early twenties. Further stated that one of the robbers displayed what appeared to be an automatic pistol as he entered the store, and said, *Give us the money or we'll kill you.* Ladd stated that Brown then reached under the counter where he kept a loaded .38 caliber pistol. Several shots followed, and Ladd threw himself to the floor.
- The robbers fled, and Ladd didn't know if any money had been taken.
- At this point, Ladd realized that Brown was unconscious on the floor and bleeding from a head wound.
- Ambulance called by Ladd, and Brown was removed by same to General Hospital.
- Personally interviewed John White, 382 Dartmouth Place, who stated he was inside store at the time of occurrence. White states that he hid behind a wine display upon hearing someone say, *Give us the money.* He then heard shots and saw two young men run from the store to a yellow car parked at the curb. White was unable to further describe auto. States the taller of the two men drove the car away while the other sat on passenger side in front.
- Recovered three spent .38 caliber bullets from premises and delivered them to Crime Lab.
- To General Hospital at 1800 hours but unable to interview Brown, who was under sedation and suffering from shock and a laceration of the head.
- Alarm #12487 transmitted for car and occupants.
- Case Active.

Based solely on the contents of the preliminary investigation submitted by Detective Dixon, select one sentence from the following groups of sentences which is MOST accurate and is grammatically correct.

1. A. Both robbers were armed.
    B. Each of the robbers were described as a male white.
    C. Neither robber was armed.
    D. Mr. Ladd stated that one of the robbers was armed.

1._____

2. A. Mr. Brown fired three shots from his revolver.
    B. Mr. Brown was shot in the head by one of the robbers.
    C. Mr. Brown suffered a gunshot wound of the head during the course of the robbery.
    D. Mr. Brown was taken to General Hospital by ambulance.

2._____

3. A. Shots were fired after one of the robbers said, *Give us* the money or we'll kill you.
    B. After one of the robbers demanded the money from Mr. Brown, he fired a shot.
    C. The preliminary investigation indicated that although Mr. Brown did not have a license for the gun, he was justified in using deadly physical force.
    D. Mr. Brown was interviewed at General Hospital.

3._____

4. A. Each of the witnesses were customers in the store at the time of occurrence.
    B. Neither of the witnesses interviewed was the owner of the liquor store.
    C. Neither of the witnesses interviewed were the owner of the store.
    D. Neither of the witnesses was employed by Mr. Brown.

4._____

5. A. Mr. Brown arrived at General Hospital at about 5:00 P.M.
    B. Neither of the robbers was injured during the robbery.
    C. The robbery occurred at 3:30 P.M. on February 10.
    D. One of the witnesses called the ambulance.

5._____

Questions 6-10.

DIRECTIONS: Each of Questions 6 through 10 consists of information given in outline form and four sentences labelled A, B, C, and D. For each question, choose the one sentence which CORRECTLY expresses the information given in outline form and which also displays PROPER English usage.

6. Client's Name - Joanna Jones
    Number of Children - 3
    Client's Income - None
    Client's Marital Status - Single

    A. Joanna Jones is an unmarried client with three children who have no income.
    B. Joanna Jones, who is single and has no income, a client she has three children.
    C. Joanna Jones, whose three children are clients, is single and has no income.
    D. Joanna Jones, who has three children, is an unmarried client with no income.

6._____

7. Client's Name - Bertha Smith
    Number of Children - 2
    Client's Rent - $105 per month
    Number of Rooms - 4

7._____

A. Bertha Smith, a client, pays $105 per month for her four rooms with two children.
B. Client Bertha Smith has two children and pays $105 per month for four rooms.
C. Client Bertha Smith is paying $105 per month for two children with four rooms.
D. For four rooms and two children client Bertha Smith pays $105 per month.

8. Name of Employee - Cynthia Dawes
   Number of Cases Assigned - 9
   Date Cases were Assigned - 12/16
   Number of Assigned Cases Completed - 8

   A. On December 16, employee Cynthia Dawes was assigned nine cases; she has completed eight of these cases.
   B. Cynthia Dawes, employee on December 16, assigned nine cases, completed eight.
   C. Being employed on December 16, Cynthia Dawes completed eight of nine assigned cases.
   D. Employee Cynthia Dawes, she was assigned nine cases and completed eight, on December 16.

9. Place of Audit - Broadway Center
   Names of Auditors - Paul Cahn, Raymond Perez
   Date of Audit - 11/20
   Number of Cases Audited - 41

   A. On November 20, at the Broadway Center 41 cases was audited by auditors Paul Cahn and Raymond Perez.
   B. Auditors Raymond Perez and Paul Cahn has audited 41 cases at the Broadway Center on November 20.
   C. At the Broadway Center, on November 20, auditors Paul Cahn and Raymond Perez audited 41 cases.
   D. Auditors Paul Cahn and Raymond Perez at the Broadway Center, on November 20, is auditing 41 cases.

10. Name of Client - Barbra Levine
    Client's Monthly Income - $210
    Client's Monthly Expenses - $452

    A. Barbra Levine is a client, her monthly income is $210 and her monthly expenses is $452.
    B. Barbra Levine's monthly income is $210 and she is a client, with whose monthly expenses are $452.
    C. Barbra Levine is a client whose monthly income is $210 and whose monthly expenses are $452.
    D. Barbra Levine, a client, is with a monthly income which is $210 and monthly expenses which are $452.

Questions 11-13.

DIRECTIONS: Questions 11 through 13 involve several statements of fact presented in a very simple way. These statements of fact are followed by 4 choices which attempt to incorporate all of the facts into one logical sentence which is properly constructed and grammatically correct.

11.   I.   Mr. Brown was sweeping the sidewalk in front of his house.   11.____
      II.   He was sweeping it because it was dirty.
      III. He swept the refuse into the street
      IV. Police Officer Green gave him a ticket.
Which one of the following BEST presents the information given above?

    A. Because his sidewalk was dirty, Mr. Brown received a ticket from Officer Green when he swept the refuse into the street.
    B. Police Officer Green gave Mr. Brown a ticket because his sidewalk was dirty and he swept the refuse into the street.
    C. Police Officer Green gave Mr. Brown a ticket for sweeping refuse into the street because his sidewalk was dirty.
    D. Mr. Brown, who was sweeping refuse from his dirty sidewalk into the street, was given a ticket by Police Officer Green.

12.   I.   Sergeant Smith radioed for help.   12.____
      II.   The sergeant did so because the crowd was getting larger.
      III. It was 10:00 A.M. when he made his call.
      IV. Sergeant Smith was not in uniform at the time of occurrence.
Which one of the following BEST presents the information given above?

    A. Sergeant Smith, although not on duty at the time, radioed for help at 10 o'clock because the crowd was getting uglier.
    B. Although not in uniform, Sergeant Smith called for help at 10:00 A.M. because the crowd was getting uglier.
    C. Sergeant Smith radioed for help at 10:00 A.M. because the crowd was getting larger.
    D. Although he was not in uniform, Sergeant Smith radioed for help at 10:00 A.M. because the crowd was getting larger.

13.   I.   The payroll office is open on Fridays.   13.____
      II.   Paychecks are distributed from 9:00 A.M. to 12 Noon.
      III. The office is open on Fridays because that's the only day the payroll staff is available.
      IV. It is open for the specified hours in order to permit employees to cash checks at the bank during lunch hour.
The choice below which MOST clearly and accurately presents the above idea is:

    A. Because the payroll office is open on Fridays from 9:00 A.M. to 12 Noon, employees can cash their checks when the payroll staff is available.
    B. Because the payroll staff is only available on Fridays until noon, employees can cash their checks during their lunch hour.
    C. Because the payroll staff is available only on Fridays, the office is open from 9:00 A.M. to 12 Noon to allow employees to cash their checks.
    D. Because of payroll staff availability, the payroll office is open on Fridays. It is open from 9:00 A.M. to 12 Noon so that distributed paychecks can be cashed at the bank while employees are on their lunch hour.

Questions 14-16.

DIRECTIONS: In each of Questions 14 through 16, the four sentences are from a paragraph in a report. They are not in the right order. Which of the following arrangements is the BEST one?

14. I.   An executive may answer a letter by writing his reply on the face of the letter itself instead of having a return letter typed.   14.____
    II. This procedure is efficient because it saves the executive's time, the typist's time, and saves office file space.
    III. Copying machines are used in small offices as well as large offices to save time and money in making brief replies to business letters.
    IV. A copy is made on a copying machine to go into the company files, while the original is mailed back to the sender.
The CORRECT answer is:

    A. I, II, IV, III   B. I, IV, II, III
    C. III, I, IV, II   D. III, IV, II, I

15. I.   Most organizations favor one of the types but always include the others to a lesser degree.   15.____
    II. However, we can detect a definite trend toward greater use of symbolic control.
    III. We suggest that our local police agencies are today primarily utilizing material control.
    IV. Control can be classified into three types: physical, material, and symbolic.
The CORRECT answer is:

    A. IV, II, III, I   B. II, I, IV, III
    C. III, IV, II, I   D. IV, I, III, II

16. I.   They can and do take advantage of ancient political and geographical boundaries, which often give them sanctuary from effective police activity.   16.____
    II. This country is essentially a country of small police forces, each operating independently within the limits of its jurisdiction.
    III. The boundaries that define and limit police operations do not hinder the movement of criminals, of course.
    IV. The machinery of law enforcement in America is fragmented, complicated, and frequently overlapping.
The CORRECT answer is:

    A. III, I, II, IV   B. II, IV, I, III
    C. IV, II, III, I   D. IV, III, II, I

17. Examine the following sentence, and then choose from below the words which should be inserted in the blank spaces to produce the best sentence.   17.____
The unit has exceeded _____ goals and the employees are satisfied with _____ accomplishments.

    A. their, it's   B. it's, it's
    C. its, there   D. its, their

18. Examine the following sentence, and then choose from below the words which should be   18.____
    inserted in the blank spaces to produce the best sentence.
    Research indicates that employees who _____ no opportunity for close social rela-
    tionships often find their work unsatisfying, and this _____ of satisfaction often
    reflects itself in low production.

    A. have, lack   B. have, excess
    C. has, lack   D. has, excess

19. Words in a sentence must be arranged properly to make sure that the intended meaning   19.____
    of the sentence is clear. The sentence below that does NOT make sense because a
    clause has been separated from the word on which its meaning depends is:

    A. To be a good writer, clarity is necessary.
    B. To be a good writer, you must write clearly.
    C. You must write clearly to be a good writer.
    D. Clarity is necessary to good writing.

Questions 20-21.

DIRECTIONS: Each of Questions 20 and 21 consists of a statement which contains a word
             (one of those underlined) that is either incorrectly used because it is not in
             keeping with the meaning the quotation is evidently intended to convey, or is
             misspelled. There is only one INCORRECT word in each quotation. Of the four
             underlined words, determine if the first one should be replaced by the word let-
             tered A, the second one replaced by the word lettered B, the third one
             replaced by the word lettered C, or the fourth one replaced by the word let-
             tered D. *PRINT THE LETTER OF THE REPLACEMENT WORD YOU HAVE
             SELECTED IN THE SPACE AT THE RIGHT.*

20. The alleged killer was occasionally permitted to excercise in the corridor.   20.____

    A. alledged   B. ocasionally
    C. permited   D. exercise

21. Defense counsel stated, in affect, that their conduct was permissible under the First   21.____
    Amendment.

    A. council   B. effect
    C. there   D. permissable

Question 22.

DIRECTIONS: Question 22 consists of one sentence. This sentence contains an incorrectly
             used word. First, decide which is the incorrectly used word. Then, from among
             the options given, decide which word, when substituted for the incorrectly used
             word, makes the meaning of the sentence clear.

22. As today's violence has no single cause, so its causes have no single scheme.   22.____

    A. deference   B. cure   C. flaw   D. relevance

119

23. In the sentence, *A man in a light-grey suit waited thirty-five minutes in the ante-room for the all-important document,* the word IMPROPERLY hyphenated is

    A. light-grey   B. thirty-five
    C. ante-room   D. all-important

23.____

24. In the sentence, *The candidate wants to file his application for preference before it is too late,* the word *before* is used as a(n)

    A. preposition   B. subordinating conjunction
    C. pronoun   D. adverb

24.____

25. In the sentence, *The perpetrators ran from the scene,* the word *from* is a

    A. preposition   B. pronoun
    C. verb   D. conjunction

25.____

KEY (CORRECT ANSWERS)

1.	D		11.	D
2.	D		12.	D
3.	A		13.	D
4.	B		14.	C
5.	D		15.	D
6.	D		16.	C
7.	B		17.	D
8.	A		18.	A
9.	C		19.	A
10.	C		20.	D

21.	B
22.	B
23.	C
24.	B
25.	A

PREPARING WRITTEN MATERIAL

PARAGRAPH REARRANGEMENT
COMMENTARY

The sentences which follow are in scrambled order. You are to rearrange them in proper order and indicate the letter choice containing the correct answer at the space at the right.

Each group of sentences in this section is actually a paragraph presented in scrambled order. Each sentence in the group has a place in that paragraph; no sentence is to be left out. You are to read each group of sentences and decide upon the best order in which to put the sentences so as to form as well-organized paragraph.

The questions in this section measure the ability to solve a problem when all the facts relevant to its solution are not given.

More specifically, certain positions of responsibility and authority require the employee to discover connections between events sometimes, apparently, unrelated. In order to do this, the employee will find it necessary to correctly infer that unspecified events have probably occurred or are likely to occur. This ability becomes especially important when action must be taken on incomplete information.

Accordingly, these questions require competitors to choose among several suggested alternatives, each of which presents a different sequential arrangement of the events. Competitors must choose the MOST logical of the suggested sequences.

In order to do so, they may be required to draw on general knowledge to infer missing concepts or events that are essential to sequencing the given events. Competitors should be careful to infer only what is essential to the sequence. The plausibility of the wrong alternatives will always require the inclusion of unlikely events or of additional chains of events which are NOT essential to sequencing the given events.

It's very important to remember that you are looking for the best of the four possible choices, and that the best choice of all may not even be one of the answers you're given to choose from.

There is no one right way to solve these problems. Many people have found it helpful to first write out the order of the sentences, as they would have arranged them, on their scrap paper before looking at the possible answers. If their optimum answer is there, this can save them some time. If it isn't, this method can still give insight into solving the problem. Others find it most helpful to just go through each of the possible choices, contrasting each as they go along. You should use whatever method feels comfortable, and works, for you.

While most of these types of questions are not that difficult, we've added a higher percentage of the difficult type, just to give you more practice. Usually there are only one or two questions on this section that contain such subtle distinctions that you're unable to answer confidently, and you then may find yourself stuck deciding between two possible choices, neither of which you're sure about.

PREPARING WRITTEN MATERIAL
EXAMINATION SECTION
TEST 1

DIRECTIONS: The sentences that follow are in scrambled order. You are to rearrange them in proper order and indicate the letter choice containing the CORRECT answer. *PRINT THE LETTER OF THE CORRECT ANSWER IN THE SPACE AT THE RIGHT.*

1. Police Officer Jenner responds to the scene of a burglary at 2106 La Vista Boulevard. He is approached by an elderly man named Richard Jenkins, whose account of the incident includes the following five sentences:

    I.   I saw that the lock on my apartment door had been smashed and the door was open.
    II.   My apartment was a shambles; my belongings were everywhere and my television set was missing.
    III. As I walked down the hallway toward the bedroom, I heard someone opening a window.
    IV. I left work at 5:30 P.M. and took the bus home.
    V.   At that time, I called the police.

    The MOST logical order for the above sentences to appear in the report is

    A.   I, V, IV, II, III
    C.   I, V, II, III, IV
    B.   IV, I, II, III, V
    D.   IV, III, II, V, I

    1.____

2. Police Officer LaJolla is writing an Incident Report in which back-up assistance was required. The report will contain the following five sentences:

    I.   The radio dispatcher asked what my location was and he then dispatched patrol cars for back-up assistance.
    II.   At approximately 9:30 P.M., while I was walking my assigned footpost, a gunman fired three shots at me.
    III. I quickly turned around and saw a white male, approximately 5'10", with black hair, wearing blue jeans, a yellow T-shirt, and white sneakers, running across the avenue carrying a handgun.
    IV. When the back-up officers arrived, we searched the area but could not find the suspect.
    V.   I advised the radio dispatcher that a gunman had just fired a gun at me, and then I gave the dispatcher a description of the man.

    The MOST logical order for the above sentences to appear in the report is

    A.   III, V, II, IV, I
    C.   III, II, IV, I, V
    B.   II, III, V, I, IV
    D.   II, V, I, III, IV

    2.____

3. Police Officer Durant is completing a report of a robbery and assault. The report will contain the following five sentences:

    I.   I went to Mount Snow Hospital to interview a man who was attacked and robbed of his wallet earlier that night.
    II.   An ambulance arrived at 82nd Street and 3rd Avenue and took an intoxicated, wounded man to Mount Snow Hospital.
    III. Two youths attacked the man and stole his wallet.
    IV. A well-dressed man left Hanratty's Bar very drunk, with his wallet hanging out of his back pocket.
    V.   A passerby dialed 911 and requested police and ambulance assistance.

    3.____

The MOST logical order for the above sentences to appear in the report is

   A. I, II, IV, III, V
   C. IV, V, II, III, I

   B. IV, III, V, II, I
   D. V, IV, III, II, I

4. Police Officer Boswell is preparing a report of an armed robbery and assault which will contain the following five sentences:

    I.   Both men approached the bartender and one of them drew a gun.
    II. The bartender immediately went to grab the phone at the bar.
    III. One of the men leaped over the counter and smashed a bottle over the bartender's head.
    IV. Two men in a blue Buick drove up to the bar and went inside.
    V. I found the cash register empty and the bartender unconscious on the floor, with the phone still dangling off the hook.

The MOST logical order for the above sentences to appear in the report is

   A. IV, I, II, III, V
   C. IV, III, II, V, I

   B. V, IV, III, I, II
   D. II, I, III, IV, V

4._____

5. Police Officer Mitzler is preparing a report of a bank robbery, which will contain the following five sentences:

    I.   The teller complied with the instructions on the note, but also hit the silent alarm.
    II. The perpetrator then fled south on Broadway.
    III. A suspicious male entered the bank at approximately 10:45 A.M.
    IV. At this time, an undetermined amount of money has been taken.
    V. He approached the teller on the far right side and handed her a note.

The MOST logical order for the above sentences to appear in the report is

   A. III, V, I, II, IV
   C. III, V, IV, I, II

   B. I, III, V, II, IV
   D. III, V, II, IV, I

5._____

6. A Police Officer is preparing an Accident Report for an accident which occurred at the intersection of East 119th Street and Lexington Avenue. The report will include the following five sentences:

    I.   On September 18, 1990, while driving ten children to school, a school bus driver passed out.
    II. Upon arriving at the scene, I notified the dispatcher to send an ambulance.
    III. I notified the parents of each child once I got to the station house.
    IV. He said the school bus, while traveling west on East 119th Street, struck a parked Ford which was on the southwest corner of East 119th Street.
    V. A witness by the name of John Ramos came up to me to describe what happened.

The MOST logical order for the above sentences to appear in the Accident Report is

   A. I, II, V, III, IV
   C. II, V, I, III, IV

   B. I, II, V, IV, III
   D. II, V, I, IV, III

6._____

7. A Police Officer is preparing a report concerning a dispute. The report will contain the following five sentences: 7.____

    I.   The passenger got out of the back of the taxi and leaned through the front window to complain to the driver about the fare.

    II. The driver of the taxi caught up with the passenger and knocked him to the ground; the passenger then kicked the driver and a scuffle ensued.

    III. The taxi drew up in front of the high-rise building and stopped.

    IV. The driver got out of the taxi and followed the passenger into the lobby of the apartment building.

    V. The doorman tried but was unable to break up the fight, at which point he called the precinct.

The MOST logical order for the above sentences to appear in the report is

  A. III, I, IV, II, V   B. III, IV, I, II, V
  C. III, IV, II, V, I   D. V, I, III, IV, II

8. Police Officer Morrow is writing an Incident Report. The report will include the following four sentences: 8.____

    I.   The man reached into his pocket and pulled out a gun.

    II. While on foot patrol, I identified a suspect, who was wanted for six robberies in the area, from a wanted picture I was carrying.

    III. I drew my weapon and fired six rounds at the suspect, killing him instantly.

    IV. I called for back-up assistance and told the man to put his hands up.

The MOST logical order for the above sentences to appear in the report is

  A. II, III, IV, I   B. IV, I, III, II
  C. IV, I, II, III   D. II, IV, I, III

9. Sergeant Allen responds to a call at 16 Grove Street regarding a missing child. At the scene, the Sergeant is met by Police Officer Samuels, who gives a brief account of the incident consisting of the following five sentences: 9.____

    I.   I transmitted the description and waited for you to arrive before I began searching the area.

    II. Mrs. Banks, the mother, reports that she last saw her daughter Julie about 7:30 A.M. when she took her to school.

    III. About 6 P.M., my partner and I arrived at this location to investigate a report of a missing 8 year-old girl.

    IV. When Mrs. Banks left her, Julie was wearing a red and white striped T-shirt, blue jeans, and white sneakers.

    V. Mrs. Banks dropped her off in front of the playground of P.S. 11.

The MOST logical order for the above sentences to appear in the report is

  A. III, V, IV, II, I   B. III, II, V, IV, I
  C. III, IV, I, II, V   D. III, II, IV, I, V

10. Police Officer Franco is completing a report of an assault. The report will contain the following five sentences: 10.____

    I.   In the park I observed an elderly man lying on the ground, bleeding from a back wound.

    II. I applied first aid to control the bleeding and radioed for an ambulance to respond.

III. The elderly man stated that he was sitting on the park bench when he was attacked from behind by two males.
IV. I received a report of a man's screams coming from inside the park, and I went to investigate.
V. The old man could not give a description of his attackers.

The MOST logical order for the above sentences to appear in the report is

A. IV, I, II, III, V
C. IV, III, V, II, I
B. V, III, I, IV, II
D. II, I, V, IV, III

11. Police Officer Williams is completing a Crime Report. The report contains the following five sentences:

I. As Police Officer Hanson and I approached the store, we noticed that the front door was broken.
II. After determining that the burglars had fled, we notified the precinct of the burglary.
III. I walked through the front door as Police Officer Hanson walked around to the back.
IV. At approximately midnight, an alarm was heard at the Apex Jewelry Store.
V. We searched the store and found no one.

The MOST logical order for the above sentences to appear in the report is

A. I, IV, II, III, V
C. IV, I, III, II, V
B. I, IV, III, V, II
D. IV, I, III, V, II

12. Police Officer Clay is giving a report to the news media regarding someone who has jumped from the Empire State Building. His report will include the following five sentences:

I. I responded to the 86th floor, where I found the person at the edge of the roof.
II. A security guard at the building had reported that a man was on the roof at the 86th floor.
III. At 5:30 P.M., the person jumped from the building.
IV. I received a call from the radio dispatcher at 4:50 P.M. to respond to the Empire State Building.
V. I tried to talk to the person and convince him not to jump.

The MOST logical order for the above sentences to appear in the report is

A. I, II, IV, III, V
C. II, IV, I, III, V
B. III, IV, I, II, V
D. IV, II, I, V, III

13. The following five sentences are part of a report of a burglary written by Police Officer Reed:

I. When I arrived at 2400 1st Avenue, I noticed that the door was slightly open.
II. I yelled out, *Police, don't move!*
III. As I entered the apartment, I saw a man with a TV set passing it through a window to another man standing on a fire escape.
IV. While on foot patrol, I was informed by the radio dispatcher that a burglary was in progress at 2400 1st Avenue.
V. However, the burglars quickly ran down the fire escape.

The MOST logical order for the above sentences to appear in the report is

A. I, III, IV, V, II
C. IV, I, III, II, V
B. IV, I, III, V, II
D. I, IV, III, II, V

14. Police Officer Jenkins is preparing a report for Lost or Stolen Property. The report will include the following five sentences:

    I. On the stairs, Mr. Harris slipped on a wet leaf and fell on the landing.

    II. It wasn't until he got to the token booth that Mr. Harris realized his wallet was no longer in his back pants pocket.

    III. A boy wearing a football jersey helped him up and brushed off the back of Mr. Harris' pants.

    IV. Mr. Harris states he was walking up the stairs to the elevated subway at Queensborough Plaza.

    V. Before Mr. Harris could thank him, the boy was running down the stairs to the street.

The MOST logical order for the above sentences to appear in the report is

  A. IV, III, V, I, II   B. IV, I, III, V, II
  C. I, IV, II, III, V   D. I, II, IV, III, V

14.____

15. Police Officer Hubbard is completing a report of a missing person. The report will contain the following five sentences:

    I. I visited the store at 7:55 P.M. and asked the employees if they had seen a girl fitting the description I had been given.

    II. She gave me a description and said she had gone into the local grocery store at about 6:15 P.M.

    III. I asked the woman for a description of her daughter.

    IV. The distraught woman called the precinct to report that her daughter, aged 12, had not returned from an errand.

    V. The storekeeper said a girl matching the description had been in the store earlier, but he could not give an exact time.

The MOST logical order for the above sentences to appear in the report is

  A. I, III, II, V, IV   B. IV, III, II, I, V
  C. V, I, II, III, IV   D. III, I, II, IV, V

15.____

16. A police officer is completing an entry in his Daily Activity Log regarding traffic summonses which he issued. The following five sentences will be included in the entry:

    I. I was on routine patrol parked 16 yards west of 170th Street and Clay Avenue.

    II. The summonses were issued for unlicensed operator and disobeying a steady red light.

    III. At 8 A.M. hours, I observed an auto traveling westbound on 170th Street not stop for a steady red light at the intersection of Clay Avenue and 170th Street.

    IV. I stopped the driver of the auto and determined that he did not have a valid driver's license.

    V. After a brief conversation, I informed the motorist that he was receiving two summonses.

The MOST logical order for the above sentences to appear in the report is

  A. I, III, IV, V, II   B. III, IV, II, V, I
  C. V, II, I, III, IV   D. IV, V, II, I, III

16.____

17. The following sentences appeared on an Incident Report:

    I. Three teenagers who had been ejected from the theater were yelling at patrons who were now entering.

    II. Police Officer Dixon told the teenagers to leave the area.

    III. The teenagers said that they were told by the manager to leave the theater because they were talking during the movie.

    IV. The theater manager called the precinct at 10:20 P.M. to report a disturbance outside the theater.

    V. A patrol car responded to the theater at 10:42 P.M. and two police officers went over to the teenagers.

The MOST logical order for the above sentences to appear in the Incident Report

    A. I, V, IV, III, II   B. IV, I, V, III, II
    C. IV, I, III, V, II   D. IV, III, I, V, II

17.____

18. Activity Log entries are completed by police officers. Police Officer Samuels has written an entry concerning vandalism and part of it contains the following five sentences:

    I. The man, in his early twenties, ran down the block and around the corner.

    II. A man passing the store threw a brick through a window of the store.

    III. I arrived on the scene and began to question the witnesses about the incident.

    IV. Malcolm Holmes, the owner of the Fast Service Shoe Repair Store, was working in the back of the store at approximately 3 P.M.

    V. After the man fled, Mr. Holmes called the police.

The MOST logical order for the above sentences to appear in the Activity Log is

    A. IV, II, I, V, III   B. II, IV, I, III, V
    C. II, I, IV, III, V   D. IV, II, V, III, I

18.____

19. Police Officer Buckley is preparing a report concerning a dispute in a restaurant. The report will contain the following five sentences:

    I. The manager, Charles Chin, and a customer, Edward Green, were standing near the register arguing over the bill.

    II. The manager refused to press any charges providing Green pay the check and leave.

    III. While on foot patrol, I was informed by a passerby of a disturbance in the Dragon Flame Restaurant.

    IV. Green paid the $7.50 check and left the restaurant.

    V. According to witnesses, the customer punched the owner in the face when Chin asked him for the amount due.

The MOST logical order for the above sentences to appear in the report is

    A. III, I, V, II, IV   B. I, II, III, IV, V
    C. V, I, III, II, IV   D. III, V, II, IV, I

19.____

20. Police Officer Wilkins is preparing a report for leaving the scene of an accident. The report will include the following five sentences:

    I. The Dodge struck the right rear fender of Mrs. Smith's 1980 Ford and continued on its way.

    II. Mrs. Smith stated she was making a left turn from 40th Street onto Third Avenue.

    III. As the car passed, Mrs. Smith noticed the dangling rear license plate #412AEJ.

    IV. Mrs. Smith complained to police of back pains and was removed by ambulance to Bellevue Hospital.

    V. An old green Dodge traveling up Third Avenue went through the red light at 40th Street and Third Avenue.

The MOST logical order for the above sentences to appear in the report is

    A. V, III, I, II, IV   B. I, III, II, V, IV
    C. IV, V, I, II, III   D. II, V, I, III, IV

20.____

21. Detective Simon is completing a Crime Report. The report contains the following five sentences:

    I. Police Officer Chin, while on foot patrol, heard the yelling and ran in the direction of the man.

    II. The man, carrying a large hunting knife, left the High Sierra Sporting Goods Store at approximately 10:30 A.M.

    III. When the man heard Police Officer Chin, he stopped, dropped the knife, and began to cry.

    IV. As Police Officer Chin approached the man, he drew his gun and yelled, *Police, freeze.*

    V. After the man left the store, he began yelling, over and over, *I am going to 'kill myself!*

The MOST logical order for the above sentences to appear in the report is

    A. V, II, I, IV, III   B. II, V, I, IV, III
    C. II, V, IV, I, III   D. II, I, V, IV, III

21.____

22. Police Officer Miller is preparing a Complaint Report which will include the following five sentences:

    I. From across the lot, he yelled to the boys to get away from his car.

    II. When he came out of the store, he noticed two teenage boys trying to break into his car.

    III. The boys fled as Mr. Johnson ran to his car.

    IV. Mr. Johnson stated that he parked his car in the municipal lot behind Tams Department Store.

    V. Mr. Johnson saw that the door lock had been broken, but nothing was missing from inside the auto.

The MOST logical order for the above sentences to appear in the report is

    A. IV, I, II, V, III   B. II, III, I, V, IV
    C. IV, II, I, III, V   D. I, II, III, V, IV

22.____

23. Police Officer O'Hara completes a Universal Summons for a motorist who has just   23._____
passed a red traffic light. The Universal Summons includes the following five sentences:
    I.   As the car passed the light, I followed in the patrol car.
    II. After the driver stopped the car, he stated that the light was yellow, not red.
    III. A blue Cadillac sedan passed the red light on the corner of 79th Street and
        3rd Avenue at 11:25 P.M.
    IV. As a result, the driver was informed that he did pass a red light and that his
        brake lights were not working.
    V. The driver in the Cadillac stopped his car as soon as he saw the patrol car,
        and I noticed that the brake lights were not working.
The MOST logical order for the above sentences to appear in the Universal Summons
is

    A. I, III, V, II, IV   B. III, I, V, II, IV
    C. Iil, I, V, IV, II   D. I, III, IV, II, V

24. Detective Egan is preparing a follow-up report regarding a homicide on 170th Street and   24._____
College Avenue. An unknown male was found at the scene. The report will contain the
following five sentences:
    I.   Police Officer Gregory wrote down the names, addresses, and phone num-
        bers of the witnesses.
    II. A 911 operator received a call of a man shot and dispatched Police Officers
        Worth and Gregory to the scene.
    III. They discovered an unidentified male dead on the street.
    IV. Police Officer Worth notified the Precinct Detective Unit immediately.
    V. At approximately 9:00 A.M., an unidentified male shot another male in the
        chest during an argument.
The MOST logical order for the above sentences to appear in the report is

    A. V, II, III, IV, I   B. II, III, V, IV, I
    C. IV, I, V, II, III   D. V, III, II, IV, I

25. Police Officer Tracey is preparing a Robbery Report which will include the following five   25._____
sentences:
    I.   I ran around the corner and observed a man pointing a gun at a taxidriver.
    II. I informed the man I was a police officer and that he should not move.
    III. I was on the corner of 125th Street and Park Avenue when I heard a scream
        coming from around the corner.
    IV. The man turned around and fired one shot at me.
    V. I fired once, shooting him in the arm and causing him to fall to the ground.
The MOST logical order for the above sentences to appear in the report is

    A. I, III, IV, II, V   B. IV, V, II, I, III
    C. III, I, II, IV, V   D. III, I, V, II, IV

KEY (CORRECT ANSWERS)

1.	B		11.	D
2.	B		12.	D
3.	B		13.	C
4.	A		14.	B
5.	A		15.	B
6.	B		16.	A
7.	A		17.	B
8.	D		18.	A
9.	B		19.	A
10.	A		20.	D

21.	B
22.	C
23.	B
24.	A
25.	C

TEST 2

DIRECTIONS: The sentences that follow are in scrambled order. You are to rearrange them in proper order and indicate the letter choice containing the CORRECT answer. *PRINT THE LETTER OF THE CORRECT ANSWER IN THE SPACE AT THE RIGHT.*

1. Police Officer Weiker is completing a Complaint Report which will contain the following five sentences:

    I. Mr. Texlor was informed that the owner of the van would receive a parking ticket and that the van would be towed away.

    II. The police tow truck arrived approximately one half hour after Mr. Texlor complained.

    III. While on foot patrol on West End Avenue, I saw the owner of Rand's Restaurant arrive to open his business.

    IV. Mr. Texlor, the owner, called to me and complained that he could not receive deliveries because a van was blocking his driveway.

    V. The van's owner later reported to the precinct that his van had been stolen, and he was then informed that it had been towed.

    The MOST logical order for the above sentences to appear in the report is

    A. III, V, I, II, IV
    B. III, IV, I, II, V
    C. IV, III, I, II, V
    D. IV, III, II, I, V

    1.____

2. Police Officer Ames is completing an entry in his Activity Log. The entry contains the following five sentences:

    I. Mr. Sands gave me a complete description of the robber.

    II. Alvin Sands, owner of the Star Delicatessen, called the precinct to report he had just been robbed.

    III. I then notified all police patrol vehicles to look for a white male in his early twenties wearing brown pants and shirt, a black leather jacket, and black and white sneakers.

    IV. I arrived on the scene after being notified by the precinct that a robbery had just occurred at the Star Delicatessen.

    V. Twenty minutes later, a man fitting the description was arrested by a police officer on patrol six blocks from the delicatessen.

    The MOST logical order for the above sentences to appear in the Activity Log is

    A. II, I, IV, III, V
    B. II, IV, III, I, V
    C. II, IV, I, III, V
    D. II, IV, I, V, III

    2.____

3. Police Officer Benson is completing a Complaint Report concerning a stolen taxicab, which will include the following five sentences:

    I. Police Officer Benson noticed that a cab was parked next to a fire hydrant.

    II. Dawson *borrowed* the cab for transportation purposes since he was in a hurry.

    III. Ed Dawson got into his car and tried to start it, but the battery was dead.

    IV. When he reached his destination, he parked the cab by a fire hydrant and placed the keys under the seat.

    V. He looked around and saw an empty cab with the engine running.

    The MOST logical order for the above sentences to appear in the report is

    3.____

A. I, III, II, IV, V
C. III, V, II, IV, I

B. III, I, II, V, IV
D. V, II, IV, III, I

4. Police Officer Hatfield is reviewing his Activity Log entry prior to completing a report. The
    entry contains the following five sentences:

    I.   When I arrived at Zand's Jewelry Store, I noticed that the door was slightly
         open.
    II. I told the burglar I was a police officer and that he should stand still or he
         would be shot.
    III. As I entered the store, I saw a man wearing a ski mask attempting to open
         the safe in the back of the store.
    IV. On December 16, 1990, at 1:38 A.M., I was informed that a burglary was in
         progress at Zand's Jewelry Store on East 59th Street.
    V.   The burglar quickly pulled a knife from his pocket when he saw me.

    The MOST logical order for the above sentences to appear in the report is

    A. IV, I, III, V, II
    C. IV, III, II, V, I

    B. I, IV, III, V, II
    D. I, III, IV, V, II

4.____

5. Police Officer Lorenz is completing a report of a murder. The report will contain the fol-
    lowing five statements made by a witness:

    I.   I was awakened by the sound of a gunshot coming from the apartment next
         door, and I decided to check.
    II. I entered the apartment and looked into the kitchen and the bathroom.
    III. I found Mr. Hubbard's body slumped in the bathtub.
    IV. The door to the apartment was open, but I didn't see anyone.
    V.   He had been shot in the head.

    The MOST logical order for the above sentences to appear in the report is

    A. I, III, II, IV, V
    C. IV, II, I, III, V

    B. I, IV, II, III, V
    D. III, I, II, IV, V

5.____

6. Police Officer Baldwin is preparing an accident report which will include the following five
    sentences:

    I.   The old man lay on the ground for a few minutes, but was not physically hurt.
    II. Charlie Watson, a construction worker, was repairing some brick work at the
         top of a building at 54th Street and Madison Avenue.
    III. Steven Green, his partner, warned him that this could be dangerous, but
         Watson ignored him.
    IV. A few minutes later, one of the bricks thrown by Watson smashed to the
         ground in front of an old man, who fainted out of fright.
    V.   Mr. Watson began throwing some of the bricks over the side of the building.

    The MOST logical order for the above sentences to appear in the report is

    A. II, V, III, IV, I
    C. III, II, IV, V, I

    B. I, IV, II, V, III
    D. II, III, I, IV, V

6.____

7. Police Officer Porter is completing an incident report concerning her rescue of a woman being held hostage by a former boyfriend. Her report will contain the following five sentences:

    I.   I saw a man holding .25 caliber gun to a woman's head, but he did not see me.

    II.   I then broke a window and gained access to the house.

    III.   As I approached the house on foot, a gunshot rang out and I heard a woman scream.

    IV.   A decoy van brought me as close as possible to the house where the woman was being held hostage.

    V.   I ordered the man to drop his gun, and he released the woman and was taken into custody.

The MOST logical order for the above sentences to appear in the report is

    A. I, III, II, IV, V   B. IV, III, II, I, V
    C. III, II, I, IV, V   D. V, I, II, III, IV

8. Police Officer Byrnes is preparing a crime report concerning a robbery. The report will consist of the following five sentences:

    I.   Mr. White, following the man's instructions, opened the car's hood, at which time the man got out of the auto, drew a revolver, and ordered White to give him all the money in his pockets.

    II.   Investigation has determined there were no witnesses to this incident.

    III.   The man asked White to check the oil and fill the tank.

    IV.   Mr. White, a gas attendant, states that he was working alone at the gas station when a black male pulled up to the gas pump in a white Mercury.

    V.   White was then bound and gagged by the male and locked in the gas station's rest room.

The MOST logical order for the above sentences to appear in the report is

    A. IV, I, III, II, V   B. III, I, II, V, IV
    C. IV, III, I, V, II   D. I, III, IV, II, V

9. Police Officer Gale is preparing a report of a crime committed against Mr. Weston. The report will consist of the following five sentences:

    I.   The man, who had a gun, told Mr. Weston not to scream for help and ordered him back into the apartment.

    II.   With Mr. Weston disposed of in this fashion, the man proceeded to ransack the apartment.

    III.   Opening the door to see who was there, Mr. Weston was confronted by a tall white male wearing a dark blue jacket and white pants.

    IV.   Mr. Weston was at home alone in his living room when the doorbell rang.

    V.   Once inside, the man bound and gagged Mr. Weston and locked him in the bathroom.

The MOST logical order for the above sentences to appear in the report is

    A. III, V, II, I, IV   B. IV, III, I, V, II
    C. III, V, IV, II, I   D. IV, III, V, I, II

7._____

8._____

9._____

10. A police officer is completing a report of a robbery, which will contain the following five sentences: 10.____
    I.   Two police officers were about to enter the Red Rose Coffee Shop on 47th Street and 8th Avenue.
    II.   They then noticed a male running up the street carrying a brown paper bag.
    III. They heard a woman standing outside the Broadway Boutique yelling that her store had just been robbed by a young man, and she was pointing up the street.
    IV.   They caught up with him and made an arrest.
    V.   The police officers pursued the male, who ran past them on 8th Avenue.
    The MOST logical order for the above sentences to appear in the report is

    A. I, III, II, V, IV   B. III, I, II, V, IV
    C. IV, V, I, II, III   D. I, V, IV, III, II

11. Police Officer Capalbo is preparing a report of a bank robbery. The report will contain the following five statements made by a witness: 11.____
    I.   Initially, all I could see were two men, dressed in maintenance uniforms, sitting in the area reserved for bank officers.
    II.   I was passing the bank at 8 P.M. and noticed that all the lights were out, except in the rear section.
    III. Then I noticed two other men in the bank, coming from the direction of the vault, carrying a large metal box.
    IV.   At this point, I decided to call the police.
    V.   I knocked on the window to get the attention of the men in the maintenance uniforms, and they chased the two men carrying the box down a flight of steps.
    The MOST logical order for the above sentences to appear in the report is

    A. IV, I, II, V, III   B. I, III, II, V, IV
    C. II, I, III, V, IV   D. II, III, I, V, IV

12. Police Officer Roberts is preparing a crime report concerning an assault and a stolen car. The report will contain the following five sentences: 12.____
    I.   Upon leaving the store to return to his car, Winters noticed that a male unknown to him was sitting in his car.
    II.   The man then re-entered Winters' car and drove away, fleeing north on 2nd Avenue.
    III. Mr. Winters stated that he parked his car in front of 235 East 25th Street and left the engine running while he went into the butcher shop at that location.
    IV.   Mr. Robert Gering, a witness, stated that the male is known in the neighborhood as Bobby Rae and is believed to reside at 323 East 114th Street.
    V.   When Winters approached the car and ordered the man to get out, the man got out of the auto and struck Winters with his fists, knocking him to the ground.
    The MOST logical order for the above sentences to appear in the report is

    A. III, II, V, I, IV   B. III, I, V, II, IV
    C. I, IV, V, II, III   D. III, II, I, V, IV

13. Police Officer Robinson is preparing a crime report concerning the robbery of Mr. Edwards' store. The report will consist of the following five sentences:

    I. When the last customer left the store, the two men drew revolvers and ordered Mr. Edwards to give them all the money in the cash register.
    II. The men proceeded to the back of the store as if they were going to do some shopping.
    III. Janet Morley, a neighborhood resident, later reported that she saw the men enter a green Ford station wagon and flee northbound on Albany Avenue.
    IV. Edwards complied after which the gunmen ran from the store.
    V. Mr. Edwards states that he was stocking merchandise behind the store counter when two white males entered the store.

The MOST logical order for the above sentences to appear in the report is

A. V, II, III, I, IV   B. V, II, I, IV, III
C. II, I, V, IV, III   D. III, V, II, I, IV

14. Police Officer Wendell is preparing an accident report for a 6-car accident that occurred at the intersection of Bath Avenue and Bay Parkway. The report will consist of the following five sentences:

    I. A 2006 Volkswagen Beetle, traveling east on Bath Avenue, swerved to the left to avoid the Impala, and struck a 2004 Ford station wagon which was traveling west on Bath Avenue.
    II. The Seville then mounted the curb on the northeast corner of Bath Avenue and Bay Parkway and struck a light pole.
    III. A 2003 Buick Lesabre, traveling northbound on Bay Parkway directly behind the Impala, struck the Impala, pushing it into the intersection of Bath Avenue and Bay Parkway.
    IV. A 2005 Chevy Impala, traveling northbound on Bay Parkway, had stopped for a red light at Bath Avenue.
    V. A 2007 Toyota, traveling westbound on Bath Avenue, swerved to the right to avoid hitting the Ford station wagon, and struck a 2007 Cadillac Seville double-parked near the corner.

The MOST logical order for the above sentences to appear in the report is

A. IV, III, V, II, I   B. III, IV, V, II, I
C. IV, III, I, V, II   D. III, IV, V, I, II

15. The following five sentences are part of an Activity Log entry Police Officer Rogers made regarding an explosion,

    I. I quickly treated the pedestrian for the injury.
    II. The explosion caused a glass window in an office building to shatter.
    III. After the pedestrian was treated, a call was placed to the precinct requesting additional police officers to evacuate the area.
    IV. After all the glass settled to the ground, I saw a pedestrian who was bleeding from the arm
    V. While on foot patrol near 5th Avenue and 53rd Street, I heard a loud explosion.

The MOST logical order for the above sentences to appear in the report is

A. II, V, IV, I, III   B. V, II, IV, III, I
C. V, II, I, IV, III   D. V, II, IV, I, III

16. Police Officer David is completing a report regarding illegal activity near the entrance to Madison Square Garden during a recent rock concert. The report will contain the following five sentences:

    I.   As I came closer to the man, he placed what appeared to be tickets in his pocket and began to walk away.

    II.   After the man stopped, I questioned him about *scalping* tickets.

    III.   While on assignment near the Madison Square Garden entrance, I observed a man apparently selling tickets.

    IV.   I stopped the man by stating that I was a police officer.

    V.   The man was then given a summons, and he left the area.

The MOST logical order for the above sentences to appear in the report is

    A. I, III, IV, II, V   B. III, I, IV, V, II
    C. III, IV, I, II, V   D. III, I, IV, II, V

17. Police Officer Sampson is preparing a report concerning a dispute in a bar. The report will contain the following five sentences:

    I.   John Evans, the bartender, ordered the two men out of the bar.

    II.   Two men dressed in dungarees entered the C and D Bar at 5:30 P.M.

    III.   The two men refused to leave and began to beat up Evans.

    IV.   A customer in the bar saw me on patrol and yelled to me to come separate the three men.

    V.   The two men became very drunk and loud within a short time.

The MOST logical order for the above sentences to appear in the report is

    A. II, I, V, III, IV   B. II, III, IV, V, I
    C. III, I, II, V, IV   D. II, V, I, III, IV

18. A police officer is completing a report concerning the response to a crime in progress. The report will include the following five sentences:

    I.   The officers saw two armed men run out of the liquor store and into a waiting car.

    II.   Police Officers Lunty and Duren received the call and responded to the liquor store.

    III.   The robbers gave up without a struggle.

    IV.   Lunty and Duren blocked the getaway car with their patrol car.

    V.   A call came into the precinct concerning a robbery in progress at Jane's Liquor Store.

The MOST logical order for the above sentences to appear in the report is

    A. V, II, I, IV, III   B. II, V, I, III, IV
    C. V, I, IV, II, III   D. I, V, II, III, IV

19. Police Officer Jenkins is preparing a Crime Report which will consist of the following five sentences:

    I.   After making inquiries in the vicinity, Smith found out that his next door neighbor, Viola Jones, had seen two local teenagers, Michael Heinz and Vincent Gaynor, smash his car's windshields with a crowbar.

    II.   Jones told Smith that the teenagers live at 8700 19th Avenue.

    III.   Mr. Smith heard a loud crash at approximately 11:00 P.M., looked out his apartment window, and saw two white males running away from his car.

    IV.   Smith then reported the incident to the precinct, and Heinz and Gaynor were arrested at the address given.

    V.   Leaving his apartment to investigate further, Smith discovered that his car's front and rear windshields had been smashed.

The MOST logical order for the above sentences to appear in the report is

A.   III, IV, V, I, II   B.   III, V, I, II, IV
C.   III, I, V, II, IV   D.   V, III, I, II, IV

20.   Sergeant Nancy Winston is reviewing a Gun Control Report which will contain the following five sentences: 20._____

    I.   The man fell to the floor when hit in the chest with three bullets from 22 caliber gun.
    II.   Merriam'22 caliber gun was seized, and he wasgiven a summons for not having a pistol permit.
    III. Christopher Merriam, the owner of A-Z Grocery, shot a man who attempted to rob him.
    IV. Police Officer Franks responded and asked Merriam for his pistol permit, which he could not produce.
    V.   Merriam phoned the police to report he had just shot a man who had attempted to rob him.

The MOST logical order for the above sentences to appear in the report is

A.   III, I, V, IV, II   B.   I, III, V, IV, II
C.   III, I, V, II, IV   D.   I, III, II, V, IV

21.   Detective John Manville is completing a report for his superior regarding the murder of an unknown male who was shot in Central Park. The report will contain the following five sentences: 21._____

    I.   Police Officers Langston and Cavers responded to the scene.
    II.   I received the assignment to investigate the murder in Central Park from Detective Sergeant Rogers.
    III. Langston notified the Detective Bureau after questioning Jason.
    IV. An unknown male, apparently murdered, was discovered in Central Park by Howard Jason, a park employee, who immediately called the police.
    V.   Langston and Cavers questioned Jason.

The MOST logical order for the above sentences to appear in the report is

A.   I, IV, V, III, II   B.   IV, I, V, II, III
C.   IV, I, V, III, II   D.   IV, V, I, III, II

22.   A police officer is completing a report concerning the arrest of a juvenile. The report will contain the following five sentences: 22._____

    I.   Sanders then telephoned Jay's parents from the precinct to inform them of their son's arrest.
    II.   The store owner resisted, and Jay then shot him and ran from the store.
    III. Jay was transported directly to the precinct by Officer Sanders.
    IV. James Jay, a juvenile, walked into a candy store and announced a hold-up.
    V.   Police Officer Sanders, while on patrol, arrested Jay a block from the candy store.

The MOST logical order for the above sentences to appear in the report is

A.   IV, V, II, I, III   B.   IV, II, V, III, I
C.   II, IV, V, III, I   D.   V, IV, II, I, III

23. Police Officer Olsen prepared a crime report for a robbery which contained the following five sentences: 23._____
    I.   Mr. Gordon was approached by this individual who then produced a gun and demanded the money from the cash register.
    II. The man then fled from the scene on foot, southbound on 5th Avenue.
    III. Mr. Gordon was working at the deli counter when a white male, 5'6", 150-160 lbs., wearing a green jacket and blue pants, entered the store.
    IV. Mr. Gordon complied with the man's demands and handed him the daily receipts.
    V.   Further investigation has determined there are no other witnesses to this robbery.

    The MOST logical order for the above sentences to appear in the report is

    A. I, III, IV, V, II   B. I, IV, II, III, V
    C. III, IV, I, V, II   D. III, I, IV, , II, V

24. Police Officer Bryant responded to 285 E. 31st Street to take a crime report of a burglary   24._____
    of Mr. Bond's home. The report will contain a brief description of the incident, consisting of the following five sentences:
    I.   When Mr. Bond attempted to stop the burglar by grabbing him, he was pushed to the floor.
    II. The burglar had apparently gained access to the home by forcing open the 2nd floor bedroom window facing the fire escape.
    III. Mr. Bond sustained a head injury in the scuffle, and the burglar exited the home through the front door.
    IV. Finding nothing in the dresser, the burglar proceeded downstairs to the first floor, where he was confronted by Mr. Bond who was reading in the dining room.
    V.   Once inside, he searched the drawers of the bedroom dresser.

    The MOST logical order for the above sentences to appear in the report is

    A. V, IV, I, II, III   B. II, V, IV, I, III
    C. II, IV, V, III, I   D. III, II, I, V, IV

25. Police Officer Derringer responded to a call of a rape-homicide case in his patrol area   25._____
    and was ordered to prepare an incident report, which will contain the following five sentences:
    I.   He pushed Miss Scott to the ground and forcibly raped her.
    II. Mary Scott was approached from behind by a white male, 5'7", 150-160 lbs. wearing dark pants and a white jacket.
    III. As Robinson approached the male, he ordered him to stop.
    IV. Screaming for help, Miss Scott alerted one John Robinson, a local grocer, who chased her assailant as he fled the scene.
    V.   The male turned and fired two shots at Robinson, who fell to the ground mortally wounded.

    The MOST logical order for the above' sentences to appear in the report is

    A. IV, III, I, II, V   B. II, IV, III, V, I
    C. II, IV, I, V, III   D. II, I, IV, III, V

KEY (CORRECT ANSWERS)

1.	B		11.	C
2.	C		12.	B
3.	C		13.	B
4.	A		14.	C
5.	B		15.	D
6.	A		16.	D
7.	B		17.	D
8.	C		18.	A
9.	B		19.	B
10.	A		20.	A

21.	C
22.	B
23.	D
24.	B
25.	D

POLICE SCIENCE NOTES

INTERVIEWS, INTERROGATION, AND RULES OF EVIDENCE

Introduction

Making investigations is a very important part of any peace officer's daily work. In the early stages of an investigation, facts often may appear to be crystal clear. The whole picture may change, however, after a thorough investigation is made. A serious crime may be disclosed. An incident, on the other hand, may appear to be very serious but, in reality, it turns out to be a minor occurrence. The peace officer's job is to investigate and get the facts.

Authorities are pretty much in agreement that more than 85 percent of police investigative time is expended in talking to people. More surprising than that, to most people, is the fact that more than 99 percent of all evidence offered during the trial of a case is oral testimony—what witnesses say under oath.

Obviously, then, an investigator must know how to get information from people and how to evaluate it. He must know something about the art of conducting an interview or an interrogation to do that. But skill in conducting an interview or an interrogation can never supplant the need to make a good investigation. A good investigation is the essence of effective police work.

Sometimes a peace officer may fail to recognize, moreover, that more than technical skills are needed if he is to discharge his duties effectively and intelligently. He must be alert at all times during the course of any investigation, whether it is a minor traffic accident or the brutal killing of another human being, to secure evidence (facts) that will be admissible in a criminal court. A working knowledge of the rules of evidence is a necessity for all law enforcement officers.

It often has been said that criminal cases are won or lost at the scene of the offense. Police officers are aware that accurate and thorough investigation is the foundation of successful prosecution. But not always are they aware that something more than sound investigation is required in order to support their case. Court dockets reveal that countless cases have been lost because some important bit of evidence laboriously collected and relied upon by the police officer to establish the case, has been thrown out because it did not satisfy the rules of evidence. Evidence must be obtained which will be admissible in court. The officer *must* understand the fundamental rules governing the admission and rejection of evidence. These are the rules which shed light on the apparent mysteries and obscurities of trial procedures and make it possible for the officer to prepare a case which will enable judge and jury to receive reliable information upon which to base a proper decision.

Interviews and Interrogation
Importance of the Subject Matter

The interviewing of witnesses and prospective informants, and the interrogation of criminal suspects, are the investigative methods most frequently used by the police. In fact, most of our serious crimes would remain unsolved if it were not for investigative leads and the proof of guilt that result from the use of these procedures. A well-designed course in police interviews and interrogations makes provision for 30 or more hours of instruction. Only the most important techniques can be considered in this lesson.

Basic Definitions

(1) To interview means to ask questions for the purpose of securing information. However, when the word "interview" is used, there is an implication that the

desired information will be voluntarily given. (2) To interrogate also means to ask questions. But, when the word "interrogate" is used, there is an implication that the investigator's request for information will be met with resistance by the subject.*

"Interrogate" as used in police work, includes the entire contact of the officer with the subject. Reactions, time lapses, attitude, emotional responses, and many other factors may be just as important to an officer as the words used by the subject.

For the balance of this lesson, the words "interview" and "interrogation" may be used interchangeably. Both situations involve conversation with a purpose. The fundamental principles apply in either case.

Basic Rule

NO ONE IS LEGALLY OBLIGED, AS A GENERAL STATEMENT, TO PROVIDE INFORMATION FOR THE POLICE. There are exceptions to this rule, but they are few. Parties involved in certain vehicular accidents must make reports to the proper police authorities. Operators of motor vehicles must furnish the police certain information when a demand is made for it. There are other circumstances in which the police must be given information. But, generally, in regard to the subject of a police interrogation, the basic rule is correct. Police officers must rely upon skill in obtaining information from people.

Most interrogation efforts must be directed at making the subject want to provide the needed information. The art, or science (caE it what you will) of interrogation, is measured by the ability of the interrogator to bring the subject to the point where he chooses to be of assistance.

*The legal trend in recent years is to restrict the opportunities of the police to acquire evidence by questioning suspects. "Interrogation" has fallen somewhat into disfavor, therefore, because it implies pressure to overcome reluctance to talk." Thus many police today void the term and utilize the word "interview" whether the subject is cooperative or hostile, witness or suspect. All persons are interviewed, none is interrogated.

Warning of Rights

The U.S. Supreme Court in the case of *Miranda v. Arizona*** held that it was unconstitutional for officers to interrogate a person in custody without first warning him of his rights. Before questioning a suspect who is detained, then, an officer must first inform him that:

1. He has a right to remain silent
2. Any statement he does make will be used as evidence against him
3. He has the right to the presence of an attorney
4. If he cannot afford an attorney one shall be retained or appointed for him

Enforcement of this rule is through the operation of the *exclusionary evidence rule*. If it is shown that the defendant did not receive the proper warning before questioning, all confessions, statements, admissions, and any other evidence discovered because of what he has said will not be permitted into evidence. Every officer should have in his immediate possession a card issued by his department or the prosecutor on which the necessary warnings are printed. He should read those warnings *word for word* before he begins any questioning of a suspect.

All confessions are not excluded if warnings are not first given. The court"s interest is in protecting persons against being compelled by police to give statements through questioning. Therefore, it is not applied where a private person questions the suspect (unless the private person is acting for the police) or the suspect blurts out his confession on his own without being questioned.

As with nearly all rights, the rights to silence and the presence of an attorney may be waived by the suspect. However, the waiver must be made voluntarily, knowingly, and intelligently. Courts are faced daily with the difficult decision of determining whether the defendant or the officer is telling the truth about a waiver of rights. Therefore, as much as is possible the officer should obtain a

*384 U.S. 436(1966).

signed waiver of rights before he begins his questioning. Every police department should have such forms printed and immediately available to all officers.

Even where a suspect has waived his right to silence, etc., and/or has made statements if at any time he indicates that he no longer wishes to talk or wishes an attorney, questioning must stop immediately.

Involuntary confessions, statements, or admissions will also be excluded from evidence. Involuntariness is induced by: promises, hopes of reward, or benefit; or coercion through violence, fear, or threats.

Privacy

The principal psychological factor contributing to successful interrogation is privacy-being alone with the person under interrogation. This we all seem to realize instinctively in our own private or social affairs, but in criminal interrogations it is generally overlooked or ignored. For instance, in asking a personal friend or acquaintance to divulge a secret, we carefully avoid making the request in the presence of other persons; we seek a time and place when the matter can be discussed in private. Likewise, when anyone harbors a troublesome problem that he would like to "get off his chest," he finds it easier to confide in another person alone rather than in the presence of a third person. This is so even though the other person may also be one to whom the disturbed individual would like to reveal the same information. In other words, if B and C are equally good friends of A, and A wants to discuss his troubles with both B and C, it will be easier for A to first talk to one of them alone, for example, to B, and then, on another occasion, to make the same disclosure to the other one. A moment's reflection by anyone upon his own past experiences will readily satisfy him regarding the privacy requirements for confidential or embarrassing disclosures. Nevertheless, in criminal interrogations, where the same mental processes are in operation, and to an even greater degree by reason of the criminality of the disclosure, interrogators generally seem to lose sight of the fact that a suspect or witness is much more apt to reveal his secrets in the privacy of a room occupied by himself and his interrogator than in the presence of an additional person or persons.

In the famous Degnan murder case in Chicago (1945046), the importance of privacy was impressively revealed *by the murderer himself.* William Heirens, a 17-year-old college student, was accused of the brutal killing of 6-year-old Suzanne Degnan. His fingerprints were found on a ransom note left in the Degnan home and the handwriting on the note was identified as his. There was also evidence that he had killed two other persons and committed 29 burglaries. His attorneys, to whom he apparently admitted his guilt, advised him to confess to the prosecuting attorney and thereby afford them an opportunity to save him from the electric chair.

Arrangements were made, by Heirens' counsel, with the Cook County State's attorney to take Heirens' confession, but at the appointed time and place Heirens refused to confess. The reason for this last-minute refusal appears in the following headline from the Chicago Daily News of August 2, 1946: "Youth asks Privacy at Conference. Blames Refusal to Talk on Large Crowd at Parley." The newspaper account further stated: "It was learned that Heirens balked at a conference arranged for last Tuesday because (the Prosecuting attorney) had invited almost 30 law enforcement officers and others to be present * * * It was at the conference between the youth and his lawyers that he told them for the first time that there were "too many" present on Tuesday. He said he would go through the confession arrangements to escape the electric chair if it could be done under different conditions. The State's attorney told reporters that he had invited the police officials to the conference because they had all played a leading part in the investigation and he felt they should be "in on the finish."

Another Chicago newspaper, the Chicago Times of August 2, 1946, reported:

"It was hinted the original confession program was a flop because the youth was frightened by the movie-like setting in (the State's attorney's) office. Presumably he was frightened out of memory, too. 'I don't remember.' His self-consciousness reportedly was deepened by the presence of several members of the police department, especially (the police officer) whose handiness with flower pots as weapons brought about Heirens' expose in a burglary attempt.

"At the second setting for the taking of Heirens' confession the number of spectators was reduced by about half, but a reading of the confession gives the impression that Heirens, though admitting his guilt, withheldfor understandable reasonsabout 50 percent of the gruesome details and true explanations of his various crimes.

"It is indeed a said commentary upon police interrogation practices when a 17-year-old boy has to impart an elementary lesson to top-ranking law enforcement officials, i.e., that it is psychologically unsound to ask a person to confess a crime in the presence of 30 spectators."

Reports and How to Ask Questions

Another cardinal rule of interrogation is "never to solicit or accept information without making it a matter of record." If you accept information you also accept responsibility. That does not mean, however, that each time a question is asked of a person that the response must be reduced to writing. The rule is construed to apply to investigative situations. In such a situation, as a matter of self-protection and as a guarantee that you fulfill your obligation, such information should be reduced to writing and made a matter of record.

Finally, in questioning a witness make use of the following basic interrogatories" (1)when, (2) where, (3) who, (4) what, (5) how, and (6) why. Another good interroga-

tory to use that can be quite fruitful is: Why not? By asking those questions, or as many of them as are applicable, enough information can be obtained to prepare a good report.

The Rules of Evidence

Evidence Defined and Described

Evidence is defined as that which tends to prove or disprove any matter or to influence the belief respecting it. It is further defined in legal acceptation and as including *all the means* by which any alleged matter of fact, the truth of which is submitted for investigation, is established or disproved. Although the term "evidence" is sometimes used interchangeably with the term "proof there is substantial distinction between the two.

Evidence and Proof Distinguished

The word "proof as used in the law of evidence is an ambiguous word. "Proof is the end result of conviction or persuasion produced by evidence. Put another way, "proof is only the effect or result of evidence, and evidence is only the medium of proof. In sum, then, evidence plus evidence plus evidence equals proof.

The Nature of the Law of Evidence

The law of evidence relates to the use of evidence before judicial tribunals, and, in its proper significance, consists of: (1) certain rules as to the exclusion of evidence, and (2) the rules which prescribe the manner of presenting evidence in the courts.

How Evidence is Brought Out

Evidence is adduced in a courtroom by: (1) oral testimony, (2) real evidence, and (3) writings. Writings as used in the law of evidence is a broad term that includes documents, affidavits, and depositions, and court records.

Evidence Classified

The term "evidence" is an exceptionally broad one—so broad, in fact, that three major classifications are now recognized: *direct* evidence, *circumstantial* evidence and *real* evidence.

Direct evidence is that means of proof which tends to show the existence of a fact in question without the intervention of the proof of any other fact. It is evidence that is based on the personal knowledge of a witness which came to him by means of one of his five senses.

Donigan and Fisher, in their book, pages 3-5, distinguish the three major classes of evidence in the following way:

If a man takes the stand and says: "I saw Joe Doake draw a gun and fire twice into the body of this man who fell over"—that is *direct* evidence. It is direct because an eyewitness is describing what he saw—facts which he knows of his own knowledge obtained by means of one of his five senses.

But suppose that a witness testifies:

"Joe Doake and John Smith went into a clothes closet together. The door closed behind them. There were no windows, airways, or other means of ingress or egress. Nobody entered or left. The closet was empty before Doake and Smith went in. Suddenly, I heard a shot. Doake rushed out of the closet with a smoking gun in his hand. I rushed into the closet and found Smith lying on the floor. He had been shot in the back, behind the shoulder blades."

That is *circumstantial* evidence as to who killed Smith. The man on the witness stand did not see Doake fire the fatal shot, and yet these facts as related by the witness are so closely associated with the fact at issue (who killed Smith) that the killing may be reasonably inferred therefrom. Thus, direct and circumstantial evidence can be easily distinguished. Direct evidence is testimony relating the immediate experience on the part of a witness. The essence of circumstantial evidence is logical inference. The existence of the principal fact is inferred from one or more circumstances which have been established directly.

Real evidence is simply physical evidence -evidence furnished by things themselves, on view or inspection. It is evidence which speaks for itself and requires no explanation, merely identification. Such evidence is extremely important, not only because of its effect on the jury but because of the range of subjects covered. There have been cases in which the aroma of whiskey and the music from an aria were admitted as real evidence. Photographs, moving pictures, X-rays, maps, diagrams, experiments and tests conducted in court, views of premises, exhibitions of the personal—all are real evidence.

Admissibility of Evidence

Before any evidence can be admitted in a court, it must meet three tests.

Evidence must be: (1) relevant, (2) material, and (3) competent. In some situations evidence will be excluded even though it meets the three general tests. The three general tests of admissibility are supplemented by other rules which for the most part simply provide different ways of trying to promote a fair and impartial trial. For example, courts usually will reject evidence that is unduly prejudicial. Evidence that a defendant has been convicted of other crimes is rejected except under certain circumstances as being unduly prejudicial. Many more examples could be given when evidence would be excluded though relevant, material, and competent.

Specific Rules of Evidence

There are no universal rules of evidence. Rulings of courts may vary from one State to another. Common law rules still exist in some States, but have been modified by statute in others, and to an increasing extent, the rules of evidence are being codified by legislative enactments. Every police officer should be acquainted with the evidentiary rules of his particular State.

The Hearsay Rule

Ask the man on the street what he knows about the law of evidence. Usually the only doctrine he will be able to mention is the one called by the old English word hearsay. In the law of evidence the word embraces what lawyers refer to as "The Hearsay Rule and Its Exceptions."

"Briefly, hearsay evidence is information relayed from one person to the witness before it reaches the ears of the court or jury. Its value, if any, is measured by the credibility to be given to some third person not sworn as a witness to the fact, and consequently not subject to cross examination." An ancient rule of evidence that is known as the *hearsay rule* forbids the use of *objectionable hearsay evidence* in judicial proceedings.

The "rule is simply that hearsay evidence is generally inadmissible in courtbecause such evidence *may not be trustworthy or reliable* and there is no way to test its trustworthiness or reliability by cross-examination of the witness who is on the stand." The hearsay rule applies not only to oral statements but to written communications as well.

The law has recognized that injustice might be done unless certain exceptions to the rule were permitted. Each of the exceptions is based on the principle that the evidence, though technically objectionable hearsay, nevertheless is considered trustworthy and reliable because of certain protective circumstances, and sometimes, that some special necessity exists for its introduction.

Police officers should be acquainted with a number of real exceptions to the hearsay rule. Four of the exceptions are of greater concern to police officers than the others. These are:

1. Admissions.
2. Confessions.
3. Dying declarations.
4. Spontaneous declarationsthe res gestae rule.

A great deal of independent study on your part will be necessary if you are to gain a fair understanding of the hearsay rule and what must be established in order to use objectionable hearsay as a real exception to that rule.

Opinion Evidence

Another important rule of evidence that should be known by any police officer is "The Opinion Rule." Next to the hearsay rule this rule of evidence has given rise to more problems in the courts than any other rule of evidence.

Generally speaking, it may be said that opinion is the exclusive province of the jury, and that witnesses will not be allowed to invade such province. A witness is to testify to facts, so that the jury may form an opinion as to such facts and render its verdict accordingly. This rule of evidence has its origin in our common law system of proof which is exacting in its insistence upon the most reliable sources of information.

The theory of the courts in restricting a witness to stating facts is that the triers of fact, either judge or jury, are as able to draw the proper inferences and conclusions as the witness, in the average case; however, the exclusion of opinion evidence does not extend to cases in which the factfinders are not as able to draw conclusions as the witness. There are subjects upon which opinion evidence is admissible.

Opinion evidence may be divided into lay opinion and expert, opinion. A great many words would be needed in order to give a reasonable explanation of the scope and application of these two sides of the opinion rule. This lesson is not the proper place to attempt to do that.

Conclusion

The aim of this lesson has been to furnish you with enough information about the two topics discussed to make you aware of their importance in law enforcement. Both topics are so broad that it has been only possible to touch them lightly. The instructor can suggest some reference material that may be used to explore either topic in greater depth and, if you can find the time to read some of it, you will find it not only informative but interesting as well.

POLICE SCIENCE NOTES

BASIC CONCEPTS OF LAW AND ARREST

Man has been puzzling over the appropriateness of community controls throughout his recorded history and undoubtedly before that. What he has been trying to decide are the answers to: "Who is/are going to run the show." "Under what restrictions must authority operate?" and "What acts by community members shall be required or prohibited?" Basic to an understanding of the complexity of answers to these questions is an awareness of the variety of systems and laws under which various societies have lived and are living. At some time some community has lived under laws directly opposite to those under which we now control ourselves, and their requirements were "right" for that time and place. In fact, we can bring to mind examples of changes which have occurred in our own United States of America during its existence—even within our own lifetime. The requirements placed upon the members of any community by its government consist of laws which filter out by prevailing over others in the market place of ideas and which are manifested by their issuance through formal governmental organizations.

Every police officer should be aware of the fact that there is no law which has not been enacted in response to and for the purpose of correcting a problem which has become significant by the degree to which some members of the community have acted in opposition to the common belief. In short, where there is no meaningful opposition to the feelings of the majority there is no law in support of those beliefs. For example, cannibalism is not prohibited in the United States because opposition to it is so pervasive that it is reasonable to say that only the mentally ill have engaged in that gruesome activity.

Individuals and communities require guidelines defining acceptable conduct and reciprocal duties and responsibilities in order to attain feelings of tranquility, a sense of well being, and a belief that conformance to group requirements will result in the society's respect for and supply of individual needs in response. Basic to any society, primitive or modern, is the necessity for compliance with authority, the necessity for disciplined behavior, and the necessity for community tranquility. Each individual must relinquish his right to act entirely for his own self-interest in return for the agreement of others not to deprive him unduly of his right to personal freedom or to impinge upon his reciprocal rights under the law. Every requirement of law acts to some degree to reduce individual freedom of action, but reasonable restrictions on absolute freedom are essential to community living and to protect individuals against others. As the danger to any community belief increases so will the group response grow in severity to reduce that threat, especially when the common belief is basic and widely accepted without reservation.

Police officers are faced with daily frustration caused by their inability to understand clearly that the freedom-loving citizens of our Nation have learned from past experiences (some of which initiated our Nation's birth) that absolute authority demands rigid compliance with even the smallest and relatively unimportant requirement and results in stultifying repression of personal freedom. The ultimately efficient government can only be one in which power is so centralized that it is dictatorial and undemocratic. Therefore, laws have developed which restrict the police to that level of efficiency which is acceptable to the citizens and which permits the greatest possible individual freedom. Again, there is no law where there is no problem. Therefore, there should be little serious doubt that one of the highest duties of a police officer is to know and follow the law because it has been developed in answer to previously existing actions which were conducted in opposition to the beliefs of the people. Officials who are responsible for law enforcement must personify lawfulness as they interact with offenders. A peace officer is endowed with awesome power over life and property, and he must not only restrict his actions to those the law but also restrain himself personally to be considered a thoughtful, objective, police professional.

It is important that every police officer understands the basics of the checks and balances system under which we govern ourselves. Our forefathers so constructed our governmental system that none of the three branches of our government, the legislative, the executive, and the judicial, could become so strong that it would be able to dominate the people completely. The basic objective of this system is to prevent one or a few people from absolute control and overwhelming power. In its operation, the checks and balances system prevents domination by providing stumbling blocks in the paths of requirements which do not meet with the approval of the great majority of the citizens. Without considerable support, legislatures will not pass laws, the executive branch will not actively enforce them, and the courts will overturn them. However, those requirements which are backed by the great majority of the people are enacted by legislatures, enforced with great universality and vigor by the executive branch, and upheld by the courts.

The individual professional police officer understands the checks and balances system and acts within the law because of this knowledge. At the operational level, even though a patrol officer is aware of a problem he does not attempt to "enforce the law" when the legislature has not passed a statute dealing with it. He neither strains to fit the facts of an incident into another statute nor makes an arrest for an unrelated offense in order to harrass the "law breaker." At the executive level, the professional police administrator or agency head allocates the resources of his department according to priorities so that enforcement of important offenses is emphasized. The accompanying spinoff is naturally the deemphasis of enforcement against those offenses which are determined to be of lesser importance. The term which applies to this assignment of priorities is *selective enforcement.*

Professional Demeanor

The appropriateness of the reasons for and the manner by which members of a community are deprived of their liberty is one of the most difficult problems to be solved by members of a society and its lawmakers. An arrest or detention is a matter of preventing the free movement of a person. In most cases what is more important to the person subject to this deprivation of liberty is the manner in which an arrest or detention is effected. There is a great difference between simply following the directions of another without the free will to do any other thing one might wish to do and that loss *plus* being searched, handcuffed, placed in obvious incarceration, and even being stripped of all clothing and dignity for the purpose of maximizing security. In fact, most people will understand the necessity of appropriate loss of liberty, but what makes them seriously upset is the public spectacle and loss of face which it can entail when improperly conducted, especially when the arresting officer shows personal antagonism toward the prisoner.

The professional officer balances the importance of each factor involved in an arrest situation. Although safety to himself, his fellow officers and the general public is very important, he is well aware that it is not always the most important factor. In fact, he knows that some persons will submit to an arrest quietly unless demeaning security precautions are utilized or personal antagonism is manifested by the arresting officer.[2]

---

[2]The use of psychological games, "loaded" words, gestures, and "body language" indicate one's true feelings. The sum or totality of these messages constitutes non-verbal communication, which is often the major influencing factor upon the feelings which exist between individuals who are experiencing personal interaction.

Unfortunately, the unprofessional officer often considers security and safety to be uppermost and controlling in nearly every case and is personally offended by lawbreakers. When these conditions prevail, arrested and detained persons are often subjected to such overwhelming threats to their psychological well being (or face) that they find it necessary to fight back against those who are creating the threat. In some cases their loss of face or distress is so great that they physically attack any person who obstructs their liberty and are willing to kill to escape rather than to suffer the public humiliation of detention or arrest. Therefore, the professional officer effects his detentions and arrests with circumspection and avoids excessive psychological distress to those being restricted. By making the arrest as easy as possible on the offender, the arresting officer also makes it as easy as possible on himself and his coworkers. The professional exerts his will over those whom he is arresting by the use of reasoning rather than his club. The officer who is involved in fights significantly more often than his coworkers, however, soon becomes well known and is avoided as a partner.

Persons usually react in three general ways to a police officer who is enforcing the law or is about to make an arrest. They may submit to his directions or the arrest without resistance. Such persons follow the directions of the officer because they believe that the officer is correct in what he is doing or they simply bow to the inevitable. The professional, skilled police officer will so conduct himself that the great majority of persons will react to his directions in this way.

Other persons may feel gravely threatened by the officer's actions and believe it necessary to attack, either verbally or physically, or flee. Whatever their action may be, it is an attempt to reduce the real or imagined threat to their physical or mental well being. Although the attack will usually be directed at the source of the threat, the officer, it may be against another person-an "innocent" third party. This is still an attempt to reduce their feelings of frustration, however, but the target will be an object or person who cannot "fight back." We have all witnessed examples of distressed persons who kick their cats, shout at their children, or drive their automobiles recklessly when frustrated. In fact, many times officers find themselves to be the "cat" whom it is necessary for the person to "kick" to compensate for a frustrating experience which occurred prior to the officer's arrival on the scene. The professional officer, because of his self confidence, is never threatened by verbal "cat kicking." He is able to control these excited persons through the use of his calm, professional, competent manner so that they soon begin to accept his directions. This same technique is usually effective with those offenders who are inclined towards physical attack. The experienced professional officer knows with reasonable accuracy those who cannot be dissuaded and with reasonable force acts to protect himself and others from physical attack.

The professional officer asks himself questions such as these: "This person is attacking me verbally, therefore, he (NOT I) is greatly threatened by somethingam I the threat, or is it something else?" "Is this attack going to be all talk, or will it turn into a physical attack?" "What can I do to reduce his feeling of distress?" The unprofessional reacts out of his own fear of the verbal attack, retaliates in kind, and the situation rapidly escalates into physical combat or the bringing of inappropriate charges out of spite. Invariably the result of retaliatory action by an officer who attacks to save his own face, no matter how poorly the offender may have acted to initiate the incident, is the salvation of the offender's conscience. This is because the offender will be able to say to himself that the officer attacked him, therefore, no matter what the offender has done, the officer has become the "bad guy" who is subject to all the blame-the "offensive cat," if you will.

The third reaction is that of ignoring or remaining unaffected by the threat. Persons who manifest this type of reaction are those who are secure, unconcerned, and believe that they truly are not endangered by the threat. They are convinced that those who are acting aggressively towards them cannot in fact harm them in any basic way. In every day language, this type of individual is called a person with "self confidence." It is this type of confidence that the professional police officer exhibits. It is a quiet confidence, as opposed to the blatant, pushy, aggressive, officious manner of those who are unsure of themselves and who try to make up for it with bluster, which is immediately recognizable as a lack of confidence.

Self confidence is the kind of attitude which makes it possible to exert one's will upon others while encountering the least resistance from them. The officer who exhibits this confidence brings the belief into the minds of those he is controlling that: "This officer will not ask anything of me which is not only lawful but also reasonable and necessary, and if I refuse to act in response to his requests, I will be not only unlawful but also unreasonable and appear foolish to others." On the other hand, if it is the person who is to be arrested who exhibits the self confidence, that person is the one who has the greatest chance of defeating the officer and taking over control of the situation. The officer who allows himself to be manipulated is in for a very uncomfortable experience. The danger to the officer is rarely that of physical attack, rather he will feel greatly threatened psychologically. He may begin to believe that he is appearing foolish and damaged in his self image (loss of face; receiving severe blows to his ego, etc.). Unless he retains his self control, he may well commit a rash or illegal act which can easily result in disciplinary action or a civil suit naming him and his department as defendants. But the experienced professional officer never loses during these encounters because:

He never presses or demands more than is absolutely necessary

Even though the law may empower him to do

more

He always acts within the law

And utilized it to accomplish its basic purpose,

not just technical requirements which were designed to accomplish some other objective.

His actions assure that his opponent becomes aware that:

What the officer requires is within the law

The full extent of the available powers are never utilized without full reason

The officer never acts out of personal vengeance

Professional Discretion

ONLY ROOKIES TRY TO ENFORCE ALL THE LAWS ALL THE TIME, AND ONLY ROOKIES CONFINE THEIR ENFORCEMENT ACTIVITY ALMOST EXCLUSIVELY TO AN ARREST. The experienced professional officer has learned that enforcement of some laws is best accomplished by simply being present and visible. Other laws can be enforced by a warning or an educationally oriented conversion with actual or potential offenders. There are certain laws which do require that offenders be processed through the criminal justice system by either a summons or physical arrest. In most jurisdictions, with rare exceptions, no officer is in fact required to arrest for an offense except when ordered to do so by a magistrate, either by the judge in person or under his written order in the form of a warrant.[3]

Criminal Law

A crime or an offense is an act or omission forbidden by law, prosecuted by the governmental officials of the jurisdiction, and punishable upon conviction. The statutes which define what acts or omissions are crimes or offenses must clearly state the

3 Administrative orders which require a particular type of enforcement action for specific offenses or offenders must be followed, however.

kind of conduct which is prohibited or required and designate the punishment which is to be applied to those adjudged guilty.

Each statute which defines a crime is constructed of elements or criteria which the prosecution must prove before a defendant may be found guilty of the charge. The words used in statutes each have very special and particular meaning under law, and an officer must be careful to be aware of these legal terms because definitions in law sometimes differ from the meanings they convey when used in informal or daily conversation. For example, larceny or theft involves the *taking* of the *personal property of another.* Each of the underlined words is an element of the offense, and they are not the only elements. The "thief has not taken if he has not gained possession, it is not personal property if it is an attachment to a house, and it is not another's if the thief is a part owner or the property has been abandoned. Furthermore, even if he does commit all those acts, he has not committed theft unless he intended to steal. For example, the acts were committed under his reasonable belief that the property was his. Also, no matter how fervent was his intention to steal, there cannot be a conviction where the item "stolen" was not subject to ownership which is protected by law, for example an illegal lottery ticket.

Detentions

Police officers are empowered to make detentions and arrests under appropriate restrictions. A detention is a temporary restriction of one's liberty during which the detaining person is permitted to make a short investigation for the purpose of determining whether or not the person detained is subject to arrest for an offense.[4] The authority and restrictions upon it which apply to this power of an officer are delineated by either court decisions or statutes, dependant upon the law which prevails within a particular

jurisdiction. This type of detention is generally referred to as "stop and frisk."[5] These three little words, however, have become the subject of thousands of pages of court decisions and statutes. This manual must cover the subject with just a few words, and readers should bear in mind that jurisdictions differ in what is permissible. Each officer should become well versed in the law on this subject as it is applied in his jurisdiction.

The stop and detention of a person is generally authorized when an officer has reasonable grounds for *suspecting* that the individual whom he intends to detain:

    Has committed a crime

    Is committing a crime

    Ia about to commit a crime

Note that the facts on which the officer bases his stop and detention are less than those necessary for him to effect an arrest, and it is essential to his authority that the person to be detained must be suspected of criminal activity. An arrest requires that the officer has reasonable grounds for *believing* that the person has committed or is committing a crime, but a detention requires the officer to have reasonable grounds for *suspecting* involvement in criminal activity. Because the officer is possessed of information short of that required to make an arrest, he may not use deadly force to stop or detain the person.[6]

An important factor in the laws dealing with detentions is that of the duration which will be permitted. In jurisdictions where the courts have delineated the law on this subject, case law permits officers to detain persons a reasonable time. The duration permitted is determined by the relative

---

4 Detention is also used to describe the incarceration of an individual in a jail or other facility after being charged with an offense.

5 The officer's authority to stop and his right to frisk are separate and distinct. In fact, in the majority of cases the officer will not have the right to frisk the person detained.

6 Of course, if the person resists by the use of deadly force the officer may respond with deadly force in self defense.

importance of permitting the officer time necessary to ascertain whether or not the person has committed a crime and the loss of freedom suffered by the person detained. Each case is decided on its own facts. Where statutes control, legislatures either permit a reasonable time, similar to court holdings, or specifically limit the duration, varying from ten minutes to two hours. Under both case law and statutes, however, an officer in every jurisdiction is required to release the person immediately after he has determined that the person has not committed a crime. Where the duration is limited to a specified time period, when the time limit has expired the officer must either arrest the person for a crime or immediately release him, even though with more time to investigate the officer might have been able to develop sufficient information to effect an arrest.

Another critical difference among the various jurisdictions is the right of the officer to transport the person detained during the course of the investigation. In some jurisdictions the officer is not permitted to remove the person from the place at which the detention was initiated. In areas where it is permitted, the transportation must be conducted only when it is reasonably necessary for the purpose of investigating the possible criminal involvement of the person detained, and unless the investigation results in the person's arrest he should be returned to the place from which he was removed. The officer may ask any pertinent question of the person detained, for example his name, an explanation of what he is doing or where he is going, the ownership of any property in his possession, etc., but the officer must constantly remain aware that the person detained is under *no* obligation to answer *any* question. The detained individual may remain absolutely silent during the whole period of detention, is under no obligation to produce any identification or other property for the officer's inspection, and the officer

has no right to take *anything* from the person except a weapon.[7]

Frisks

The frisk is a very limited search which may be conducted by an officer who has detained a person. It may be performed only when the officer:

Knows that the person has a weapon in his immediate possession

Reasonably suspects that the person has a weapon in his immediate possession.

Note that the frisk is for weapons only, and that the officer must be able to state the facts which caused the development of his belief that the person possessed a weapon. The frisk:

Must be only for the purpose of locating the weapon

Must be initially restricted to touching or grasping only the *outer* clothing of the individual

May be continued inside the outer clothing, pockets, etc., only after the officer has felt something which reasonably causes him to believe that a weapon is contained within.

If the officer finds a weapon he may remove it from the person's possession. If the possession of the weapon on the part of the person constitutes a crime the officer may arrest for that offense and retain the weapon as evidence. If the person is not

---

7 Refusal to identify oneself or being passively uncooperative makes the investigation more difficult and in some jurisdictions will extend the permitted duration of the detention, but the person commits no offense.

Exceptions would be circumstances under which the person detained is performing some activity or possesses something which is subject to licensing. For example, driving an auto-mobile, in which case the officer has the right to demand the person's driver's license and vehicle registration. Refusal to product these items upon demand is a crime which subjects the person to arrest, but prior to effecting the arrest the officer has no right to search for or take these items.

arrested the officer shall return the weapon at the end of the detention.[8]

Arrests

An arrest is the deprivation of one's liberty by another for the purpose of initiating the arrested person's processing through the justice system, usually the criminal justice system. An arrest must be made in compliance with the restrictions which surround such an action. Otherwise it is considered a false arrest and will cause the loss of the admissibility of any resulting evidence and possible loss of a conviction. The arresting officer may also possibly be subject to a suit for civil damages and be charged with a crime. An "arrest"" which is made without the intention of processing the party into or through the justice system would be kidnapping within the statutes of most jurisdictions. Arrests can be made either under the authority of an arrest warrant or with out a warrant, and the arresting person can be either a police officer or a person.[9]

An arrest involves the following elements:

---

[8] If the person has a right to possess the weapon generally but committed the offense by the facts existing at the time, for example carrying a handgun concealed without a permit, the officer may return the weapon if the person ceases to commit the offense. Under the aforementioned facts, if the person continues on his way while carrying the handgun openly. However, if the weapon is contraband, i.e., he is prohibited from possessing the weapon under any circumstances, the officer should retain the weapon for the purpose of turning it in to the police department for eventual destruction. Examples of contraband weapons are switchblades, brass knuckles, sling shot, sword canes, machineguns, explosive and gas grenades, etc.

[9] An arrest made by a person is usually called a "citizen's arrest," but it is not required that the person be a citizen of the United States of America. There is no age requirement to be met by the person; juveniles and even children may effect an arrest. Police officers have no immunity from arrest, although they need not give up their weapons except to another officer.

1. The arresting party "intends" to take the arrested person into custody. Although in most cases the arresting party's actual intention is to take the person into custody, and the best way to express this is by stating words such as, "You are under arrest for...," courts determine the intention from all the defend himself from false arrest liability by simply claiming that he had no intention to arrest.

2. The arresting party acts under the belief that he has legal authority. If the arresting party is correct in his belief the arrest is valid, but if he actually does not have the authority it is an illegal arrest. Examples of lack of authority would be arrests made under a void or nonexistent warrant, even though the officer had been informed that there was a warrant, and arresting for a misdemeanor not committed in his presence, if this is not permitted in his jurisdiction.

3. The arresting party gains custody and control of the arrested person. An arrest is not complete until the arrested person comes within the custody and control of the arresting party, and this state exists when either the person submits or his resistance is overcome. It is not necessary that the person be touched or that any force be applied if he understands that he is in the power of the arresting person and submits to control; that his liberty is restrained is sufficient. On the other hand, if the officer's words "You are under arrest for .. ." are immediately followed by the suspect's running away there has been no arrest. In fact, unless the flight includes some physical contact or the application of force between the suspect and the

arresting party, the flight does not constitute resisting arrest.[10]

An arrest warrant is an order of a court directing police officers to arrest and bring before the court the person named in the warrant.[11] If it is practicable an officer should obtain a warrant before making an arrest. The basic purpose served by the warrant process is to protect persons from unjustified arrests and prosecutions. The warrant is one of the manifestations of the checks and balances system in that a member of the judicial branch
passes upon the legitimacy of actions intended by the executive branch. Given the same circumstances or facts known to an officer, if he arrests after obtaining a warrant the courts will in all probability sustain the arrest, but if he arrests without one his action will be much more closely scrutinized for probable cause.

Following are common requirements for a valid arrest warrant:

1. Probable cause.

The magistrate issuing the warrant must make an impartial judgment on the basis of the evidence presented that probable cause exists that a crime has been committed by the person to be arrested. Probable cause is more than mere suspicion on the part of the officer requesting the warrant, but he is not required to present proof beyond a reasonable doubt of the person"s guilt. Information supplied by informants may be used, even if their identity is not disclosed, but officers must be able to state facts which indicate the probable reliability of such information which they have not acquired through their own observation.

2. Affidavit supported by oath or affirmation. Some person must swear to his belief in the truth of the statements contained in the affidavit.

---

[10] Flight in a motor vehicle is a crime in most jurisdictions, however, because of the extreme hazards involved in such actions.

[11] Most warrants are directed only to police officers. A private person can arrest under the authority of a warrant only if he is specifically named in it.

3. Person particularly described.

The description must be such that the officer serving the warrant is supplied with information sufficient for him to believe with reasonable certainty that the person whom he is about to arrest is the person described. Ordinarily the warrant includes the name of the person, but sometimes this is not known. In such cases a physical description, occupation or place of employment, residence address or other information may be utilized to particularly describe the person.

4. Nature of the offense.

Although the language need not describe the offense with the same detail as in an indictment or information, it must be sufficient to inform the person of the subject of the accusation.

5. Officers designated.

The warrant may direct an individual officer or a class of officers to arrest the person. For example, the warrant may be addressed to all police officers in the state.

6. Issued in the name of the jurisdiction.

Warrants must be issued either in the name of the state under which the issuing magistrate's authority exists or in the name of the United States when issued by a federal official.

7. Signed by the issuing official.

Only an official authorized by law may sign a warrant, and he must be a neutral and impartial person, a magistrate or judicial officer.

Requirements to be followed in serving a warrant:

1. Person serving warrant must be named in it. Either the officer or person serving the warrant must be specifically named in the warrant or he must be within the class of persons designated.

2. Must be served within the jurisdiction.

A warrant issued in one state may not be served in another unless the second state has authorized this service by statute. An officer in the second state may arrest if he has knowledge of the warrant's issuance, however, his knowledge constituting the reasonable grounds for his belief that a felony has been committed by the person.

3. Officer make known his purpose.

Unless the information will imperil the arrest or the person flees or resists before the officer can convey his intention, the officer must inform the person of his intention to arrest and the cause for it.

4. Show the warrant or inform person it exists. Under common law the officer must possess the warrant and show it to the person if he demands it, but most modern codes have relaxed this requirement under the needs of today's society. However, the officer's belief in the existence of the warrant must be reasonable, and it shall be shown to the person as soon as practicable if he so requests.

Arrests can be made without a warrant by both officers and private persons. The authority of a police officer is more extensive, but not as much so as most people believe.

1. Both an officer and a private person can arrest for a felony committed in their presence and for a felony which has actually been committed but not in their presence.[12]

2. An officer can arrest for a felony which he reasonably believes has been committed by the individual to be arrested, even though the crime has not been committed, but a private person may not. Stated in another way, the officer is protected if he makes a reasonable mistake, but the private person is not.

3. In all jurisdictions an officer can arrest for a misdemeanor which is committed in his presence, but in some jurisdictions a private person may not.

---

12 An offense may be a felony in one jurisdiction and a misdemeanor in another. Generally a crime punishable by either death or imprisonment in a state prison is a felony, and most states do not provide for imprisonment in their state prisons for terms of less than one year. The laws in each jurisdiction should be consulted, and if the statute declares that the offense is a felony or punishment is death or imprisonment in the state prison the offense is a felony.

4. In some jurisdictions an officer may arrest for a misdemeanor not committed in his presence when he has reasonable cause to believe that it has been committed by the suspect, but a private person may not do so in any jurisdiction.

The Constitution, statutes, and court decisions refer to the necessity of the "reasonable cause" and "probable cause" which must exist before the authority to arrest arises. This degree of proof, evidence, or information to be possessed by the officer who intends an arrest must be more than good faith suspicion (enough to effect a detention for investigation), but it need not be proof beyond a reasonable doubt of the person's guilt. The reasonable cause is determined as of the time the arrest is effected. Evidence acquired after the arrest may not be utilized to validate a preceding arrest. In fact, if the arrest is not based on probable cause that evidence will be excluded no matter how condemning and conclusive it might have been in proving the defendant's guilt.

The standards by which an officer's reasonable cause to arrest is ascertained is determined individually for each case. That is, the information in his possession and its relationship to the development of probable cause in his mind (as opposed to a reasonable man test) in the light of his personal experience and the circumstances of the case before the court will all be considered by the court in arriving at its holding that there was or was not probable cause to arrest. Actions which do not attract the attention of untrained or inexperienced persons or officers may convince the experienced and trained officer that a particular offense is being committed. This experience may include not only the activity but also the person performing it. An officer who knows of the past criminal record of a suspect may consider that history along with other facts in developing reasonable cause, but the officer may not arrest on only the basis of one's previous criminal record.

The following are sources which can develop reasonable cause to arrest for the officer:

1. Complaints from victims and information from witnesses.

Statements and information received which indicate that a crime has been committed and which provide evidence by which the offender can be ascertained by developing reasonable cause to arrest. An officer must bear in mind that if the crime complained of is less than a felony no arrest will be valid unless a warrant is first issued, unless their jurisdiction is one in which officers are permitted to arrest for misdemeanors on reasonable cause. But if the jurisdiction is one in which private persons can arrest for misdemeanors, the victim or a witness can make the arrest and turn the prisoner over to the officer.

2. Information from an informant.

The reliability of the informant is an important factor. An officer should maintain records on the cases in which the particular informant's information has proven to be accurate, and whenever possible the officer should make further investigation to determine that the information is correct prior to making his arrest without a warrant.

3. Observation of the officer.

When the officer witnesses the actual commission of the crime there is reasonable grounds to arrest without serious question. But when his observations lead him to a reasonable suspicion only, then he must first detain until his investigation leads to reasonable cause to arrest. When all the circumstances lead the officer to the reasonable belief that a felony has been committed he may arrest under his reasonable belief in any jurisdiction, but for a misdemeanor only if his jurisdiction permits that type of arrest. An officer can always obtain a warrant and effect the arrest later for the misdemeanor.

4. Physical evidence.

Fingerprints, identification dropped at the scene of the crime, footprints leading from the scene of the crime to the place of apprehension, and other physical evidence closely tying the suspect to the crime would be sufficient to give rise to reasonable cause to arrest.

5. Information received from the officer's department or from another agency.

Information received over the police radio, at briefings, or from wanted circulars or lists may form the basis for reasonable cause, however, persons initiating these messages must have reasonable cause for doing so.

CITATION/SUMMONS PROCESS

The processing of offenders into the justice system is ordinarily begun when he is contacted by the police. At this point the person may be "physically" arrested and taken to jail or other place of detention to await his appearance before the court. Very few defendants want to spend time in jail, and the purpose of such incarceration is only to assure the appearance of the defendant before the magistrate.[13] Originally, under our criminal law, incarceration to await court appearance was the only process utilized no matter what the degree of the offense. Beginning with the widespread use of the automobile and the numerous offenses committed by motorists, spurred by the growth of more liberal feelings toward offenders by both the general community and persons involved in the administration of justice, and because of the great savings in time and money which the method causes, written notification to an offender of the charge to be made and the time and place to appear before a magistrate has now become prevalent. Commonly called "a ticket," the citation or summons process is now not only used universally for traffic code offenses but has expanded to include many other types as well, such as theft, assault,

---

[13] Although the only purpose under law is to assure appearance in court, jailing is often utilized to serve other purposes. For example, detention of persons likely to harm themselves or others, detention to prevent obvious offenders from committing further crimes, and detention to provide additional time in which to conduct an investigation. In practice this is usually accomplished by setting bail too high for the defendant to meet.

battery, a variety of regulatory statutes, and other misdemeanor offenses. Whenever possible or permitted an officer should use this process.

The "ticket" procedure can proceed in three ways, an arrest followed by release, a detention followed by release, or the delivery of a notice of charges to be filed to the person charged. Although definitions differ somewhat, the citation process is that which involves an arrest by an officer followed by the offender's signing on the citation that he promises to appear in court at the time indicated, at which time he is given a copy of the citation and released from arrest. The defendant's signature and promise is his "bail". Should he fail to appear he commits an offense which is separate from that of the original charge. The offender may refuse to sign the citation, but if he chooses to exert this right the officer is required to incarcerate him.

In jurisdictions in which the summons process is utilized, the offender is detained (not arrested) for a period necessary for the officer to determine the defendant's identity and write the summons, a copy is given to the person (he is not required to take it), and he is then released from detention. The suspect is not required to sign the summons, he commits no offense if he does not appear, and upon his non-appearance the court simply issues a warrant of arrest for the charge made.[14]

The notice process involves leaving a written notice to be discovered by the person to be charged or otherwise delivering such notice, for example by mail. The vast majority of cases in which this process is used involves parking offenses, but it can also be utilized for many other offenses. Whether the person receives the notice or not, the charge is filed before the court, and if the defendant does not appear as directed in the notice an arrest warrant will be issued by the court. Each officer must be aware of the law concerning these processes in his area because in many jurisdictions numerous offenses have been required by statutes and departmental regulations to be so handled. Therefore, an officer who incarcerates a person who is entitled under law or departmental regulation to be offered a citation or summons will be subject to prosecution, civil suit, and/or disciplinary action.

---

14 Of course, the defendant who deliberately fails to appear cannot reasonably expect the judge to be pleased, but he can reasonably expect little consideration from the court if its finding on the charge is "guilty."

POLICE SCIENCE NOTES

PATROL

Introduction

Patrol is commonly referred to as the "backbone" of police activity. It serves as the foundation upon which all other police functions rest. It is the fundamental operation which contributes greatly to the successful curtailment of criminal activities. Police patrol is also a basic factor in providing the public with the type of police service that it has a right to expect.

The word "patrol" comes from the French "Pattrouiller" meaning "to go through puddles." This is an excellent description of the task because good patrolling means going through puddles, through garbage-filled alleys, and up rickety back stairs in all kinds of weather and at all times of day or night.

While patrol is neither glamorous nor exciting at all times, it can be interesting and rewarding for the individual officer. It gives the officer an opportunity to observe a wide variety of people and supplies insight into their problems. By being alert and understanding, he can analyze his beat area and render effective public service.

The continuous patrol of an area, whether on foot or in a vehicle, makes or breaks a law enforcement agency. Nothing contributes more to police efficiency and the belief of the community in its security and protection by its police than the manner in which patrol duty is performed. Patrol is truly the police department's first line of defense against crime.

Purposes of Patrol

The general purposes of patrol might be stated as follows:

1. The protection of life and property.

2. The preservation of the peace.

3. The prevention of crime.

4. The detection and apprehension of criminals.

5. The regulation of conduct (noncriminal).

6. The performance of required services such as giving aid and information.

These are the tangible, definite things for which police patrols are designed, but on the other side, there are certain intangible things that are very important, but cannot be reduced to exact actions. The policeman on the street is more than just an officer on patrol; he is the police department in the eyes of many of the people and indeed, he represents all of government to a large portion of the public. This factor indicates the leadership role which the policeman is called upon to play in time of civil defense emergency or natural disaster. So, it is doubly important that he know and execute his task well. In no area of his work is the policeman required to exercise tact, good judgment, and leadership as often as while he is patrolling.

Types of Patrol

There are three general classifications of police patrol which are pertinent here. They are foot patrol, vehicular patrol, and plainclothes patrol.

Every patrolman is a foot patrolman at one time or another. There are two types of foot patrol, moving and fixed. An officer on moving patrol is assigned to a designated route or beat to cover. This route is generally in an area where there is a concentration of police hazards. An officer on a fixed post has primary assignment at one location, such as traffic direction at a specific intersection. Much of the work to be done falls within this category.

Vehicular patrol includes the performance of many of the same functions that are required of the foot patrolman. The basic difference can be found among these factors:

1. The use of some mode of transportation, i.e., bicycle, motorcycle, horse, boat, aircraft, or most often, automobile.

2. The ability to cover a larger geographic area.

3. The existence of constant radio contact in most instances.

While vehicular patrol may also involve moving or fixed assignments, fixed vehicular patrol is normally only employed when communications contact is imperative.

Plainclothes patrol may be foot or vehicular, moving or fixed. It is normally used only to handle special problems such as the control of criminal activities in areas of high-crime frequency or surveillance of specific persons or locations.

Police Patrol Techniques

Efficiency in patrol can be attained only through considerable experience. There are, however, a number of tested techniques that the auxiliary policeman should know and practice.

While patrolling his assigned area the patrolman should "be systematically unsystematic." The officer should frequently backtrack and take an unexpected route whether in a vehicle or on foot. He should maneuver so as to observe the people and locations on his beat without in turn being observed. This can be done properly only if the patrolman has knowledge of his beat.

Knowledge of the patrol area is a prime requirement of good police work. The officer must familiarize himself with his area as completely as possible. Geographic familiarity is an absolute necessity. The patrol officer, whether on foot or motorized, is often called upon to get to a given location at a moment's notice. He must, therefore, be aware of shortcuts, dead ends, construction work and any other factor which might cause delay. The patrolman must also have knowledge of the legitimate activities and crime potentialities of his area.

The location of stores, service stations, other houses of business and their hours, is vital knowledge to the; beat officer. Knowledge of these things will enable him to more readily recognize some unusual activity that may possess criminal implications. This knowledge is also useful to the officer because it will enable him to intelligently direct persons asking for information. It is, thus, essential for the officer to know the area which he is patrolling.

Observation is also an important tool for the patrolman. It includes the utilization of all of his senses in ascertaining just what is occurring in his area of responsibility. Observation is a result of intelligent curiosity, and it can and should be developed. The officer should carefully take in all aspects of life around him as he walks his beat. When anything out of the ordinary takes place, he should evaluate it and take the steps that are necessary. The required evaluation is of the utmost importance and it will necessitate years of experience before the officer's faculties are developed to a peak of efficiency. The officer should, however, constantly practice his observational technique because only through such constant exercise can he expect to achieve effectiveness.

Particular care should be taken when observing individuals. Personal description is critical to the patrolman's task. Every officer should learn the procedure employed by his department for identifying suspects or wanted persons.

Some Things to Watch for While on Patrol

While patrolling an area, an officer should be careful to observe the following things:

1. Doors and windows in buildings those are not secure. If any are found, the officer should search the premises, secure the premises with any means at hand, and notify the owner through appropriate channels.

2. Conditions conducive to crime such as: improperly secured buildings, partitions between stores, things of value left unattended, and window displays and counter displays of unusual value.

3. Suspicious persons or known criminals. The officer should also observe suspicious behavior such as: loitering around banks, warehouses, shipping rooms, dock terminals, schools, hotels, stores, etc.; door-to-door peddling, begging, delivery services strange to the area; and persons with no apparent destination or purpose.

4. Business places. These should be scrutinized carefully on each tour. The officer should ascertain the following information concerning each of them: location of safes and cash registers; location and type of night lights, and alarm systems; habits of the staff; exits; means of locking doors, windows, gratings, skylights, basements, etc.

5. Vehicles. The patrolling officer will find them important to his work. They will often be the thing most likely observable in connection with criminal activities. Many excellent arrests and much fine police work have resulted from observation of vehicles. Traffic enforcement, of course," requires close observation of vehicles, but the officer on patrol must not confine his interests only to traffic violations.

6. Signs of disorder, excitement or unusual activity such as: large groups of people, hysteria at the scene of a fire or other disaster, drunk or quarrelsome persons, persons running away from

   or toward some incident or location, or people avoiding the police or watching police activity.

7. Conditions which are hazardous or require actions such as the repair of sidewalks, streets, street lights, and various fire hazards. In some instances the officer should take remedial action himself. In other cases, he should report the condition through the proper channels.

Information and Assistance

Besides his various activities in the area of crime control, the police officer is called upon by the public for information and assistance. It is important that he handle these requests with dispatch and accuracy. This is especially true in time of emergency and disaster. The correct performance of such actions also tends to result in greater public cooperativeness.

At Crisis Locations

Patrol duties in fallout and crisis locations, while involving the same basic principles discussed above, will also be concerned with situations peculiar to crowded and unfamiliar conditions. The following list of such situations is suggestive, not exhaustive:

1. Hazardous conditions, such as insufficient ventilation, fire hazards, etc.

2. Violations of regulations, such as smoking at unauthorized times or places, unnecessary noise while others are trying to sleep, horseplay, scuffling, etc.

3. Evidences of poor morale or emotional disturbances.

4. In general, all situations about which the authorities should be kept informed, such as evidence of boredom, illness, behavior problems of small children, etc.

Conclusion

Patrol is the backbone of police service. Without constant vigilance on the part of the basic patrol unit, the patrolman, the police cannot hope to accomplish their objectives under normal or emergency conditions. It is, then, critical that the individual officer extend himself as far as possible in the performance of this indispensable police activity.

***

POLICE SCIENCE NOTES

DRIVING POLICE VEHICLES

Importance of Safe Driving

The great majority of police officers assigned to field duties operate police vehicles. The ability to drive motor vehicles safely is an extremely important requirement among the many skills necessary to the professional police officer today. It is imperative that officers understand that the ability to drive over the streets and highways at the ultimate speed of which their vehicles are capable is not the most important attribute contributing to the makeup of superior patrol vehicle operators. The belief that safety comes first is, and this belief is manifested by an intense interest in the development of defensive driving attitudes and techniques. These include adult behavior behind the wheel, conscious attention to the driving environment at all times, avoiding the dangers caused by the potential or actual mistakes of others, and the continuous development and honing of driving skills. The professional police officer sets an example of skillful and safe driving for the community in his operation of his police vehicle.

Types of Police Vehicle Operation

An officer will ordinarily operate his patrol vehicle for one of these four purposes: transportation, patrol, answering an emergency call, or pursuit of another vehicle. The factors which differentiate these types of operation are prior knowledge of the route and destination and whether or not the emergency lights and siren are operated during the trip. For a transportation drive the officer will have prior knowledge of both his route and destination. When he is patrolling his purpose is surveillance of the beat, so his route and destination are flexible and change constantly according to what he observes. Answering an emergency call is a transportation trip made quickly and ordinarily while operating the emergency lights and siren. In a pursuit, especially at high speed, the emergency lights and siren are operated, but the route and destination are determined by the person being chased.

While engaged in each type of patrol car operation the police driver should remain aware of dangers peculiar to its nature. For example, during a transportation trip the driver's attention may wander so much that he fails to notice a developing accident situation in time to avoid collision. As he patrols, an officer's intense interest in possible criminal activity may so distract his attention from driving that he collides with stopped vehicles or runs off the road. The dangers inherent in emergency runs and pursuits are great, and the officer who exceeds his abilities, the capabilities of his vehicle, or believes that all persons will see his emergency lights and hear his siren or react appropriately to them is heading for disaster. The law requires that others yield the right of way to an approaching emergency vehicle, but it by no means guarantees that all will do so and erects no physical barrier to protect the patrol car.

Every officer should put himself in the position of other drivers and pedestrians as he operates his emergency vehicle. As an ordinary driver (a substandard one) or pedestrian (a crippled, deaf or blind one), would he be sufficiently alert to detect and react in time to avoid a police car going two or three times the speed limit, racing through a red light or blind intersection without slowing, or passing or rounding a curve on the left side of the road?

Although it is true that the law requires the right of way to be yielded to the emergency vehicle, it presupposes that there is a reasonable opportunity to do so. There is absolutely no right given to an officer to crash negligently or recklessly into another to take a right of way which has not been yielded.

In addition to the death, injury and/or damage resulting from crashing an emergency vehicle, the officer on an emergency call will not arrive to provide the desperately needed service, and the officer in pursuit will fail to apprehend.

Choice of Route to Emergency Scene

The route chosen by an officer assigned to answer an emergency call should be planned for and deliberately chosen by the officer to accomplish several objectives. The first factor to be considered is safety. The officer should choose the route which will be least congested according to the time of day and day of week and any other conditions which may affect traffic flow. Unless unusual conditions dictate otherwise, the route should traverse arterial streets as much as possible so that the effects and dangers of cross traffic and uncontrolled blind intersections can be avoided. The second factor to consider is that route which will permit him to make the best time, since the call is an emergency. He should be aware of any streets which have been temporarily closed or obstructed and of those routes which may be blocked by trains or special events such as parades. A third factor depends on the type of case involved. If persons are or may be fleeing from the scene of a crime, the officer may be able to proceed toward the scene in answer to the call over the same route those escaping can be expected to use.

Vehicle, Skill, Beat Knowledge

The speed at which a highway can be negotiated with reasonable safety depends upon the vehicle driven, the general skill of the driver, and the knowledge by the driver of the particular route traversed. Police department budgets do not permit the purchase of race cars for patrol vehicles, but present-day production of police package vehicles with heavy duty suspension and engines of reasonable power permit the acquisition of vehicles with good speed capabilities by police departments. The police officer's skill in operating a vehicle at speed is generally superior to the ordinary driver because the officer has greater opportunities for developing his capabilities through training and experience. Although it is always possible for a person pursued by an officer to have a superior car and greater skill, the advantage of knowing the route traversed will ordinarily lie with the officer. Every officer should, therefore, consciously make the effort to traverse all the routes on his beat so that he will be aware of every hazard which they contain and how he can best drive over them safely not only in an emergency or in pursuit but also in ordinary driving.

Appropriate Degree of Urgency in Responding to Call for Service

Many police departments have provided for the appropriate urgency to be followed by an officer assigned a call according to the type of complaint, crime, or service to be provided. Written orders designating the degree of urgency by the type of call are preferred to operations wherein such decisions are left to the unsupervised decision of the patrol officer assigned to the call.

There are generally four kinds of responses. The least imperative are to be handled by the assigned officer at some time during his assigned tour of duty which has become available in the absence of other assignments. In some instances the officer will fmd no time available, and the task must be left for the next day or be assigned to another officer on the oncoming shift.

The next more important type of call is to be answered immediately by the officer assigned, but by driving without his emergency lights and siren and while obeying all traffic regulations.

The most important and urgent calls are those emergencies where the officer's response is immediate and while utilizing the patrol vehicle's emergency lights and siren and under the exemptions permitted from the usual traffic regulations.

The fourth call made is answered by each individual officer in the same manner as an emergency service call, but many units are sent to the scene. In these cases each officer must take great care to avoid collision with another emergency vehicle also being operated with emergency lights and siren.

Defensive Driving

The best driver is one whose ability consists of a combination of superiority in skillful manipulation of a vehicle, the ability to operate the machine to its ultimate under all conditions, and a defensive attitude, under which he is well aware of and compensates for, his own limitations and those of others. In other words, a person could be very skillful but be unsafe because he exceeds his limitations or fails to consider those of others on the highway. Some elderly persons have lost much of their ability to nimbly operate their cars because advancing age has slowed their reactions, but they may be still safe drivers by increasing their caution and remaining constantly aware of their limitations.

The superior safe driver is a defensive driver, one who is constantly aware of the accident potential existing at all times by correct interpretation of prevailing conditions and who compensates for and/or reduces that potential by appropriate defensive action.

The following are some defensive driving techniques which can be easily practiced by police officers:

Check lights, brakes, tires, windows, horn, steering, gasoline in tank, and emergency equipment before leaving the station.

Cleaning the inside of all glass will not only be safer, but will permit better surveillance in all directions with less strain. Especially important for night duty or during inclement weather.

Remain constantly aware of traffic conditions in all directions, but know where to concentrate attention for the greatest potential hazard as conditions change.

The changing effects of weather, time of day and day of week on the traffic and roadway conditions should be known for every part of the beat.

Eye contact should be made with any driver or pedestrian who may enter the path of the patrol vehicle so that the officer can judge whether or not his approach is noticed. If the person appears unaware, the officer should slow, swerve, give warning with horn or lights, or even stop to avoid collision.

The presence of a driver, the operation of brake, back up or turn signal lamps of a parked car, or visible exhaust from it, all should warn of possible imminent movement.

The intentions of other vehicle operators should not be judged solely by the signals given by them or the lack thereof.

The intention to turn, stop, start or reverse should also be judged by the speed of the vehicle, the direction in which the driver or passengers are looking, the availability of a driveway, street, or parking space, the position of the vehicle on the road, an obstruction in the vehicle's path, etc.

The slower a vehicle is moving the more abruptly it can be and is likely to be turned.

The police driver should signal his intentions before beginning any unusual movement.

When following another vehicle the fact that its brake lights do or do not work and their sensitivity should be noted at the earliest opportunity.

Following too closely is hazardous, but when the vehicle being followed cannot be seen through or around the distance should be greatly increased.

The stopping distance of a vehicle which hits another will be absolutely astonishing to any unwary officer who follows it too closely.

When driving in heavy, stop-and-go traffic an officer should not only consider the braking pressure necessary to stop for the vehicle ahead, but also leave sufficient extra room to stop more gradually in case the person at his rear is in attentive. The driver to the rear should be observed almost as closely as the one in front.

An officer approaching a crosswalk or any other place where pedestrians can be expected, should look for them through the windows of adjacent passenger cars or beneath the frames of adjacent trucks for their feet.

Whenever it is reasonable to do so, signal drivers to be stopped with emergency lights, headlights, horn, hand signals or gestures before employing the siren.

Drivers are often unaware that they are about to be pulled over, and some become so startled by a siren that they lock their brakes and skid to a stop without turning to the shoulder or curb. Stay well back when stopping drivers. The roof lights of a patrol car which is too close, often cannot be seen in his mirror by the driver to be stopped, and a few drivers will deliberately brake as hard as possible in an attempt to cause the officer to crash.

If the officer is too close the suspect may escape apprehension by abruptly turning into another road and disappearing before the officer can back up or turn around to pursue.

EMERGENCY LIGHTS AND SIRENS DO NOT PHYSICALLY HALT OR REMOVE ANYTHING FROM A PATROL CAR'S PATH. EVERY PROFESSSIONAL OFFICER WILL DRIVE ACCORDINGLY.

NOBODY IS PERFECT, AND NO PROFESSSIONAL OFFICER EXPECTS TO APPREHEND EVERY DRIVER WHO ATTEMPTS TO ESCAPE BY DRIVING WITH EXTREME RECKLESSNESS AT THE HIGHEST POSSIBLE SPEED.

Unfortunately, there have been some officers who have tried to maintain a perfect record. The deaths of officers, the innocent, and the pursued have resulted.

Written Pursuit Policy

The International Association of Chiefs of Police (IACP) passed a resolution more than 30 years ago urging the adoption by law enforcement agencies of a written pursuit policy for the direction of agency personnel engaged in the pursuit of high speed vehicle pursuits of persons attempting to evade arrest. The following is the policy adopted by IACP's Highway Safety Committee:

Pursuit Policy

I. *When to Initiate a Vehicular Pursuit*

Pursuits should only be initiated when a law violator clearly exhibits the intention of avoiding arrest.

Officers intending to make stops shall endeavor to be in close proximity to the violator's vehicle before activating emergency equipment thus eliminating the violator's temptation to attempt evasion.

II. *Pursuit Procedures*

The emergency equipment (red lights and siren) must be activated not only to warn the pursued but also to protect the officers and others.

A. *Number of Police Units Participating*

The pursuit shall be limited to the initial unit and a secondary unit. All other units shall stay clear of the pursuit.

EXCEPTION: If the pursuit is initiated by a two wheel motorcycle officer he shall abandon the pursuit when a four wheel unit joins the pursuit. The motor officer shall proceed to the termination point of the pursuit if the suspect is apprehended.

The senior officer of the unit initiating the pursuit may request additional units to join the pursuit if he deems it necessary.

B. *Control of the pursuit unit initiating the Pursuit*

The first responsibility of the unit initiating (primary unit) the pursuit is the apprehension of the suspects without unnecessary danger to themselves or other persons. Unless relieved by a supervisor, the senior officer in the primary unit shall be responsible for the broadcasting of the progress of the pursuit, controlling the pursuit tactics and deciding if the pursuit should be abandoned. If the primary unit is unable to continue the pursuit the secondary unit shall become the primary unit.

Secondary Unit

Officers in the secondary unit shall make the necessary notifications to assure that no additional units join the pursuit.

C. *Pursuit Driving Tactics*

1. There shall be no paralleling of the pursuit route, unless the pursuit passes through a unit's assigned area. The paralleling unit shall not be operated under emergency conditions (red lights and siren).

2. The primary and secondary units shall be the only units operating under emergency conditions (red lights and siren) unless other units are assigned to the pursuit.

3. There shall be no caravanning of units paralleling the pursuit or attempting to join the pursuit.

4. Officers involved in a pursuit, or paralleling a pursuit shall not attempt to pass other units unless requested to do so by the primary unit.

D. *Helicopter Assistance*

If the law enforcement agency involved has a helicopter, the following shall apply:

1. When feasible the helicopter shall join the pursuit.

2. The helicopter shall advise the pursuing unit that the helicopter has joined the pursuit.

3. The ground unit shall relay all necessary information to assist the helicopter unit.

4. The helicopter, when practicable, shall advise the ground unit of upcoming traffic congestion, road hazards, and other factors which might endanger the safety of the pursuing unit or others.

5. When the pursued vehicle is lost or the pursuit terminates and the suspect flees on foot, the helicopter unit shall broadcast information which may assist the ground unit.

E. *Communications*

After a broadcast has been given as to the location and other information indicating the vehicle has been lost or the vehicular pursuit terminated, the units which have been involved shall take the steps necessary to coordinate the search for the pursued vehicle or suspects fleeing on foot.

F. *Loss of Pursued Vehicle*

When the pursued vehicle is lost, the primary unit shall broadcast necessary information to assist other units in locating suspects or returning to normal duty. The primary unit shall be responsible for coordinating any further search for either the pursued vehicle or suspects fleeing on foot.

G. *Termination of the Pursuit*

Officers of the primary unit are responsible for the arrest of the suspect when the suspect voluntarily terminates the pursuit, or becomes involved in a traffic accident. The secondary unit shall be responsible for backing up the primary unit and making the necessary broadcast to terminate the vehicular pursuit. If the officers of the primary unit become involved in a foot pursuit the senior officer of the secondary unit or the responding supervisor shall be responsible for coordinating any further activity.

H. *Discontinuing the Pursuit*

1. Officers involved in a pursuit must continually question whether the seriousness of the violation reasonably warrants continuation of the pursuit.

2. A pursuit shall be discontinued when there is a clear danger to the pursuing officers or the public.

   Example: When the speeds dangerously exceed normal traffic flow or when pedestrians or vehicular traffic necessitates unsafe maneuvering of the vehicle.

   The pursuing officers must consider present danger, seriousness of the crime, length of pursuit and the possibility of identifying the suspect at a later time when determining whether or not to continue the pursuit.

3. When a helicopter is available and has visual contact with the pursued vehicle the primary unit should consider discontinuing emergency operation (red lights and siren) and allow the helicopter to continue surveillance of the suspect and assume the responsibility of directing the ground units so as to apprehend the suspect without the dangers involved in a pursuit.

4. All officers involved in vehicular pursuits will be held accountable for the continuation of a pursuit when circumstances indicate the pursuit should be discontinued. Since the driver officer is primarily concerned with the safe operation of the police vehicle, the passenger officer is particularly responsible for advising the driver officer when he feels the pursuit is exceeding reasonable limits.

III. *Supervisor's Responsibility*

A field supervisor, if available, shall respond immediately to the termination point and assume responsibility for police action at the scene. The supervisor shall critique the concerned pursuit regarding adherence to policy.

POLICE SCIENCE NOTES

FORCE, SEARCH, AND SEIZURE

Use of Force

The right to use force against another varies according to the reasonable and apparent necessity that it be applied. The most important factors considered in the determination of how much force may be used by an officer are the following:

1. Is the force used or contemplated essential, or could the actor reasonably foresee that less force would be sufficient?

2. Does the crime to be prevented or the arrest to be attempted involve a felony or misdemeanor?

3. Does the act or crime to be prevented by force endanger property rights or human life and limb, and to what extent?

4. What are the responsibilities under law between the actor and what or whom he is attempting to protect with force?

5. Do departmental regulations restrict officers to less force than that permitted by statutes and court decisions?

When necessary, a police officer is permitted to use force in the performance of his duty to accomplish the following objectives:

1. To preserve the peace, prevent commission of offenses, or prevent suicide or self-inflicted injury.

2. To make *lawful* arrests and searches, to overcome resistance to such arrests and searches, and to prevent escapes from custody.

3. To defend himself or another against unlawful violence to his person or property.

4. To interrupt an intrusion on or interference with the lawful possession of property.

Lawful force is an aggressive act committed by a police officer in the performance of his duty when it is necessary to accomplish any of the objectives listed above. Deadly force is that which under the prevailing circumstances is capable of or intended to cause death or great bodily injury. Although lawful, or necessary, force is ti *minimum* amount sufficient to achieve a legitimate poh objective, this does not mean that an officer is permitted to escalate the force he uses without limit until the police objective is accomplished. For example, it would be illegal and immoral for an officer to use deadly force to prevent a person from unlawfully interfering with or even destroying anothers personal property such as an automobile, even if under the circumstances, shooting the person would be the only way the destruction could be stopped.

Deadly force may be used to prevent a felony which threatens the life or safety of a person. However, when the felony does not involve such danger, the tendency of the law among jurisdictions to prohibit such extreme measures is steadily growing. Even in those jurisdictions in which the statutes and court cases continue to permit deadly force to be used to prevent felonies in which life is not endangered police departments are prohibiting it through their policies and regulations.

Once a crime has been committed the chief law enforcement interest is the apprehension of the offender. Although laws vary, deadly force may generally be used to effect the arrest of a dangerous criminal who is endangering or has threatened human life, but this amount of force may not be used on a thief no matter how much he stole. No jurisdiction punishes theft with the death penalty, so no officer should apply "capital punishment" to a thief.[1]

---

[1] It is still permissible in some jurisdictions to apply deadly force when necessary to effect the arrest of any felon, and some jurisdictions have even enacted such laws recently. See Florida Statutes 776.05, 051, 1975, Nevada Revised Statutes 200.140, 1975.

In no jurisdiction is deadly force permitted to effect an arrest for a misdemeanor. If the subject resists, the officer may escalate the amount of his force until it becomes deadly if this is necessary to protect himself from death or great bodily injury, and the officer is not required to retreat. However, the use of deadly force is not justified to apprehend a misdemeanant even though he is in flight and there is no other way to capture him.

The right of self-defense is based on the necessity of permitting a person who is attacked to take reasonable steps to prevent harm to himself. This right permits him to use any reasonable force to prevent threatened harm, offensive bodily contact or confinement. Since it is a defense to a charge or accusation of use of force, the burden is on the actor to show the facts which caused him to use force and that it was reasonable.

The privilege to act to defend oneself arises not only when the danger is real but even when the danger does not in fact exist, providing that the belief in the presence and degree of danger is reasonable. For example, if after a long, high speed, wild and reckless attempt on the part of a motorist to escape an officer the offender stops, leaps from his car and whips his hand inside his jacket, it would be reasonable for the officer to believe that he was about to be fired upon. It would be lawful use of deadly force for the officer to draw and fire his sidearm at the offender even if, in fact, the motorist was unarmed and reaching for only his wallet and driver license. The belief that he is threatened, however, must be that which a reasonable man would have under the circumstances. The person defending himself is not required to restrain himself with outstanding bravery, but on the other hand the reasonable man standard does not permit an abject coward to attack when there is no reasonable ground for his belief that he is in danger.

If force is continued after an attacker is disarmed, defeated, helpless, or the danger has passed, it is unlawful. No matter how gross the provovation had been on the part of the original attacker, there is no right to continue the use of force for revenge or punishment.

No officer should possess or use any weapon or incapacitating device which is neither issued nor approved by his department, including the ammunition in his firearm. Naturally, issued or approved weapons which have been materially altered to increase the force which they may apply should also not be possessed or used.

Under normal circumstances only the methods or weapons listed below should be used to apply force. It is the officers responsibility to first exhaust every reasonable means of employing lesser force before escalating to a more severe application of force. The following methods are listed in ascending order from the least severe to the most drastic:

1. Physical strength and skill.
2. Approved noxious substance, mace, gas, etc.
3. Approved baton, sap, or blackjack.
4. Approved sidearm or other firearm loaded with approved ammunition.

Weapons should never be brandished or displayed as a threat unless their use under the circumstances would be reasonable and lawful.

Only those security devices or measures issued or approved by the department should be used to restrain those in custory, and the devices and measures should be used reasonably and only for the purpose of preventing:

1. Escape
2. Destruction of evidence
3. Attack
4. Self-inflicted injury
5. Commission of an offense

An officer who, out of anger or for the purpose of inflicting punishment or pain, cinches handcuffs too tightly, places a person in s straight jacket, strips a prisoner naked, puts an offender into a padded cell, incarcerates an offender with others who may attack him, or continues security measures when they are no longer reasonably necessary is acting unlawfully and reprehensibly.[2] It is the responsibility of the courts to punish, not the police.

The decision of an officer to use handcuffs or not is a difficult one. Opinions on this subject vary among experienced, professional officers. Where departmental regulations have been issued which state the circumstances under which handcuffs shall, may or must not be utilized they should be followed. However, because of the difficulty involved in covering all the possible situations in a regulation, they have not been written for officers guidance in many agencies. The officer must then utilize his professional discretion.

The officer who decides whether or not to use handcuffs on the basis of his answer to, "If I were this prisoner, would I realize or could I be lead to understand that handcuffs are reasonable and necessary?" will arrive at the appropriate conclusion. An officer who states that "I handcuff everybody I arrest," does not, it is to be hoped, really do so. It is obviously ridiculous to handcuff "little oP ladies" and small children without exception. On the other hand, the officer who fails to restrain dangerous felons, persons in a state of rage, or others who can be reasonably expected to do any of the acts which security measures are designed to prevent certainly should be handcuffed.

An officer who fails to use his cuffs when it is appropriate endangers himself, his coworkers, the prisoner and others.[3]

---

[2] An officer who deliberately deprives a person of his constitutional rights violates 18 U.S.C. 242, a federal criminal statute. Intentional unnecessary violence has been held to deprive a prisoner of the right to due process before punishment. United States v. Stokes, 506 F.2d 771, 1975.

[3] Officers have been killed and injured by children of astonishingly tender ages. The ability to accurately determine from the circumstances, including nonverbal communications and body language, the inclinations of persons contacted is an important skill to be developed by every officer.

Persons who are restrained by security devices are helpless, and officers must remain constantly aware of the possibility that such prisoners may be injured or suffer needlessly if precautions are not utilized. Therefore, secured persons must not be left unattended unnecessarily or otherwise subjected to needless danger or discomfort. The variety of possible situations to be avoided are too numerous to mention, but two must be. Prisoners should never be handcuffed to a vehicle which is used to transport them. If the vehicle is involved in an accident they cannot be removed from it if the officer is incapacitated or otherwise incapable of releasing them. It is appropriate to restrain handcuffed prisoners with safety belts because anybody can release the belts. However, if the person is handcuffed to the vehicle, only an officer can provide the key to the cuffs. Prisoners who indicate that they need to relieve themselves must be permitted to do so as soon as possible. The officer who refuses to permit his prisoner to use toilet facilities or to aid the nauseated person who must vomit is inflicting cruel and unusual punishment upon him.

Search and Seizure*

The most important factor relating to the law of search and seizure, and what each officer should seriously consider before he begins any search for or collection of evidence, is that WHENEVER POSSIBLE A SEARCH WARRANT SHOULD BE OBTAINED BEFORE SEARCHING FOR OR SEIZING EVIDENCE.

Both State and federal constitutions guarantee to everybody protection against unreasonable searches and seizures. This protection extends to their person, houses, papers and other property. No search warrant may be issued without probable cause, supported by oath or affirmation, and every warrant must

---

*For a thorough discussion of current issues in search and seizure law see Israel, *Legislative Regulation of Searches and Seizures: The Michigan Proposals*, 73 Mich. L. Rev. 222 (1975).

particularly describe the place to be searched and the persons or things to be seized.[4]

The protection given by the Fourth Amendment arose from the unpleasant experiences suffered by colonial Americans when searches by English soldiers were conducted under the authority of "writs of assistance" or "general warrants" These writs and warrants were issued with little restraint, without probable cause, and empowered authorities to conduct searches virtually any place on the mere suspicion that goods subject to seizure might be discovered.

The words of the Fourth Amendment must be interpreted by the courts so that the meaning of the law can be applied to the fact situations of each case presented. Thousands of cases have defined "person" "houses" "probable cause" "search" and other words which appear in the Amendment.

Although persons subjected to unlawful searches and seizures have recourse to civil actions against officials who violate their rights,[5] the most common procedure by which they protect themselves is through the application of the exclusionary evidence rule. The exclusionary rule is simply that evidence

obtained by unreasonable searches and seizures will not be admitted upon trial, usually upon objection raised by the defendant at a pre-trial "suppression hearing." The rule is not provided for in the Constitution, rather it was developed by the courts as their solution to the means by which the provision of the Amendment would be enforced not adopt it. Today, however, it is universally applied in both federal and state courts because of the holding of the Supreme Court of the United Stated in the case of Mapp v. Ohio in 1961.[6] The purpose to be fulfilled by the rule is that officers will be deterred from illegally searching for or seizing evidence when they know that it cannot be used against the defendant to prove his guilt.7

Search Warrants

A search warrant is an order written in the name of the State, signed by a judicial officer in the proper exercise of his authority, directing a sheriff, constable, or other officer to search a specified place for evidence, stolen property or other "fruits" of a crime, or contraband, and to bring the articles enumerated before the court if they are discovered.

The following are criteria or requirements which must be met before a valid search warrant may be issued:

1. *Probable Cause*

If the facts in the affidavit are sufficient to lead a reasonable and prudent man to believe that a crime has been committed and that the articles described can be found at the place specified, then issuance of a search warrant is justified.[8] Information received by an officer from an undisclosed

---

[4]The Fourth Amendment to the Constitution reads: "The right of the people to be secure in their persons, houses, papers, and effects against unreasonable searches and seizures, shall not be violated, and no Warrants shall issue, but upon probable cause, supported by Oath or affirmation, and particularly describing the place to be searched, and the persons or things to be seized." The protection provided is both to the person, restricting arrests and detentions, and to his property, restricting searches for and seizures of things.

[5]42 U.S.C. 1983 allows a civil suit for damages when a person acting under color of state law deprives another person of "any rights, privileges, or immunities secured by the Constitution and laws." See *Monroe* v. *Pope*, 365 U.S. 167, 1961.

[6]*Mapp v. Ohio*, 367 U.S. 643 (1961). The federal courts have operated under the exclusionary rule since *Weeks* v. *United States*, 232 U.S. 383 (1914).

[7] Other common law courts, such as the English, have not adopted the exclusionary rule.

[8]For an often quoted discussion of probable cause see *Brinegar v. United States*, 338 U.S. 160, 1949.

informant may be used as the basis for a search warrant, but the applicant for the warrant must be able to give the judicial officer substantial reasons to support the probable validity of the information which has been provided. The underlying circumstances upon which the applicant bases his belief must be specified by him. It is not sufficient to merely state, even with fervor, the police officers belief. The facts of which he is aware which led to the development of that belief must also be stated.[9]

2. Oath or Affirmation

If this requirement is not fulfilled, the evidence obtained will not be admitted. The presumption that the magistrate had sworn the applicant is rebuttable by the defendant, and if no oath was administered the warrant is invalid and the evidence will be lost (excluded).

3. Particular Description of Place and Things

Whatever the wording to describe the place to be searched, the objective to be served is that the officers who are commanded to conduct the search will not, if they follow the description included in the warrant, search the wrong premises and disturb the rights of the innocent. If the warrant does not identify the property to be seized, it will not justify any seizure of that property. Contraband such as prohibited arms, explosive devices, and gambling equipment will ordinarily not be required to be as specifically described as stolen goods, since contraband is S3izable by any officer lawfully observing it. When warrants are obtained for contraband the best description possible under the circumstances should always be attempted.

---

[9] The so-called Spinnelli-Aguilar rule was formulated in *Spinelli v. United States,* 394 U.S. 410, 1969, and *Aquilar v. Texas,* 378 U.S. 108, 1964.

4. Issuing Official

The purpose served by requiring warrants is to assure that the innocent will not be disturbed by uncontrolled and unreasonable actions of officials of the executive branch of government. Therefore, the impartial and objective consideration by the judiciary of the probable cause and the reasonableness of the contemplated action is interposed as a restraint. Attempts to bypass this objective, even to accomplish other well founded purposes such as the efficient issuance of warrants, have generally been found unconstitutional by the courts.[10]

5. Property Subject to Seizure

Under early law, only stolen property could be seized under a search warrant. However, types of articles subject to seizure have been greatly expanded. Limitations still exist in some states such as requiring that only stolen or embezzled property (fruits of the crime), articles used to commit the crime (instrumentalities), or articles which are prohibited or controlled by statutes (contraband) may be seized. Such restrictions prevent officers from taking objects which are important as evidence, such as shoes worn by a suspect which could be compared with footprints found at the scene, but which fail to meet the definition of statutory restrictions. The United States Supreme Court in *Warden v. Hoyden* held in 1967,[11] that statutes which permitted search warrants to issue for "mere evidence" are constitutional. It is up to those states which still follow the old rule to change their statutes or court decisions to permit seizure of evidence, but they are not

---

[10]Efficiencies are clearly possible within this requirement. California and Arizona allow officers to secure search warrants by phonw, making it possible in some areas to get 65% of all warrants in under one hour and most of the rest within two hours. Miller, "Telephonic Search Warrants: The San Diego Experience," 9 *The Prosecutor* 385, 1974.

[11] 387 U.S. 294, 1967.

required to do so.

Only those items specified in the warrant may be seized. If other property is seized it must be under authority other than that provided by the warrant.

6. *Execution Only By Those Ordered*

A search warrant may only be executed by those commanded by it to act, but the person designated may be specifically by either name or class (peace officers, for example). The person designated may be assisted by others, however.[12]

7. *Time Limit*

A search warrant must be executed within a reasonable time or it will fail to meet constitutional requirements. The amount of time which is reasonable varies, of course, according to the circumstances of each case. Most jurisdictions have by statute limited the time in which a search warrant may be executed, and the permissible period varies from a number of hours to more than a week. Some jurisdictions require special judicial authorization for warrants to be served at night.

8. *Prior Notice, Demand, and Forcible Entry*

If the local law allows and the warrant is for the seizure of items which can be destroyed quickly or if officers are aware of facts which reasonably lead them to believe notice to occupants would lead to danger of attack, entry may usually be effected without notice. Otherwise they are first required to notify persons within the premises of their identity and right to enter and make a demand that they be permitted to enter. Reasonable and necessary force may be used to effect entry when officers must act quickly to avoid evidence destruction or

attack, or if they are denied entry after notice has been given and their demand had been refused. Force may also be used to enter unoccupied premises or when the denial is passive, for example, when occupants remain silent and do not open the door.

Warrantless Searches and Seizures

Three factors have influenced and caused the development of those laws under which warrantless searches are permitted. They are permitted and lawful:
1. By consent
2. When necessity or emergency require immediate action
3. Where no right to protection exists

Consent Searches

A general principle of law is that one can waive any right or privilege to which he is entitled. However, because rights and privileges have arisen from previously experienced problems, courts observe very carefully the evidence presented in support of contentions that a defendant consented to a search.

Consent must be voluntary, the prosecution has the burden of proving consent clearly, and some sort of positive action by the person waiving must be shown.[13] For example, unless the person positively states his consent or makes some clearly understood gesture, the consent will not be held to be voluntary.

The search cannot extend beyond that granted by the terms of the consent in either area or time. That is, consent to search a room will not permit other rooms or the whole house to be searched, and the person may stop the search at any time simply by revoking his consent.[14]

---

[12] Nonfederal officers should always be assisted by federal officers when serving a search warrant based on probable cause for a search relating to a strictly federal crime. United States v. Townsend, 394 F.Supp. 736, 1975

[13] See *Schneckloth v. Bustamonte,* 412 U.S. 218, 1973.

[14] Some states hold otherwise, that once given, consent cannot be withdrawn, but the trend of cases is that searches must stop immediately upon any revocation.

The person consenting must have the capacity to do so. A person who has the right to possess premises or things may give consent, but others may not. For example, the occupant of a hotel room may consent to its search but not the management;[15] a parent can consent to a search of a minor childs room but not that of an adult child if the room is exclusively that childs, although permission to search areas used in common by the family is valid; a minor childs consent is unlikely to be held valid, but an adult child can consent to a search of at least jointly used areas; a spouse can consent if the premises are occupied by both spouses; and a person caring for the personal property of another may permit search of it.[16]

Immediate Action Required

The most prevalent situations under which this exception is granted are searches made incident to a lawful arrest. Necessity is the motivating factor in permitting these searches. The two purposes served are to protect the arresting officer from attack and to prevent the person from access to things which would facilitate his escape, and to assure that evidence will not be destroyed by the defendant.[17]

Should any of the following criteria not be met the evidence discovered will be excluded:

1. The arrest must be lawful.

2. The search must be made for the purposes listed above (protection, security, evidence).

* An arrest for an unlicensed vehicle, to be followed by a citation, may not be the basis for a search for drugs as there is no relationship between the offense and the purpose of the search.

3. The arrest must not be a sham or subterfuge made only to initiate a search not based on reasonable cause.[18]

* An arrest warrant sworn out by officers (who merely suspect a burglary by the subject) charging the defendant with spitting on the sidewalk for the purpose of gaining entrance to his residence when they execute it-evidence of the burglary would be excluded.

Both the area searched and the time during which the search will be permitted are limited. Officers may make a reasonable search of areas within the persons reach or the distance through which he might be able to quickly leap in order to obtain a weapon for attack or evidence to destroy. Searching for evidence during an arrest beyond this area is no longer permitted without a search warrant.[19] The search must be made contemporaneously with the arrest. After the subject has been removed from the scene and/or confined in jail the necessity of immediate action no longer prevails, and the officer must obtain a search warrant to search the area of the arrest.[20] An arrestees person may be immediately fully searched, as opposed to a mere pat-down for weapons, incident to an arrest for which he is actually being taken into custody, or the search may be delayed until booking.[21]

[18] Of course, if an officer can point to facts which, in the light of his experience, lead to the reasonable inference that the person whom he has stopped for a traffic offense is armed, he may search for the weapon to protect himself, *Terry v. Ohio*, 392 U.S. 88, 1968; but if he merely suspects that the person may be armed and *then* stops the person for a traffic violation as an excuse to search, the weapon will not be admissible.

[19]*Chimel v. California*, 395 U.S. 752, 1969, overruled the older rule allowing broader searches found in *Harris v. United States*, 331 U.S. 145, 1947, and *United States* v. *Rabinowitz*, 339 U.S. 56, 1960.

[20] United States v. Davis, 423 F.2d 974, 1970.

[21] United States v. Robinson, 414 U.S. 218, 1973, and Gustafson v. Florida, 414 U.S. 260, 1973. New York, California and Hawaiis State supreme courts have limited this recent expansion of police search freedom, however.

[15]*Stoner v. California*, 376 U.S. 483, 1964.

[16]*Frazier v. Cupp*, 394 U.S. 731, 1969.

[17]*Chimel v. California*, 395 U.S. 752, 1969. Note that the same limitations on what types of articled (fruits of the crime, etc.) may be seized under a search warrant also apply in warrantless searches according to the law in the particular jurisdiction.

8

Once in jail, an arrestee or his property room effects may be researched without a warrant where the searches are not unreasonably made, i.e., harassment searches.[22]

The right of officers to search a car beyond the reach of the subject being arrested, for example in the closed trunk or even the locked glove compartment, would have to be based on grounds other than the arrest itself, i.e., on probable cause to search those areas, on consent, or "plain sight," or on a valid inventory.

When probable cause exists and the evidence is contained within a moving (or about to be moved) vehicle, officers may search.[23] There is a significant difference in the necessity for immediate action between searches of buildings and searches of vehicles which may speedily be moved out of the jurisdiction before a search warrant can be obtained. An occupied car on a highway is movable, and the persons within it are alerted to the presence of officers. The evidence may never again be located if courts were to require officers to obtain a warrant to search under these circumstances. To conduct a warrantless search of a "moving" vehicle, the officer should have that amount of information which would cause a court to readily issue a search warrant if there were time to procure one. The officer may make the search without first arresting the person. The search will be upheld under the vehicle exception if the essential requirements of probable cause are shown to have existed prior to the search.[24]

Where No Right to Protection Exists

Seizures of evidence without a search is not a violation of the Fourth Amendment

when officers are lawfully present and the article seized is seen by them. Courts do not require officers to leave obvious evidence to be destroyed, but officers must not be trespassers at the time the evidence isobserved. Furthermore, if an officer is a trespasser when he does see evidence, he cannot then procure a search warrant on the basis of the information he acquired as a trespasser.[25]

The protection offered by constitutional provisions are to protect persons against the acts of government officers, not private parties. Therefore, if a private person obtains evidence through unlawful entrance or burglary the evidence may be used against the criminal defendant. Of course, if an officer initiated the private persons action or participated in it, the evidence would be excluded. Searches and seizures are unlawful when they unreasonably intrude into areas where the person can reasonably expect privacy, but not outside those areas. Open fields, public streets and other places of similar description are outside the restrictions of the Fourth Amendment.[26]

Inventories of vehicles which come into the hands of the police through impounding procedures are permitted. The inventory made of the vehicle is for the purpose of making an inventory of its contents to protect the owner rather than a search for evidence of an offense. The officers intrusion is only justifiable if it is a good faith attempt to protect the property in the car. In effect, the evidence is discovered "accidentally" while the officer is doing what he has a right to do and where he has legitimate cause to be.[27]

[22]United States v. Edwards, U.S. , 1974. Severalstates have more limited rules.

[23] Texas v. White, U.S. ,1975.

[24]Carrol v. United States, 267 U.S. 132, 1925; Chambers v. Maroney, 399 U.S. 42, 1970. If the car should more properly be considered to be a part of a household, for instance it is parked in a persons driveway, and there is no danger that it will bemoved, a warrant is necessary. Coolidge v. New Hampshire, 403 U.S. 443, 1971.

[25]The "plain view" doctrine was discussed in Coolidge v. New Hampshire, 403 U.S. 443, 1971.

[26]The reasonable expectation of privacy analysis, discussed at length in Katz v. United States, 389 U.S. 347, 1967, greatly limits some uses of the "plain view" doctrine. For instance, police look in defendants window from a fire escape. They are not trespassing, but may violate the defendants reasonable expectation that no one would look in his window.

[27]Cooper v. California, 386 U.S. 58, 1967; Harris v. United States, 390 U.S. 234, 1968; Cady v. Dombrowski, 413 U.S. 1074, 1973.

POLICE SCIENCE NOTES

FIREARMS-CARE, MAINTENANCE, AND FAMILIARIZATION

Importance of Police Firearms

The police are the action group called upon to enforce the regulations of the lawfully constituted government of the community. Unfortunately, laws are sometimes actively resisted, occasionally with deadly force. Such life-endangering incidents require the police to overcome the resistance with equal or superior force, the ultimate being through use of firearms.

Most officers go through their entire careers without the necessity of firing their weapons at a person, and some without ever being required to even draw their weapons. Daily, however, other police officers somewhere are faced with the dire necessity to protect themselves or others by the use of their firearms. One is reminded of the rhyme from the early days of the repeating handgun:

Be not afraid of any man
　　no matter what his size.
When danger threatens call on me,
　　and I will equalize.

But no officer should suffer under the mistaken belief that he becomes "equal" simply because he carries a firearm. Rather, he must be well trained and practiced in order to accomplish these two important objectives:

1. The professional police officer must know the circumstances under which the use of his firearm is *essential* so that he will utilize its deadly force *only* under such conditions.
2. The professional police officer must, through practice, become proficient in the use of firearms so that he will be superior to those few opponents who attack with deadly force.

Police professionals look forward to the time when advanced weapons are available which will instantly incapacitate attackers without deadly force, and such are being presently developed. However, until then officers must utilize firearms which kill when immediate incapacitation of an aggressor is essential to protect life.

Proficiency in the use of firearms can be developed only through periodic practice performed at least monthly if at all possible. There are essentially two types of shooting practice utilized by police. The first is shooting at stationary bulls eye targets, which requires considerable accuracy as the target is small. Shooting at this type of target with a handgun is performed entirely by operating the weapon single action. The second type of practice is that of combat or "practical" courses in which the targets are human silhouettes and/or moving or disappearing. When this type of course is performed with a handgun it is ordinarily fired double action.

Each officer should avail himself of every opportunity to increase his skill with the firearms utilized by his department, even if it is only by dry firing. Combat situations arise unexpectedly, and there is little time to think. Unless the proper habits and skills have been well developed by constant practice, the officer may fail in his attempt to protect his own life or that of another. There may be opportunity for only one shot before it is too late it must be a good one.

It is not possible here to provide a detailed explanation of how to shoot well or to provide comprehensive instruction in firearms. That must be learned from expert instructors and perfected through practice. It is hoped, however, that each officer will come to know his weapons, use them accurately, and fire them only under appropriate and lawful circumstances. Those are the marks of the professional officer.

Police Firearms

At present, police firearms are all small arms and include handguns (also termed "sidearms"), shotguns (also called "riot guns" when equipped-as they usually are with barrel shorter than those used for hunting purposes), tear gas guns, automatic weapons, and rifles. Hand and tear gas guns can be thought of as "defensive" weapons, although some handguns are now available which fire bullets at velocitie: formerly possible only with shoulder weapons. The remaining firearms are "offensive" weapons fired from the shoulder. An offensive weapon is one which would be utilized against an extremely dangerous and well-armed aggressor because of its larger caliber, higher muzzle velocity, longer range, greater accuracy or rapid rate of fire. Offensive weapons are used when it is necessary to attack and kill.

The following are some of the terms used to identify or describe police firearms:

Small arm--firearm capable of being fired while hand held or held with the hands and braced against the shoulder

Shoulder weapon--firearm normally fired while held with the hands and braced against the shoulder

Rifle--shoulder weapon with a rifled bore

Shotgun--smoothbore shoulder weapon; generally loaded with shot shells but rifled slugs also used

Handgun/sidearm--firearm normally held, aimed and fired with one hand

Pistol--handgun with integral chamber and barrel

Revolver--handgun with a cylinder containing several chambers which, are moved successively into line with the barrel to be fired

Automatic/machine pistol/submachine gun/machine gun--self-loading firearm capable of continuous fire as long as the trigger remains pulled

Semi-automatic/autoloader--self-loading firearm which will fire only one shot each time the trigger is pulled and not another until it is first released

NOTE: When a weapon is called a machine gun, machine pistol, or submachine gun it will always be a truly automatic firearm capable of continuous fire until the trigger is released. However, the terms "automatic pistol" or "automatic shotgun" are commonly used in referring to weapons which are actually semi-automatics (autoloaders). A true "automatic rifle" is a machine gun, but the term is popularly used for semi-automatic rifles also. A rare handgun is the automatic revolver; few have been manufactured, and the police do not use them.

The energy utilized for the self-loading operation of an automatic or autoloader weapon is that of the previously fired round's recoil or its gas pressure acting upon a piston. Therefore, auto weapons are referred to as being either recoil or gas operated.

Caliber--the measurement in decimal (expressed in hundredths, i.e., .22, .32., etc., or thousandths, i.e., .223, .300, .357, etc.) parts of an inch of a firearm's bore diameter between opposite lands

Gauge--the size of a shotgun's bore expressed by the number of lead spheres, each precisely fitting that bore, which would weigh one pound

Grooves/rifling--the spiral channels (usually numbering from four to six) which have been cut into the bore to impart rotation to the bullet during its passage. The gyroscopic action of the spinning bullet prevents its tumbling during flight and increases accuracy.

Lands--the surface of the bore between adjacent grooves

Single action--cocking a handgun manually before each shot, or a handgun which must be manually cocked (for the first shot if it is an autoloader)

Double action--a firearm designed so that operating the trigger cocks the weapon (for the first shot if it is an auto loader), or the firing of a weapon by employing its double action capability.

Dry firing--practicing with an unloaded weapon; sighting, squeezing the trigger, cocking, etc.

Care of Firearms

The critical factor for the proper maintenance of police firearms is simply that of firing them under a planned, periodic schedule. Not only does such use prove each weapon's ability to function properly (or not), but the officers become more proficient through the practice involved.

Quality firearms which are well maintained last for more than a lifetime, and the wear caused by firing them is usually the least important factor in causing malfunctions. If a police firearm fails to shoot as it should, the cause is most likely to be negligence in its care by the officer to whom it has been issued. Maintenance is simple. The officer need only keep a *light* coating of oil on exposed and moving parts and run a swab through the barrel and cylinders weekly and perform these easy tasks immediately after the gun's exposure to unusual dampness or dirt. In short, it should simply be kept clean and rust free.

Faulty ammunition is the next most likely cause for malfunction. Cartridges more than a year old should not be carried on duty. Excessive oiling of the weapon at any point where that oil can contact and seep into the rounds must be avoided to prevent cartridge malfunction. Although rounds should be kept free of dirt, moisture and corrosion, they should be neither oiled nor polished, merely wiped clean with a dry rag.

Inability to fire or inaccuracy can be caused by accidental damage inflicted by dropping a weapon or other impacts received by it. Such blows can bend or break parts of the weapon or damage and misalign the sights. Immediately after a firearm is dropped, struck or otherwise receives an impact, it should be carefully examined for damage. Any problem should be corrected immediately. Unless it is obvious that the repair required is minimal and within the capability of the person performing it, the weapon should be sent to a gunsmith.

Another common cause of malfunction is that of work performed for repair or to "improve" a weapon by a person who is insufficiently skilled in the craft of the gunsmith. Too often trigger pulls are lightened or spring tensions changed, to improve accuracy on the target range, to the point at which the gun becomes extremely dangerous to handle or fails to fire at all. Firearms are finely machined devices which can be ruined by the inexperienced.

Safety Rules

A gun is a machine designed to kill and it will do so whether or not the person possessing it intends such a result when he fires the weapon or permits its accidental discharge. There is an old saying among experienced police officers that, "More policemen are shot by policemen than by criminals."* Following the suggestions below will prevent most accidental deaths and injuries caused by firearms.

No person should fire a weapon unless and until he is aware of where the bullet may strike. This includes the target at which he is aiming *and* any other person or thing likely to be hit if he misses or the bullet passes through the target.

Every gun should be assumed as being loaded by every person who has not had the opportunity to personally inspect it.

Whenever possible, if a firearm is to be passed to another, it should be either unloaded or the action opened (or the cylinder of a revolver swung out). If it is loaded when passed, however, the statement, "This is loaded," should be expressed *and* acknowledged.

Guns should be kept away from children and the inexperienced either by being locked away or immobilized with a locking device on the weapons themselves. Various types of gun locks are available and a revolver can be "locked" by swinging the cylinder out and locking handcuffs through the frame in its place.

Firing or fingering the trigger while on the run is extremely hazardous and to be consciously avoided even during combat.

A gun should *never* be pointed at a person unless firing it would be necessary and lawful under the conditions existing or imminently expected to arise.

Holding a person at bay with a cocked double-action firearm is extremely hazardous because of the great possibility of accidental discharge, and is to be consciously avoided.

ON THE FIRING RANGE:

The gun should not be loaded until time for firing or, if there is a range master, by command.

A loaded weapon should never be pointed in any direction except downrange toward the target.
No shooter should turn to leave his firing position unless his weapon is first unloaded and its action opened or the gun holstered.
A shooter should not continue to shoot after a misfire or short round (insufficient or no powder).
NOTE: The gun should remain pointed downrange with its action closed for one or two minutes in case the misfire goes off late. After a short round the barrel must be inspected to make certain that the bullet has cleared it.
Each shooter should remain alert for those who disregard safety and range regulations. Such negligent persons should be either personally requested to mend their ways or reported to the range master.

Decisions Commonly Made by Agencies on Firearms

Executives of police departments are faced with the need to study their agency's firearm requirements and to make appropriate decisions concerning the weapons which their officers will be required or permitted to utilize. Following are some of the matters which must be determined:

Sidearm--specified make or model, revolver or autoloader, barrel length, target grips or standard (some target grips interfere with reloading or shooting with either hand), type of finish, caliber, single or double action, sensitivity of trigger pull, type of sights, and "back-up" or second gun.

Ammunition--magnum or standard, specified brand(s), weight of bullet, special reloads or factory only, bullet configuration (round, semiwadcutter, hollowpoint, shot packet, jacketed, etc.), age, size of shot and/ or rifled slug for shotguns, number of extra rounds or clips to be carried, and type of holder in which additional ammunition is carried.

Sidearm holsters--belt, swivel, cross-draw, shoulder, spring, full cover, hammer strap, concealed, and spring-opening.

Shoulder weapons--shotgun, rifle, gauge or caliber, barrel length, hand or auto-load, full automatic, type of sights, carried in passenger compartment or trunk, readily visible or concealed, secured by locking device or simple holder only, equipped with breakable seal, carried with chambered round or not, and supplied to each patrol car or only carried by supervisors or retained at headquarters.

The critical decision is always that which determines whether or not human life will be taken or placed in grave peril. It is hoped that every officer faced with such a decision will act morally and lawfully because of his professional training and experience.

POLICE SCIENCE NOTES

CROWD AND RIOT CONTROL

Every police officer who spends enough time on the job will eventually be faced with the difficult task of controlling or subduing a "crazy mad" individual who has lost his capacity for rational control of his emotions and goes on the attack, often with the "strength of ten." It is only the well trained officer who keeps his head and cooly proceeds to act appropriately who will be able to overcome and defeat such an attacker with the minimum force necessarily and effectively applied. In fact, in many cases the professional officer will be able to reduce the emotional stress being suffered by his opponent to the point at which force becomes unnecessary. However, the mistakes made by untrained and unprofessional officers who have acted out of personal antagonism or even rage can, and often have, escalated incidents into terribly destructive battles involving deadly force.

The same factors and influences are involved whether the police and those who must be controlled are acting as individuals or groups. The well trained, well directed, cooly professional group of officers working as a team will succeed, but a mob of enraged police will not. Success does not consist only of eventual control, but rather how and at what expense in lives, property, and antagonism it was attained.

During a period of civil unrest, tension, and overt disturbances, police capabilities are tested to the limit. There is no more trying situation or challenge to the professional performance of the police organization than the control of an unruly crowd or riotous mob. Auxiliary police officers must be trained and prepared to participate in the control of such disturbances and civil disorders because it is under such crisis situations that every available professionally trained officer is required to protect the community.

Crises Requiring Additional Manpower for Effective Control

The crisis situations requiring the concentration of available police manpower or the mobilization of reserves to effect control can be categorized under four headings:

Disasters initiated by human activities-large fires, explosions, structural collapses, etc.

Natural disasters-tornadoes, floods, earthquakes, etc.

Civil disorders and disturbances-violence which is geographically limited in effect and initiated by economic, racial, social, or political tensions.

War or revolution-violence penetrated by the military forces of a foreign nation or the resident population in sufficient strength that orderly governmental processes at the state and/or national level are threatened.

Any type of disaster will affect the stability of some persons in the community and cause them to act aggressively and irrationally to the detriment of other individuals, groups, or even the whole community. Law and order is necessary to the protection of individuals and the public, therefore such must be maintained by the police until and unless the problem becomes so pervasive and severe that the military forces must take over.

Crowds, Mobs, and Riots

It is useful to draw distinctions among various types of crowds, since they do not all require the active intervention of the police. It is as important for the police to know when not to intervene with active control methods as it is to know when and how much overt exercise of the police authority is required. It is necessary that the police be able to recognize the type of crowd with which they are dealing in order to take appropriate and timely preventive action before it evolves into into an uncontrollable mob.

A crowd is a large number of persons collected into a close body without order. As a group, such will be unorganized and without leadership, hesitant to act cohesively, respectful of the law, and ruled by reason. A physical or casual crowd is characterized by their denseness and lack of group behavior. For example, pedestrians at an intersection of a downtown shopping district. A psychological crowd, however, consists of persons with a common interest. For instance, a stadium of football fans. A psychological crowd can be hostile or aggressive. Should an official at the football game make an apparently erroneous decision the crowd could well become hostile at a hotly contended contest.

A mob is a disorderly crowd after its members have lost their sense of responsibility and their respect for the law. A mob is characterized by organization, leadership, common motive for action, and irrational, emotional, or enraged behavior. Mobs can be of three types according to their objectives, although there is often an intermingling of these purposes or effects. A mob which is motivated by the desire to attack or destroy people or property is an *aggressive* mob. An example would be a lynch mob or one which overturns and sets fire to vehicles. An *acquisitive* mob attacks for the purpose of obtaining some sort of property by force, such as food, clothing, arms, etc. An *escape* mob's purpose is to flee from danger, and they act in panic. The panicky escape mob has perceived a threat, believes they are entrapped, is faced with a partial or complete breakdown of an escape route, and suffers from lack of communication between those nearest the possible escape route and those farthest away. Orchestrating the emotions of a crowd for the purpose of inciting a riot is a leadership skill which has been deliberately acquired by some persons who are attempting to subvert ordinary governmental processes to gain an end. Some of the methods utilized to incite a riot are extensive preparatory propaganda, planned demonstrations, harangue by one

or more fiery speakers, and deliberately caused inflammatory incidents. The following are some of the influences which favor the agitator: novelty, suggestion, contagion, imitation, anonymity, release from repressed emotions, sense of power, sense of righteousness.

Principles of Crowd Control

A crowd is an essential prerequisite to the formation of a mob; thus, the proper control of it is indispensible to prevent its evolution into a mob. The following are some principles of crowd control:

As soon as possible after becoming aware of a crowd or the potential for a large gathering, acquire full information on the nature and character of the crowd.

Make plans for a definite course of action, including plans to cover any changes in the situation which may be foreseen.

Provide for an adequate force of personnel supplied with sufficient materials and equipment.

Have all equipment checked and repaired or replenished to assure proper function condition. Be in position before the arrival of the crowd. Establish a communication system among all police units.

Establish definite boundaries for the crowd. Bearing in mind applicable laws and the constitutional limitations on personal liberties, isolate and quickly remove or reduce causes of tension such as: Influence of agitators Presence of a hated person or symbol Acts of violence committed by crowd members Antagonistic police actions which are not essential to maintaining control.

Demonstration and Strike Control

Demonstrations are public exhibitions of sympathy with or in opposition to some political, economic, or social movement. Demonstrations do not develop over matters which are unopposed by others, therefore, antagonistic feelings are usually high because of the fervency of the beliefs held by the opposing parties. The intent of demonstrators is to focus attention on a problem and the persons or establishments against which action is believed necessary. The social and legal implications inherent in these situations are such that the law enforcement agency has neither the authority nor the legal responsibility to adjudicate or solve. However, the demonstrators, the opposition, and the community must be protected by the police in the public interest.

No single standard procedure can be established for all demonstrations. They will vary in their nature and the problems presented because of the character of the participants, their size, and the atmosphere in which they occur. Thus, plans must have sufficient flexibility to adjust to the situation as it develops. Deployment will be either by a show of force or strength in reserve approach. The show of force approach exists when the deployment of manpower is visible and mainly at the the scene. Generally, officers act as a barricade between the opposing factions. The advantages of this type of action is that the police may gain immediate control of a bad situation, aggressive acts by demonstrators are discouraged, and inexperienced demonstrators may be bluffed out. The disadvantages of such deployment are that the officers are subjected to long tours of duty, the majority of police strength is visible to the leaders of the antagonistic groups. The show of strength will usually be most effective when demonstrators are few in number and inexperienced, and the danger to destruction of property is imminent.

The strength in reserve approach provides for a token force at the scene with a reserve force on hand nearby. The advantages to this system is that the police do not expose the total of their force to view, fresh manpower is available because of constant relief of the men on the line, and commanding officers have greater flexibility and mobility for their total operation. On the other hand, when few officers are in sight fights or other disturbances may start and the officers at the scene will not be strong enough to immediately effect control. When demonstrators are numerous, experienced, well-trained, and properly disciplined, the strength in reserve approach may well be preferable.

Civil Disobedience Arrest

Time is not usually of major importance in making arrests of civil disobedience demonstrators; there should be no more haste than necessary. In fact, the same methodical procedure which will be described here should also be used in non-violent situations to effect arrests made during a regular tour of duty on patrol. The procedure involves a statement by the officer to each person who is violating the law asking that the unlawful activity cease, followed by an opportunity for compliance, a declaration of arrest, a request that the arrested person walk to the transport vehicle, and humane physical removal of the lawbreaker. A typical arrest, assuming non-compliance at each stage, would be:

You are interfering with the free movement of vehicular and pedestrian traffic. Please move, (wait a few seconds for responsive action, but without engaging in debate concerning the merits or lawfulness of the person's action) Will you move?

Your act prohibits the safe and peaceful movement of persons and vehicles in the public streets and prevents access to buildings. This is a violation of (state section number and code applicable) and amounts to disturbing the peace (or other short description of the violation being committed). Will you please move? (wait for compliance a few seconds)

You are now under arrest and charged with disturbing the peace (or other offense). Will you please walk to the patrol wagon?

Do you want to be carried to the patrol wagon? If you do not walk to the wagon you will be in violation of (state section number and code applicable) and the additional charge of resisting arrest will be placed against you.

Will you please walk to the patrol wagon? (remove the demonstrator on a stretcher-subject may be

strapped to stretcher, and stretchers require fewer officers to effect the removal)

Strikes

A strike is a concerted and sustained refusal of employees to perform all of the services for which they were hired. Basically it is a demonstration, therefore all the suggestions made with relation to demonstrations are applicable to strikes. Peaceful picketing is the lawful congregation of workers on *public* grounds near the premises of the employer with whom they have a controversy. Picketing becomes illegal if it blocks streets or interferes with the free and immediate use of the sidewalk or with ingress or egress to any place.

The do's of strike control by police: be absolutely impartial and neutral; limit conversations to picket line captain and ranking company official; keep general public away from dispute as much as reasonable; place responsibility by issuing instructions to either picket line captain or ranking company official; be aware of professional agitators; forward all information to those command primarily concerned with labor dispute; give *verbal* instructions when asked direction by a disputant; be cautious in breaking lines to handle vehicles; give union officials an opportunity to take care of drunken or aggressive pickets; arrange for periodic relief of police on the line.

The don'ts of strike control by police: give impression by overt act (waving, smirking, etc.) of biased feelings; become provoked by derogatory remarks; drive or otherwise go onto company property unless action is necessary to enforce the law; talk over merits of the dispute with persons from either side; give any advice pertaining to injunctions; eat in establishments frequented by disputants; accept gifts, such as donuts or coffee, or other favors from disputants or their supporters; indicate in any way sympathy for either side.

Crowd Control Formations

There are several formations which the police employ to disperse mobs and crowds. The first is the *wedge*. It is the basic formation used to break up, split, or strike into a crowd. The second formation is the *diagonal*. This particular formation is used to move a crowd away from the side of a building, a wall or other object, and is also used to turn the direction of movement of a crowd. The third common formation is the *line*. The line is used as a holding formation to deny an area to a crowd, and is also used to drive a crowd from a confined area.

It is essential that a sufficient number of officers are utilized in the formation so that the particular objective to be achieved can be attained. For example, unless the crowd is small, a squad wedge will be unsuccessful because it will be swallowed up immediately and surrounded as it penetrates the group to be controlled. A line of officers which fails to cover an exit completely will be unable to restrain some persons of the crowd from passing either through or around the ends of the line.

The appropriate interval between adjacent officers in any of the formations depends upon the type of crowd or mob being subject to control. A passive crowd can be controlled by officers at arms' length, either both arms or one arm depending on the degree of control necessary. Densely packed crowds may require the officers to be at close order (elbow's length). The interval necessary to restrain or control a mob will necessitate the officers standing shoulder to shoulder.

An important part of the training of officers in mob control is the proper use of the police baton. It is not to be used by swinging it or as a flail. Since the officers will be shoulder to shoulder, such will result in officers clubbing each other as much as the mob, and when swung the baton is likely to be torn from the one-handed grasp and then used to attack the police. In addition, when the baton is swung down upon the head and shoulders of opponents, three unfavorable results are likely to follow:

During the backswing the officer's whole body is open to attack.

The wildly swinging baton creates an extremely unfavorable appearance to the public.

The baton blows to the head leave opponents cut and bleeding, leading again to unfavorable public opinion.

The basic baton position is the "port" position. In this position, the handle end of the baton is just above the right hip and the tip approximately at the height of the left shoulder; angle to the ground is approximately 45 degrees. The arms are held bent at the elbows, the right hand grasps the handle end from the top and the left hand grasps the tip end from the bottom side. Both hands should be so close to their respective end of the baton that only one or two inches remain exposed, not enough to be grabbed and held by an opponent. The only part of the baton which an opponent can grasp is the center, therefore the officer can twist it away because the location of his hands (at the ends) gives him the superior leverage. Blows with the baton are applied by pushing, swinging, or punching toward an opponent with the center section or the ends while retaining the two handed grip. The vital target areas of the body are illustrated.

When in immediate contact with a mob, officers in formation and utilizing the baton move forward by stepping ahead with their left foot then dragging their right foot forward. The left foot always is in the leading position with the right trailing for best balance at all times; a sort of stamp and shuffle movement.

The movements in formation and use of the police baton for riot control previously described is not used in combating a mob armed with and utilizing forearms. Such conditions required armed combat tactics and weapons.

POLICE SCIENCE NOTES

POLICE-COMMUNITY RELATIONS

A few years ago the terminology used in describing the communication effort or system operating between the police and the community was "Police Public Relations," but today the appropriate words are "Police-Community Relations" (PCR). The single word change indicates an extremely different viewpoint as to what the appropriate communications should be between the police and the public they serve. In fact, even the hyphen between the words "police" and "community" is heavy with meaning.

PCR is a crime fighting, law enforcement concept in which the police and their community members, the citizens of the areas in which the police agency operates, involve themselves in communicating their objectives and problems to each other. Each group benefits from the wholesome exchange of viewpoints, and the objective toward which both move is a cooperative effort in which the police provide enforcement for and to the community according to professional and public requirements and the public assists in this effort. It is a human relations effort by both parties.

PCR is based on the human relations concept. Human relations is the whole area of study and practice aimed at establishing cooperative rather than antagonistic relationships between persons or groups. Human relations is based on effective communication so that with full and accurate knowledge of the situations all parties face, and based on realistic and rational methods of operation, all parties involved will benefit through an exchange relationship rather than one which is exploitive or superior-subordinate.

PCR involves the police department as an organization and its relationships with various segments of the community, and each member of the department and his relationships are developed through his individual contacts as a peace officer. The image conveyed by the individual officer conveys an image of the department as a whole; the image of the police agency becomes part of that which is seen by persons who individually contact each officer.

There have been at least three important changes in the relationships between the police and the community in recent years. The first is that police contacts are no longer nearly exclusively with professional criminals. The advent of the motor car and its development into the agency by which most people transport themselves has caused the police to come into contact with persons from all walks of life. This increased contact has given the police increased realization that the need for support from the law abiding citizens of the community is imperative, which backing is soon lost when contacts by unprofessional officers are too frequent.

The second change is that to service oriented police operations which are demanded by the community and provided by the police. In some areas the police agency has become the governmental unit through which many and varied requests for services from government and private groups are channelized for reference to the appropriate organization which will provide the desired assistance.

The change is that of the role of the professional police as arbitrators of competing demands by special interest groups or individuals in the society. The job of the police remains repressive in many instances, but this must be performed in a society which is basically permissive and expressivefreedom of dissent is an extremely important right in a democratic society such as ours. It must be protected, and the police are often the only agency which is immediately available to offer such a service.

PCR aims toward community involvement with the police in their efforts to provide effective law enforcement. Although it would be more pleasant if more persons within the society were to like the police, and this can be accomplished to a certain extent by an effective PCR program, the more important objective of a PCR program is to convince the various individuals and groups in the society to work with the police. It may be necessary to obtain compliance by force and repression in some instances, but it is much to be preferred to win the willing compliance of persons and groups and their assistance in repression of unlawful behavior.

Democracy can function only when the rule of law is deemed by the majority to be the appropriate procedure to follow in obtaining protection and domestic tranquil-ity. Democracy cannot function where anarchy and violence prevail to the point at which the system of designated, governmental, community controls become ineffective.

Officers must not neglect the fact that PCR programs involve the willingness and necessity to change on the part of the police in answer to beliefs held in the community. PCR is not a one-way street as was the public relations system. PCR programs and their objectives include at least the following:

Information exchange forums, meetings, and programs by which the police and various community groups and their representatives (some of whom will display very antagonistic feelings toward the police and the lawfully constituted government) communicate their objectives and beliefs.

Communications systems through which the police and minority groups involve themselves with mutual solutions to problems facing each other.

Programs designed to: inform the public of crime problems facing the police; provide information to the community which will enable them to protect themselves from being victims of criminals; and promote the inflow of information to the police which will enable them to more effectively repress criminal activity.

Enlightening sessions designed to educate individual officers so that they will become aware of the fact (and believe in the efficacy of the basic construction of our social system) that he as an officer is working for the community and should not act as a free agent in interpreting laws or forcing citizens to conform to rules of conduct which have not been formalized by officially recognized governmental action.

Personal Conduct

The individual actions taken or motivations and beliefs shown by an officer during his contacts with the public reflect upon the competence of the whole police department. Word of unprofessional conduct by individual officers spreads quickly like the waves of the sea and affect the responses of nearly unbelievable numbers of others in short order. These suggestions should be carefully considered and followed by all officers:

The professional officer is courteous, sincere, and friendly even when those whom he is contacting are abrasive, demanding or insincere.

The professional officer is able to be at ease with all types of persons and communicate and interact with them with consideration, tact and poise.

The professional officer shows respect to not only his superiors but also to his coworkers and subordinates.

The professional officer's person, uniform and equipment are always clean, presentable and/or in good condition and repair.

The professional officer is always willing to provide any reasonable service to those in need.

The professional officer's conduct is exemplary whether he is on duty or not.

Our law enforcement system is based on the premis that every peace officer is also a citizen-a member of the community who is serving the community needs rather than operating to attain his own personal objectives exclusively. The role is a sacred one and must be upheld by each and every member of the police profession.